Using Art Media in Psychotherapy

Using Art Media in Psychotherapy makes a thoughtful and contextual argument for using graphic art materials in psychotherapy, providing historical context for art materials and their uses and incorporating them with contemporary practices and theories. Written with an analytic focus, many of the psychological references nod to Jung and post-Jungian thought with keen attention to image and to symbolic function. This book jettisons the idea of reductionist, cookbook approaches and instead provides an integrated and contextual understanding of the origins of each art form as well as an insightful use for each in its application in mental health healing practices. *Using Art Media in Psychotherapy* gives clinicians and students alike the tools they need to offer psychologically minded and clinically astute choices that honor their clients.

Michelle L. Dean, MA, is the cofounder of the Center for Psyche & the Arts (www.psychearts.org). She is a board-certified art therapist, a licensed professional counselor, and a certified group psychotherapist. In her clinical practice, she provides a warm and compassionate approach in which to explore and heal. She is also a clinical supervisor and an esteemed, nationally recognized educator and consultant. Her work has been recognized through many distinguished awards and several interviews in print, radio, and television.

"With this book, Michelle Dean has added her voice to an ever-growing chorus of art therapists, counselors, and psychotherapists who are committed to including art making in the complex process of psychotherapy. Dean avoids the temptation to provide easy, prescriptive tasks that inevitably lead to superficial incorporation, opting instead for a much deeper and richer discussion of the art process in psychotherapy that is quite literally beyond the bounds of linear discursive language."

Bruce L. Moon, PhD, ATR-BC, HLM, LPC,
professor of art therapy at Mount Mary University

"*Using Art Media in Psychotherapy* offers us the depth of meaning that comes through the lens of historical example, and welcomes back the voice of soul in art psychotherapy. I am delighted to use this both with students and on my own; it is a text that infuses art therapy intervention with the richness offered by engagement with mystery."

Abbe Miller, MS, ATR-BC, LPC, director of the graduate
art therapy program and associate professor in the department
of psychology at Albertus Magnus College

"Michelle Dean delivers invigorating, contemporary scholarship with *Using Art Media in Psychotherapy*. She masterfully fuses psychotherapeutic theory to reflective practices within sacred myth and symbol. The clinical and media examples describe an epic of evolution for the nuanced use of crafted materials. This book regenerates lacuna between art and psychotherapy, between activated imagination and meaningful care of the soul. Will art therapists enact venturesome journeys from positivistic worlds to the phenomenological shores of 'integrating things anew'?"

Natalie Rae Carlton, PhD, art therapy educator

"This thoughtful addition to the literature of art therapy elucidates the roots of visual imagery via a cultural framework that includes aesthetics, mythology, iconography, religion, and philosophy within an analytic approach. Michelle Dean's refreshing contribution, at times elegantly crafted, will be useful not only for the beginning clinician but will enliven the thinking of the professional. Detailed and easy-to-follow descriptions of art materials and art interventions are generously offered."

Elizabeth Stone Matho, MA, ATR-BC, LP, LCAT, psychoanalyst,
art therapist in private practice, and faculty at the Ecole
de Psychologues Praticiens in Lyon, France

"This is an extremely well-written and comprehensive text that describes the use of media and methods of application while elucidating the value of imagery as an active and integral component of psychotherapy. Michelle Dean beautifully synthesizes historical artistic expression with philosophy, psychology, myth, culture, and the processes of creativity while maintaining the integrity of the therapeutic relationship in the description of sound clinical interventions."

Juliet King, MA, ATR-BC, LPC, director art therapy,
assistant professor, Herron School of Art and Design, IUPUI

Using Art Media in Psychotherapy

Bringing the Power of
Creativity to Practice

Michelle L. Dean

Routledge
Taylor & Francis Group

NEW YORK AND LONDON

First published 2016
by Routledge
711 Third Avenue, New York, NY 10017

and by Routledge
2 Park Square, Milton Park, Abingdon, Oxon, OX14 4RN

Routledge is an imprint of the Taylor & Francis Group, an informa business

Library of Congress Cataloging-in-Publication Data
Dean, Michelle L.
  Using art media in psychotherapy : bringing the power of creativity to practice / Michelle L. Dean.
    pages cm
  Includes bibliographical references and index.
  ISBN 978-1-138-81621-3 (hardback : alk. paper) —
  ISBN 978-1-138-81622-0 (pbk. : alk. paper) — ISBN 978-1-315-74625-8 (ebook)
  1. Arts—Therapeutic use. 2. Psychotherapy. 3. Psychotherapist and patient. I. Title.
  RC489.A7D43 2016
  616.89'1656—dc23
  2015024931

ISBN: 978-1-138-81621-3 (hbk)
ISBN: 978-1-138-81622-0 (pbk)
ISBN: 978-1-315-74625-8 (ebk)

Typeset in Sabon
by Apex CoVantage, LLC

Printed and bound in the United States of America by Publishers Graphics, LLC on sustainably sourced paper.

To Mark, Matthew, and William
With love

CONTENTS

FIGURES

PREFACE

Interest in utilizing art and the creative process in psychotherapy practice has surged in recent years. I perceive that this increased interest is bringing with it an increasing dichotomy between theory and practice, leading to larger schisms among professional camps of helping professionals as to how and when to include art and creative processes in psychotherapy practice. Many clinicians are confused or uncertain about the therapeutic benefits of arts that promote wellness as well as about practices that promote increased awareness or consciousness and expression in a psychotherapy process. Questions about who may or may not be an appropriate clinician of art-based psychotherapy remain, and thus, I feel moved to share my thoughts on my clinical and professional experience as an artist and as an art psychotherapist and hope to provide some clarity and inspirations for this approach.

I developed and researched the concepts and historical background presented in this book over my two decades of clinical practice and nearly as many years teaching an undergraduate course, Art Therapy: Media and Applications, at Arcadia University, Glenside, Pennsylvania. I have also modified and taught some of this course material in numerous continuing education programs for professionals, art therapists, mental health clinicians, and art educators. As a guest lecturer for undergraduate and graduate programs as well as at national conferences for mental health professionals, I have experienced a real hunger for practice that is "alive" and holds the essence of what attracted many to the professions of psychotherapy or art making. There is a *zeitgeist*, a belief, idea, or spirit of our time, that embraces the arts as having a healing function in physical and psychological health, but its potential is not yet fully realized. Thus, many of the passionate individuals who have entered into the arts in health care or psychological practice have found their pursuits in the current professional climate full of deadening standards and methods. Let it be clear, I am not for anarchy when it comes to regulations or standards for professional practice, but I do believe the standards must be consistent and in keeping with the work, not something that creates extraneous work, credentials, or bureaucratic procedures. I disagree with standards that do not serve as standards should: to protect the public and enhance care. Lear (1999), a philosophy professor and psychoanalyst, speaks of this issue as it relates to professions' seeking the highest standards. He notes that rigid standards impose rigidity on practice: "It enables the profession to stop thinking critically about how it ought to go on precisely because the standards present themselves as already answered the question. The profession can then act as though it *already knows* what high standards are. This is a form of deadness" (p. 3–4). In creative and psychoanalytic processes, spaces exist for both knowing and not knowing, which is necessary to allow for the emergence of new awareness, change, and most importantly, aliveness. The type of knowing I am referring to is an intimate knowing that our English language does not adequately express. This difference may be seen more clearly in some of the Romantic languages such as French where the two verbs *savoir* and *connaître* both mean "to know" but have very different meanings. *Savoir* means to know how to do something, like to change a diaper or pick up a child properly, or to know the facts of a situation. But the verb *connaître* means to know and understand a person or to be intimately familiar with something. If a baby were crying, it would not help to know the procedure to change a diaper as much as it would to know the child and understand what the cries are for, such as the need for comfort or feeding. In therapy, we may *savoir*—know techniques and facts that are tested by our standards—but to engage in human relationships and "alive-ening" psychotherapeutic practices, we must *connaître*—know intimately—our patients and their needs in order to respond and offer interventions appropriate to each situation. We must also be open to not knowing, such as not knowing what may emerge in the images of our patients because they hold the potential for uniqueness and individuality. Each unique opportunity holds the potent unfolding that the images created by our patients exist in that particular space and time. If we insist that a tree be drawn in a certain way, we risk chastising the expressive element at the core of individuality and psychological processes. It is my hope that this book will encourage the readers to ponder the enlivening and emergent quality of utilizing arts in psychotherapy, encompassing both aspects of knowing while suspending preconceived ideas that may thwart creative processes, and opening to the mysteries of these processes.

This book fills a gap in the current book market for art therapy and creativity in psychology. It offers a rich, in-depth view of incorporating innovative art-based practices into psychotherapy and provides a resource for the reader to consider by providing historical and cultural context, meaning, and purpose. This is the book I would have liked to have read as a graduate student and to have assigned as a teacher. I intend it to be a useful resource for courses on engagement of the arts in a therapeutic context applicable for art therapists, mental health professionals, and anyone interested in a deeper understanding of the transformative powers of image and art.

I feel this book may also be timely because the profession of art therapy seems once again to be going through a bit of an identity crisis or, in developmental terms, a bit of an adolescent crisis, as it struggles to find its own solidified identity through finding independence via independent licensure and research with the arts as its core. I would like to add my thoughts and support to the concept of art therapy as an independent practice with its roots firmly planted in the image as a conduit of knowing in the processes of psychotherapy. In particular, my preference is to use art therapy in depth-oriented, psychoanalytic, and object relations approaches framed by such scholars as Freud, Jung, Hillman, Bolby, and Winnicott. Although art therapy as a profession has had its own inner dichotomy that began in the split between art psychotherapy and art as therapy, I see within the profession room for both of these ideologies. What concerns me most is the reduction of the profession of art therapy to activities and techniques employed to keep patients entertained and active. Although arts used on their own accord as a form of self-help are undoubtedly beneficial, this is not the same process as working in a psychotherapeutic frame. Part of the confusion comes from the mechanization of psychology or counseling as techniques and tools. When these are employed from only a product or skill perspective, it takes us away from meaningful process work, which is flexible, cyclical, personal, and able to encompass a multitude of theoretical orientations and practice approaches. In this sense, it is not the tool that builds a cabinet, it is the carpenter. It is the art psychotherapist who employs the tools based on the individual and situation and who defines the practice. It is not the tools, even though our current culture often clings to methods and techniques over process. Tools, like specific art media, can structure, limit, or support therapy but should not be the reason a method is employed. Instead, psychotherapy is meant to be a process that takes place within a relational context. The individual's personal psychology comprises the driving factors of the process. There are many purported reasons for technique to reign supreme over process in our current cultural climate; a major factor is that, often, those who define treatment are not actually in clinical practice but are instead policy makers or agencies with ties to economic gain who use this piecemeal empirical research as concrete, measurable steps, and outcomes to define standards of therapeutic process. This stifles the process and hamstrings therapy. There is a disconnect from the process of clinical practice when one is doing research, and with good reason—in order to be objective and set definable measurements and goals. However, the very criteria that are limiting by virtue of setting measures, controls, and scope of practice in a lab do not always translate well into the multifactorial practice of working with complex issues and factors that are inherent in an individual's life. Additionally, researchers who postulate about techniques often are not neutral when conducting research or advocating for their use in many circumstances. As Paulo Freirea stated, "Techniques cannot be neutral. Those who talk of neutrality are precisely those who are afraid of losing their right to use neutrality to their own advantage" (as cited in Chalquist, 2013). Further, clinicians may develop the inclination to distance themselves from the intense emotional aspects of clinical work by focusing on employing techniques rather than fully engaging in the empathic engagement required of clinical and relational practice.

I personally feel the term *art psychotherapist* clearly and appropriately defines my work and the work of many others. I believe it clarifies the services and theoretical orientation I provide because the work I do comes from my education and interest in psychodynamic and depth psychology. Although my current credential defines me professionally as a board certified art therapist, my preferred term *psychotherapist* provides an important distinction: *Psychology* means the study of the spirit or soul, so the prefix *psycho* provides a core, defining aspect of the art psychotherapist.

I have always believed the title *art therapist* does not fully convey the depth and complexity of the psychological work that is done in most psychotherapy sessions that utilize art (at least in my practice). In fact, there is no mention of psychological process in the title *art therapist*, and so questions such as "What is art therapy?" endlessly arise. This is often quickly followed by, "Do you draw pictures for your patients to make them feel better?" As in a typical adjective–noun combination, it is the *art* that is describing the *therapist*. So the questions are understandable. But it is not *my* art that produces the therapeutic intervention in my patients, and I am not conducting therapy with art alone. I am also facilitating a psychological space and a relationship while performing psychological insight-oriented work that holds space for transformation between myself and the patient. This work includes art making that arises out of this psychological process. Schaverien (1992) introduced the term *analytical art psychotherapy* because "neither art therapy nor art psychotherapy satisfactorily expresses the *full* import of the pictured image as an object of transference *itself*, within the transference and countertransference relationship" (p. 6). Simply, it is the psychotherapeutic process in which the art is employed that makes the art psychotherapeutic, not the converse. While art engaged on one's own can be beneficial and therapeutic, it is not a psychotherapy practice. This text addresses art psychotherapy as a mental health profession and practice in which the therapeutic relationship is one of the holding and transformative elements.

A word of caution follows for those picking up this book to employ some of the methods in clinical practice. Springham (2008) showed how the arts have the capability to help as well as harm through the power of suspension of disbelief, which makes us feel as if we are experiencing something beyond the concrete presence of the art object. Evidence from the arts suggests that objects and images can become real and alive to a range of degree, such as an experience we can have when feeling emotionally moved by a film or by photographs of an injured child in a faraway place. We may feel moved to tears or transformed by the sight of a painting that we encounter in a museum. Or respond with wonder and awe to urban graffiti art we pass by on a train car. These responses can elicit memories or transport us to places *as if* we were in the cinema or in a war-torn country, standing there like the injured child. In a legal case, a risk in the arts and health field was described when a patient was injured by a practitioner working beyond his or her competence (Springham, 2008). This report stated that the technique used was too strong. The therapist used a technique instead of a person-informed intervention without a full understanding of what was being asked of the patient, and therefore, the recognition of the power of art to make inner states real was the basis of the proof that harm was done. Art psychotherapy is concerned with exactly this process, the moderation between the real and the imaginary and what is felt to be real and known not to be real. This "as if" state is one for which the art therapist must have the expertise to understand, assess, and work with in clinical practice.

ACKNOWLEDGMENTS

This book is a culmination of ideas and experiences that have germinated over the first 20 years of my career. I have learned from and been inspired by more people than I shall ever be able to mention in this section, so if you have been a teacher, mentor, or a friend to me, I thank you. I wish to thank Art Resource, The Artists Rights Society, and The Museum of Fine Arts in Boston for granting permission rights permission for their images. Specific credit details may be found under the description of the images accompanying the images. I wish to acknowledge the great contribution made to the completion of this book by my husband, Mark Dean. His dedication and patience, as well as his good sense, were indispensible in all phases of the preparation of this manuscript. A special thanks is given to Heather Gary for her unwavering support and encouragement and for our friendship, which is steeped in imagery, art, and storytelling. Natalie Carlton, who engaged in lively discussions about our shared profession and was a great sounding board for several chapters in this book, as well as Beth Sirota and Johanna Kane for their boundless enthusiasm and support. A heartfelt thanks is given to Abbe Miller and David Gussak for their valuable feedback of the initial proposal and to Routledge's editors, Anna Moore and Zoey Peresman, for helping to make this book a reality. I extend a profound sense of gratitude to my patients, supervisees, and my students, especially those at Arcadia University, who have inspired me and graciously allowed the use of their artwork. It is very much an honor to be entrusted with your stories and images. As the recipient of the American Art Therapy Association's 2015 Pearlie Roberson Award, I am extremely grateful. This award financially aided the procurement of many of the historic images used in this text.

AUTHOR'S NOTE

Using art in therapy does not replace the need for specific education and training in psychotherapy processes as well as understanding of and personal experience with art making. Nor is it meant to be used as a replacement for professional mental health services; it requires comprehensive education in the arts, including process and theory of image, and in the processes of psychotherapy. My hope is that this text will spark further interest and education in art psychotherapy as it provides a nuanced view of the rich and transformative use of images and the art-making process as means to understand human creativity and its role in healing and transformation. Although human artistic creations span centuries, it is my desire to ground some of the current uses of art in a cultural context. I realize this is an enormous task, and due to limitations of length, this text only begins to explore art that can be used in a therapeutic context. I hope that additional editions or volumes of this text will include more art forms, including fiber arts, handcrafts, and community art projects, as well as additional variations of the themes explored in this edition.

Regarding the historical images presented in the interior of this text, because the printing of this book will be in black and white, I have chosen whenever possible images that I believe will translate to this monochromatic presentation successfully. In choosing examples to fully illuminate the ideas, I have done what I could to reach a compromise between the subject matter, historical context, and current display methods that I believe will give the reader an appreciation of the historical art. Note that the images in the case examples were originally produced in color. It is my hope that future editions will present the images with the important element of color because color is essential for most in order to see the full spectrum of emotion and expression. And while I would have loved to have included images for every section in every chapter, printing limitations and, sometimes, thought to the therapeutic relationship had to be considered: before asking permission for patient artwork to be used in this book, the potential for changing the therapeutic alliance was considered.

The citations for C. G. Jung's *Collected Works* in the body of this text refer to volume and paragraph and will be noted as (CW: volume: paragraph). This is in keeping with the *Collected Works* numbered paragraphs system, which more closely corresponds to the referenced source than page numbers do. The full citation of each volume, including the original publication date when available, is given in the references list.

I refer to the individuals I work with as patients even though, for many, this term has fallen out of favor starting in the mid-1970s, with preference for the more commercialized term *client* or, to my abhorrence, *customer*. After listening to an impassioned talk that psychologist and Jungian analyst James Hillman delivered on the subject many years ago, I have been convinced that *patient* is a term that holds the dignity of the individual in the psychotherapeutic relationship. The term *patient* comes from *patiens*, meaning "I am suffering," and allows the person to fully own his or her struggles without false pretense or glossing over the suffering that is inherent in life. To do *therapy* means "to be attentive to." Using the terms *patient* and *therapist* provides the context for the therapeutic relationship without the pressure to produce or consume, leaves the relationship open to receive what unfolds in the psyche and the image, and allows both parties to attend to, honor, and give voice or form to the suffering. In my opinion, *patient* is a term that empowers the person to be engaged in the process rather than being passive, contracting services, or receiving a scripted outcome. Therapy is not something that is done to the person but instead creates the space to attend to the process, transformation, and production of imagery and artwork. This perspective restores the relational aspect of therapy back into a psychological (individual) process.

I am honored to be able to share with you the courageous work of my patients, students, and colleagues. They have my heartfelt appreciation for sharing their lives with me as well as their most personal stories and images. With their permission, I share in this book some of their stories and images. Their identities are kept confidential through the use of pseudonyms and fictitious descriptions attributed to their works of art so that identifiable, personal material is obscured. At times, the life story of a patient I present may actually be a montage of several people, thus describing the struggles of several in one case vignette. I employ this method to describe the essence of the situation while concealing personal and identifying information.

CHAPTER 1

INTRODUCTION
The Use of Art Media in Therapy

Art in a psychotherapy practice is much more than a quiver full of directives or a series of ingredients rattled off like a recipe in a cookbook. Although a set of ingredients may get the beginner into the kitchen, what separates the novice from a chef is a discerning appreciation for the individual ingredients and their synergetic effects. Likewise, the ability to be receptive and to engage images and the application of art and imagery into attentive and skillful intervention in a psychotherapy practice requires competent providers who are able to understand the transformative effects of imagery within the art process. The differences between art techniques and art as an emergent means of communication and knowledge spanning millennia are often confused.

Art therapy is often described as nonverbal therapy because, like sand tray therapy, some of the process may be done in silence. As a result, the session remains unfettered by cognitive processing, and the patient may stay close to the lived experience of the creative process, as the therapist holds the space like a silent witness. But as Moon (2008) stated, art therapy is really a meta-verbal therapy, a therapy that goes *beyond* traditional talk therapy. The Greek prefix *meta-* means "beyond," and while art therapy does include language, it also includes the dynamics of image and the relational aspects of a therapeutic alliance. And art therapy goes beyond the obvious hybrid of art and psychology; it encompasses much more, including cognitive, behavioral, developmental, psychological, cultural, anthropological, historical, and imagistic considerations such as archetypes. An archetype, from a Jungian perspective, refers to a collectively inherited unconscious idea, pattern, thought, or image that is universally known by a group of individuals. Archetypes commonly present as reoccurring motifs or symbols in art and literature and may be thought of as deriving from a first mold from which others are patterned. Examples of archetypes are images of mother, father, self, shadow, trickster, and hero, as well as hundreds of others. Through these symbols, matter and energy meet and psyche and body connect across time and space (Rowland, 2015).

Artwork is not an alien encounter; rather, we meet the artwork in the world and the world in the artwork. We come to understand ourselves in it and through it, and for this reason, we must come into a relationship with it (Gadamer, 2012). The art presents both an immediate reality of the individual and a historical context of the human condition. As Gadamer (2012) states, "art is knowledge and experiencing an artwork means sharing in that knowledge" (p. 84). Through the creative process, the artwork is not just an object but instead an experience—an experience that changes both the creator and the viewer. This transformation occurs through play or through the peak experience sometimes described as flow, which has its own essence, outside of consciousness. Art uses the language of symbols, metaphors, and relationship to best express itself. Art is not science. While each makes significant contributions to awareness, they are different modes of knowing.

Psychological assessment and treatment are often described through a particular lens, theory, or technique, such as cognitive or behavioral, and are often tied to fluctuating criteria for mental illness. Few of these frameworks approach images as a means of expression, health, or psychological function. Because an image enables us to consider and reflect on personal, familial, and societal health, meaning, and significance and to include relevant historical, cultural, and individual factors, the image and its expression in art in a therapeutic setting are crucial to psychological assessment and treatment. As a theoretical frame, depth psychology appears to fully encompass the human condition. This approach encourages the use of art and imagery due to their ability to hold a multitude of aspects including personal, cultural, historic, imagistic, archetypal, religious, and mythic frameworks. I concur with Schaverien (1992), who states that the process is generally equally as important as the product, although the relative importance varies across particular persons and their expressions. I also believe the relational aspect of the therapeutic process is essential because it provides the framework that holds space for the emergent material to manifest.

Through this text, I hope to present a full representation of the significance and impetus for using art in the psychotherapy process and the importance of the historical and cultural context of this material. Dunn-Snow and Joy-Smellie (2000) agreed with Congdon (1990) and Jung (1968b) when they said, "An exemplary art experiential also needs a historically based component that art therapists can refer to when discussions about artwork evolve [and] that art experiential steeped in history brings both a personal and collective meaning to the art therapy experience" (p. 125). A part of the personal process and artistic expression is the emergence of Image. Image and symbolism are integral parts of psychoanalysis. From the beginning, psychology has addressed imagery, such as through Freud's theories of dreams and through Jung's images and his encouragement of his patients to create art about their dreams and fantasies. The way imagery is regarded is of great significance, but often, due to its esoteric nature, imagery has come to be minimized in the current trends in many mental health practices to purport positivist science or empiricism. According to Berry (2008), a Jungian analyst,

> What we don't learn is a psychology of the Image, comparable to what students of archeology, iconography, aesthetics, or textual criticism would learn about the image in their fields. But we can't even discover what would be a psychology of the image so long as we in psychology are exploiting the image for what we take to be our therapeutic aims. Perhaps the other way around would be more appropriate: discover what the image wants and from that determine our therapy [p. 76].

The current text focuses on the use of image and art, or graphic representations, as a means of self-exploration and therapeutic insight and change. Although there are merits in empiricism, the many efforts to quantify the image are unable to capture the essential contribution that it makes in work with individuals and their emergent symbolism. In this book, I attempt to hold the dialectical ideas of human struggles, such as those with truth, beauty, good, evil, dread, and hate as it emerges in an image form. Such an image contains wonder and awe within its confines. I intend this text to provide readers with some of the essential history and contextual importance of image and art. The history of art predates its use for human development, regulation, and mediation, and it underpins well-being and specifically art's application in psychotherapy practice. I will explain the distinction between image and picture and give examples of their application within a therapeutic construct.

Each chapter describes a popular art medium, including a summation of its origin, its cultural and technological advances, and how it may be thought about and applied in psychotherapy. Most chapters also provide a brief illustrative case example highlighting some considerations for the use of art in psychotherapy. The number of chapters in this text is limited to ten. Although this is a humble beginning, I hope to provide depth more than breadth. In this book, I discuss the use of art in therapy but in no way do I intend this text to substitute for specific education and training in psychotherapy processes, nor do I mean it to be used as a replacement for professional help and mental health services. It is, however, a deep and well-supported view into the rich and transformative use of art and the art-making process as means to understand human creativity and its role in healing and transformation.

Drawing on the historical context of art, I describe art psychotherapy's inclusive psychological framework, symbolism, and functions. I discuss the inception of specific art media as well as how significant cultural changes have influenced their methods. This book does not merely provide a list of activities but does describe many methods commonly used in art therapy within an interpersonal psychotherapy practice of a trained clinician. Attention is given to the importance of context in the psychotherapy practice utilizing art. Any specific interventions that are given in this text are done so out of necessity because there are times when additional support or directions are helpful to the patient. The times I find more direct intervention helpful are when patients feel paralyzed by self-doubt or present as psychically impoverished due to neglect of their inner world or the result of traumatic events. Again, context is key in delivery and method. This text is meant to encourage individuals to connect to the creative process as a means of igniting their own creativity and ability to navigate many of life's challenges and to support well-being. It is also meant to open discussion of the arts as a larger psychological construct that has historical roots in human development and phenomena. Art in psychotherapy is focused on relational aspects and expressive elements, and it promotes intra/interpersonal connectivity through the therapeutic relationship (Hass-Cohen & Carr, 2008).

I begin this book by describing some of the psychological and aesthetic frameworks and influences that I find compelling because they have laid the foundation for contemporary thinking about the arts and creative process. Their inclusion is by no means a comprehensive discussion of the philosophical ideals but is meant to build a framework upon which a rationale is supported for incorporating the arts in therapy and for enhancing well-being. I hope this discussion will also shed light on the historical influences on image, art, and aesthetics as seen today. Discussion of aesthetics in the field of art therapy is minimal, with few exceptions. However, because artwork changes both the creator and the viewer by being as much an experience as it is a product, aesthetics must be considered for its emotional and subjective aspects.

I am advocating for the arts to be used in psychotherapeutic practice as a means for greater consciousness and awareness, which can sometimes only be achieved through an image, which is a source of thought and knowing. Congruent with this belief, I have found a natural affinity with the theory and teachings of depth psychology. Written with an analytic focus, many of the psychological references in this book pay homage to Jung and post-Jungian thought, as well as early philosophical writers who contemplated the roles of aesthetics and art in people's lives. Attention to image and symbolic function has been included in places. And although image and picture are often used interchangeably, there is a difference. It can be easy to conflate the picture, or product, with function, or the image creation process, and thereby inadvertently degrade the distinct value of the image and its creative expression in educational and psychotherapeutic work, which is as a potent, emergent deliverer and holder having significant psychological process.

This book jettisons the idea of a formulaic cookbook of activities. Although some might want to view a cookbook approach to therapy as a simple solution meeting the current demand for standardized methods of therapy, such a perspective would undermine the individual and his or her creative process if these activities were applied without thought. I caution that a cookbook method is dishonest to both the patient and the therapist and misses essential opportunities for connection, reverie, and emergent psychological material that are highly personal, idiosyncratic, and possibly esoteric. Clinicians and student clinicians who might reach haphazardly into a bag of tricks, grab for worksheets, or rattle off activities and techniques to keep patients busy will hopefully use this book to ground their understanding of the arts in psychotherapy with theories and ideas that have long historical, analytic, and relational roots. I believe such grounding can be an antidote to the compulsive frenzy of busywork, which is so pervasive today in mental health settings, that stresses looking at limited aspects of human functioning, often the cognitive function due to its fit with the current trends and its ability to distance the clinician from the therapeutic relationship. I hope that, by understanding the inherent nature and function of art along with its specific characteristics, origins, and capacity for expression and relatedness, mental health therapists will find meaningful applications in the therapeutic process and beyond. I encourage therapists to use this book to implement art-based interventions that arise from psychologically minded and clinically astute choices, informed with depth and integrity, which honor patients and the tradition of imagistic knowing and not knowing. By the not-knowing aspects of art, I am referring to the numinous: elements that surpass comprehension and understanding and may have spiritual and synchronistic factors.

This text supports the concept of authentic relational and transmutative opportunities in a psychotherapeutic framework by providing an integrated and contextual understanding of the origins of each art form and some insightful applications. I aim to provide thoughtful and well-researched implementations of art forms along with their historic uses in societal, cultural, and clinical contexts for engaging in personal and collective emergent material for personal psychic and collective archetypal realms. Presenting the historical context in an accessible manner informs the applicability of the art media and its ability to express, contain, and document or bear witness to suffering, and it provides opportunities for the reader to more fully grasp the potential for transcendence and transformation in a therapeutic setting. It provides for an *alive-ening* or awakening personal experience—a process for questioning and a kind of knowing that is personal and simultaneously a collective, archetypal awareness and knowledge. Life is a creative process, which integrates many philosophical questions about how we live it. The arts are a practice and as such are able to teach us much about discipline, affect regulation, patience, organization, imagination, relationships, and engagement. The image-making process can be akin to meditation and spiritual practices, offering mental and physical health benefits. Image is everywhere: in our waking life, in our dreams, in our memories, and in our language. Imagery is exulted in our arts and provides a malleable medium for reflection and examination. Socrates is famous for stating, "An unexamined life is not worth living: it is not a form of living, but that form of deadness" (as cited in Lear, 1999, p. 4). Through the examination of images, I hope to enliven the reader to study and relate to the images, invite them to employ graphic representation, and utilize the power of art in psychotherapy practice.

Brief Origins and Functions of Art and Image

Art has been used throughout time as a means of expression and to record ideas and events. Some of the earliest known expressions date back to prints made between 30,000 and 32,000 years ago, discovered in the Chauvet Cave in Southern France in 1994 (Herzog, Nelson, Ciuffo, Harding, Hobbs, & McKillop, 2010). On the cave walls, accompanied by images of prehistoric ice-age animals, are some of the earliest art productions of early humans: sets of handprints believed to be part of a spiritual practice. They are unique and identifiable to a single artist, a unique identity known only through the art he or she left behind to be preserved across the millennia (Dean, 2015; Herzog et al., 2010).

In addition to the fascinating aspects of these early expressions by our ancestral relatives is the idea that the process was not merely a means of concretely recording daily life or keeping accounts of events but was a spiritual practice or ritual. Looking at the long relationship between spiritual practice and the arts, whether it be the Paleolithic cave paintings of Chauvet, the cliff paintings of Africa (9000–8000 BCE) or the Lithic work of the Americas (11,000 BCE), one begins to ponder the importance of not only the spiritual or meditative aspect of the arts but also humans' abilities to think abstractly about our existential experience and its relationship to greater consciousness.

Art as a Universal Experience

Art is a universal process among children in cultures around the world and is something that all adults possess the capacity for into old age. All people may call themselves artists if they create artwork, reserving the term *professional artist* for those who receive money for their work. Developmentally, there is a universally accepted progression of art-making skills and schema that coincide with physical, emotional, and cognitive developmental milestones; these include such typical shapes as a circle, cross, square, and rectangle (Lowenfeld & Brittain, 1987). The content of a child's drawing may focus on certain motifs (e.g., trees, houses, or people) and is significantly correlated with gender. But equally as important as the content is the manner in which it is created. It is accepted that exceptions or deviations from typical artistic milestones in children may be attributed to personal factors, such as the two psychological types: visual (ideoplastic) and haptic (physioplastic) types of creative expression (Read, 1966). Although one type does not create superior artists, it is important to note the type because it produces a significant difference in presentation and aesthetic. Therefore, there is a natural dichotomy in art expression based on these two types. The visual type represents items in artwork close to the way they appear in space with attention to nuance and realism, much like a spectator, while the haptic type tends to display expressiveness, including exaggerations, related to internal somatic sensations and emotionality (Lowenfeld, 1965; Lowenfeld & Brittain, 1987; Read, 1962, 1966). According to Read (1966) these types were first recorded by Vernworn in 1914, who noted correlations for the visual type with concerns about conceptualization, and for the haptic type with sensations of the body; this idea is similar to Kühn's imaginative and sensorial types described in 1923.

Artistic Development Stages

As Lowenfeld and Brittain (1987) discussed in *Creative and Mental Growth*, children progress through specific stages of artistic development, based on their physical and cognitive development. Based on their research, Lowenfeld and Brittain assigned the following names to these stages: scribble, preschematic, schematic, dawning of realism (the gang stage), the age of reason (the pseudo-naturalistic stage), and last, the period of decision, which covers adolescent art. I refer the reader to Lowenfeld and Brittain for an extensive description of children's developmental artistic stages. The stages represent a general progression of development; keep in mind that children will not all begin and end a stage at a specified time because there are always variations in development. The stages are merely general guidelines; also, the characteristics of more than one stage can be apparent in a child at a given time. These artistic stages correspond closely to the cognitive, physical, and emotional growth of the child. What is most important, as with any academic or technical skill, is that the child should not be forced to do work beyond their developmental level because that could lead to frustration and cause psychological distress and harm (Bjorklund & Krebs, 1985; Strauss, 2015).

The Scribble Stage

The first stage described by Lowenfeld and Brittain (1987), the scribble stage, begins when the child is old enough to hold materials, such as crayons, without placing them in the mouth; generally this stage starts at around 18 months and continues until approximately 4 years of age. Because so much rapid development occurs during this time, the scribble stage is further divided into three subgroups: the disorganized, organized, and named scribble subtypes. The disorganized subtype presents with varied line quality and random marks, as seen in Figures 1.1, 1.2, and 1.3. This child often seems unaware of making the marks and does not hold the drawing or painting utensil in a consistent manner nor reflect a dominant hand preference. Typically, a more controlled line is possible by the age of 2 years due to physical changes and greater control over hand and arm movements. This artistic developmental subtype is named the controlled scribble stage. An example is shown in Figure 1.4, where more control over the lines can be seen. Children in this subtype have developed greater awareness of the environment and their mark-making activities. Insight into the connection between the motions of the hand and the marks on the page begin around this time. The last phase of the scribble stage is the named scribble subtype, which develops around the age of 3 years. Kellogg (1970) observed that children as young as 24 months often guide their marks into patterns. By this time, children may be able to copy a circle

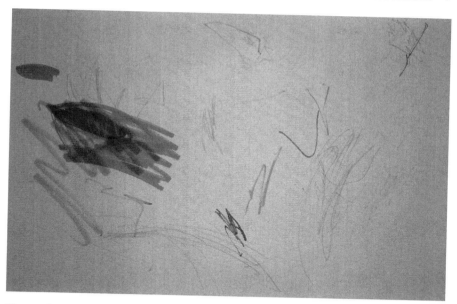

Figure 1.1 Scribble drawing in the disorganized phase when the young boy was 14 months old. © 2016 Michelle L. Dean.

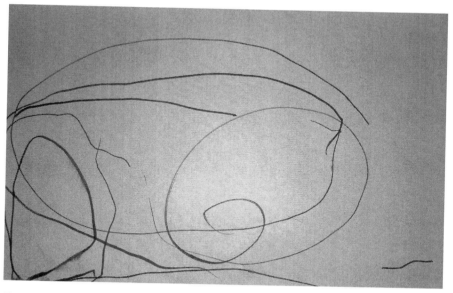

Figure 1.2 A disorganized scribble made by the same boy in Figure 1.1 at 18 months old. © 2016 Michelle L. Dean.

but not a square, they develop a basis for visual retention, they create lines that represent edges of forms, and they have greater awareness of recording feelings and things in the environment around them. Circles emerge, followed by radial lines that are both a kind of mandala and a sun (Kellogg, 1970). The radial lines provide a sense of rays and, when drawn from a baseline, form a fan-like shape;

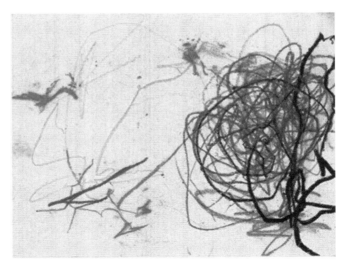

Figure 1.3 A disorganized scribble made by the same boy in Figure 1.1 at 21 months old. Several colors are chosen to create the image as well as intent. Right hand dominance is apparent as the right side of the page is more heavily colored. © 2016 Michelle L. Dean.

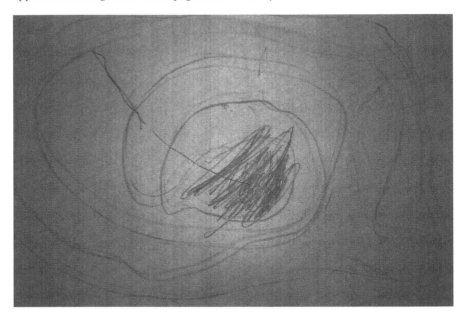

Figure 1.4 Controlled scribbling. Boy's drawing at 23 months old. © 2016 Michelle L. Dean.

when placed atop a trunk, they make some of the earliest depictions of trees along with the circle- or mandala-topped trunks. Hence, this is the time of naming the pictures, although the content of the image many not be recognizable, and the name is not always consistent. For example, Figure 1.5 shows a painting named a robot by the child, but it may be named something different when the child looks at it again at a later time because object constancy is not fully developed.

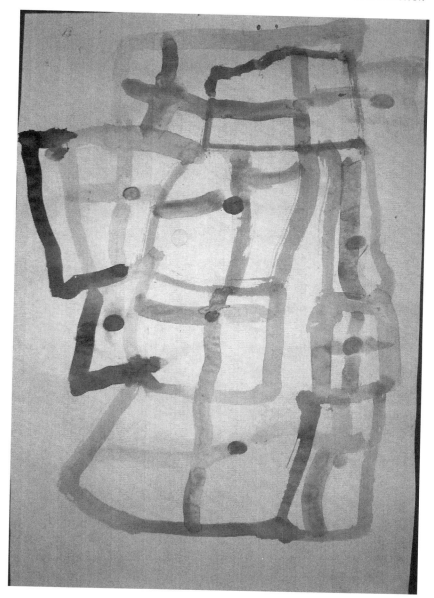

Figure 1.5 Named scribble, *The Robot*. © 2016 Michelle L. Dean.

Preschematic Stage

In the preschematic stage, the lines that had become edges begin to take recognizable forms. This is often seen starting around the age of 4 years. Colors show little relationship between objects because the form is most important. It is not uncommon for random or favorite colors to be used instead of more naturalistic colors. The use of space may appear haphazard, with objects floating on the

Figure 1.6 End stage preschematic stage drawing. © 2016 Michelle L. Dean.

page, and size can be rendered based on importance rather than realism. This can be an exciting time for artistic pursuits because it is the beginning of graphic communication, and the child may take great satisfaction in such communicating and sharing their images with others. There are recognizable forms (although they may be difficult to determine) by age 4, and by age 5, people, houses, and trees may be distinguished, as shown in Figure 1.6, which is a later stage image as demonstrated by a baseline. By age 6, the artwork may take on a clearly recognizable theme and purpose. Human drawings emerge from the circles, growing legs like tadpoles at first, and then additional appendages will follow with greater detail. By age 7, as children begin to move out of the preschematic stage into the schematic stage, a defined way of depicting certain objects emerges like a kind of shorthand, and drawings become less flexible.

Schematic Stage

Schema are highly individualized as the child moves into the schematic stage around the age of 7. During this time, artistic expressions offer windows into the child's private and rich imaginary world. The child draws with more meaning and uses consistent color for objects. A continuation of growing perception and awareness of the world is incorporated into the child's drawings and other artistic works. As other significant breakthroughs emerge, the child's newfound awareness blossoms from approximately the ages of 7 to 9 years. Some of these developments are the inclusion of a baseline, which can be seen as a foundation for objects such as trees and people to stand on. Grass is no longer randomly placed on the page but instead becomes the base or the support for trees and other pictorial elements. Multiple perspectives may be seen through the device of

X-ray vision, which is incorporated into drawings so that both the interior and exterior of buildings can be seen simultaneously. Sequence and storytelling with the pictures emerge and multiple pictures, as shown in Figures 1.7 and 1.8, may be used to tell a story like comics. The first image in this two-part drawing, a recreation of the original, begins with a castle, warriors, and knights as shown in Figure 1.7. The lines were rapidly drawn by a young boy describing the ensuing battle.

Figure 1.7 The Castle (top) is created in two images in order to provide sequence to the storytelling of a child's play. © 2016 Michelle L. Dean.

Figure 1.8 The Castle (bottom) is the second addition used to tell the story of the castle and the soldiers within. Age 6. © 2016 Michelle L. Dean.

Accompanied by sound, the child made quickly drawn bricks with a marker in a grid-like fashion. Upon filling the page, he used another piece of paper to draw the drawbridge and moat, shown in Figure 1.8, which were important to the play and telling of this particular story. As the child approaches the next stage of artistic development around the age of 9, the child employs greater flexibility in the schema to portray significance: there may be exaggerations of important parts, neglect or omission of unimportant or suppressed parts, and changes in symbols for significant parts of a figure or drawing.

Dawning of Realism

As they progress developmentally, children increasingly discover they are members of society and peer groups. They take greater interest and responsibility in their communities and in society. This stage lays the groundwork for working and cooperating with peers in adult life. They seek out greater peer interaction, and so their artistic development stage, the dawning of realism, also called the gang stage, is greatly influenced by their peers. During this time, color usage becomes rigid, and the color–object relationship remains consistent with greater sensitivity to color differences. The space usage moves from concrete to abstract, the single baseline becomes a plane, and objects may appear to recede into space while the skyline may extend to the horizon. Schema are no longer adequate, so those rigid forms give way to more personalized styles. As the child's body develops, they develop greater awareness to these changes, and this growth is reflected in their drawings, including differences between figures in clothing and gender characteristics. Peer feedback about drawing becomes increasingly important, and criticism is often taken to heart. The previously accepted convention of X-ray vision is now criticized as being unnatural and is rarely seen, unless utilized for a special application. Drawings become the result of careful visualization and observation as peers play an increasingly important role in the child's life.

Age of Reason or the Pseudo-Naturalistic Stage

Lowenfeld and Brittain (1987) reported the changes that occur as children reach early adolescence, 12–14 years old, such as their becoming more critical of themselves and their artistic abilities. This is called the age of reason or the pseudo-naturalistic stage. During this time, adolescents' drawings tend to become shorthand notations with decreasing spontaneous art activity. Details become increasingly important as their ability to focus on selected parts of the environment increases. There is a projection of non-literal, personal meaning into objects. When it comes to human representations, they pay closer attention to correct proportions and have greater awareness of joint and body actions and facial expressions. Drawings become more detailed and varied to express meaning. Cartooning is popular, and people in drawings now may be represented by less than the entire figure. As puberty sets in and the children's bodies are in the throes of hormonal and growth changes, their drawings often overemphasize sexual characteristics.

Period of Decision or Adolescent Art

The period of decision, or adolescent art, ages 14–17 years, includes conscious development of artistic skills, and most children have extended attention spans and are able to master any material. When the child is ready, perspective can be learned and utilized. Human representations continue to increase as their naturalistic attempts improve, utilizing greater awareness of proportions, actions, and visible details. They make imaginative use of figures for satire, including exaggeration of detail for emphasis and impact in communicating their ideas, thoughts, and feelings. Figures 1.9 and 1.10 illustrate this, showing an adolescent girl who was preparing for discharge from an eating disorder facility. The images depict a satirical view of how she felt as she prepared to leave the treatment facility and return home. Although this piece is a sculpture and not a drawing, many of the same developmental characteristics apply to three-dimensional works. In the front view, Figure 1.9, her bags are packed to leave. She appears to be sitting on a bench with luggage placed on both sides. However, in the back view, Figure 1.10, her "emotional baggage," including her body, is distorted, as the bench becomes a part of her body.

During our group discussion about her creation, she stated, "I will be bringing my baggage with me—my real bags of stuff and my emotional baggage that I will

Figure 1.9 Emotional Baggage (front). The sculpture depicts a satirical view of her "emotional bags" appearing one way from the front and another from the back (see Figure 1.10). © 2016 Michelle L. Dean.

Figure 1.10 Emotional Baggage (back). © 2016 Michelle L. Dean.

continue to work on in outpatient therapy." Her satire and wit are reflected in her ability to simultaneously represent multiple perspectives of how she felt.

Most adults' artistic skills remain at what is considered the developmental level of a 9- to 12-year-old unless they have further education in the arts. For young and old, the arts play a role in expressing internal realities such as thoughts and emotions, as well as being a way to record events and objects in the outer world or environment. The child's idea of art often combines the teaching methods and formulas passed down from one generation to the next in a chaotic collision. When well-meaning teachers coax young children to draw real-life objects, they may be stifling their efforts and the pride, pleasure, and confidence necessary for growth and sustaining the creative spirit (Kellogg & O'Dell, 1967). This is a missed opportunity, coupled with the unfortunate reality that, in many educational systems, the arts are considered extracurricular or "special" due to funding cuts and cultural bias. Thus, the arts have been relegated to something that only a few—the few who demonstrate "talent"—feel worthy to pursue into adulthood. This is a misguided thought with dire consequences, because the arts not only provide benefits to educational settings and outcomes but also hold the capacity to create unique experiences that are larger than the sum of their parts. As represented in Bloom's taxonomy of learning, shown in Figure 1.11, a higher order of learning incorporates analytic, evaluative, and creative thought (Anderson & Krathwohl, 2001).

The arts hold the ability to synthesize diverse knowledge, concepts, and ideals and give them voice or form. Art allows for organizing thoughts and actions, and mediating and regulating feelings. It improves inter- and intrapersonal awareness, conflict resolution, problem-solving skills, analytic skills, and the ability to synthesize complex ideas to create new outcomes (Arieti, 1976; Lowenfeld & Brittain, 1987; Wadeson, 1980). The arts provide a foundation for relating to the world around us and the relationship that we have with that space or environment

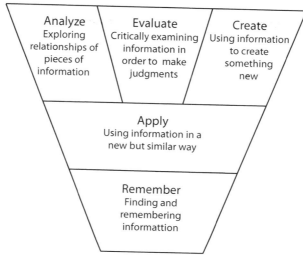

Figure 1.11 The cognitive process dimension of the revised version of Bloom's taxonomy as described by Anderson & Krathwohl (2001). This illustration depicts the belief that remembering is a prerequisite for understanding and that understanding is a prerequisite for application.

while considering the individual, familial, cultural, and archetypal. The arts are an engagement in intrinsic and extrinsic awareness unfolded into the art and the aesthetic in all things we create: the objects, technological inventions, and urban development that shape our families and communities.

What has gotten in the way of more individuals pursuing art as a natural means of knowing and expressing seems to be a culturally based valuing of technique and product over expression and process. Imagery, once at the core of psychology, is largely ignored. In its place, cognitive and behavioral schools of thought have become favored. Disturbingly, there is an amnesia regarding psychology's roots and core concepts with respect to the role of imagery that is not seen in other fields, which typically build on their earlier theories (Arieti, 1976; Hustvedt, 2011).

Additionally, there is often confusion about the distinction between what a picture is and what an image is. A picture is a representation of an object, idea, or place. It is created through perception and experience and relies on external senses (Arieti, 1976). In contrast, an image is an internal process that appears in the mind's eye; it is a representation that presents through dreams, daydreams, doodles, and other imaginative processes. Imagery evokes what is not present and enables us to recall emotional dispositions toward that absent object or person. Imagery forms the foundation of our inner reality, an essential part of human psychology, helping us to understand our world (Arieti, 1976). The arts in psychotherapy may be seen through two main lenses: philosophical and psychological. A brief explanation follows.

Philosophical and Psychological Considerations of Art

Originally, the psychology of art was concerned with the views of the artist and the percipient, or viewer. But according to Read (1966), art, which was often considered to include music and drama, was never specifically defined, and so, until comparatively recent times, discussions of art centered on beauty and the associated feelings of pleasure or displeasure. Much of how we come to understand the function of art and aesthetics and its role in humanity has grown out of the works of Plato and subsequent philosophers—Aristotle, Kant, Descartes, Hegel, Hume, and Nietzsche—as well as the founders of psychological thought—Freud and Jung. Discussions about aesthetics are rare in the practice of art psychotherapy, and as Rowland (2015) suggests, there is a *"perceived* 'gap' between art as conducted as part of institutionalized healing, or therapy, and art done by artists . . ." (p. 82). And although the artwork of some patients may not reflect the technical skill deemed culturally acceptable or desirable, it is no less worthy of discussion regarding its aesthetic properties and ability to express and elicit an emotional response from the viewer. A cultural insult has created a perceived special class of people called artists. And although we have, since the Romantic period of the 18th century, rejected the long-held preconception that art was to respect tradition (Rowland, 2015), this view has not come far enough nor is it inclusive enough. Those who do not fit the current cultural paradigm for artistic technique are often split off or judged unworthy of calling themselves *artists*. All humans have the inherent ability to express emotion and relate subjectively to art. This draws our discussion to aesthetics because, like many who shy away from the term *artist*, so too do art psychotherapists deny the value of aesthetics in the art of our patients, even though their works, like many of the Masters' works, provoke emotion and reaction. The disavowal of tradition in the arts has opened a quest for a new mythology of forms and their meanings (Rowland, 2015). These forms and meanings may be further explored through image and art in a psychotherapeutic context. Aesthetics are culturally bound, and within each time period and society there are different ideals. As can be seen in the aesthetic ideals of a pleasing body and those for certain types of art, preferences are shaped by the culture we live in and have changed over the centuries.

In our current Western culture, the arts have been relegated to a subordinate role, as have the founding ideals of psychology. The benefits of the arts, including educational, interpersonal, developmental, neurological, biological, and psychological, are minimized or denied (Hass-Cohen, 2003; Hass-Cohen & Carr, 2008; Kaplan, 2000) while the sciences are elevated. This schism within ourselves leads to a split that is projected outward, manifesting in devaluing cultural values and ideals. This is a turning away from the recognition that the sciences and the arts, while different, both offer redeeming and life-affirming attributes. Culture creates a lens through which all things are tinted. Historically, the roles of both artists and the scientists, when practiced at the highest levels, breach the confines of the blinding and potentially stifling norms. Both art and science can lead us to new perspectives, imagination, and emergent qualities. In the current one-sided valuing of science but not art, or blindness, I am reminded of Plato's *Allegory of the Cave*.

Plato's Allegory of the Cave

Originally, *imagination* referred to direct perception rather than fantasies conjured up in our minds. For the early philosophers, imagination occupied a middle ground between body and intellect. Bound with emotion and memory, it included the conscious forms of image, narrative, and stories, all vital to our subjective mental landscape.

The Greek philosopher Plato (c. 423–347 BCE) wrote *The Republic* (Plato, 1974), which attempts to articulate how we experience the forms or ideas of the material world known through sensation, as well as our ability to transcend the mundane aspects of human life or the "world of the being." In his *Allegory of the Cave*, Plato grappled with the idea of *"image and its relation to self and reality"* (Kugler, 2008, p. 78). It is through engagement with something beyond our complete understanding, like the elusive ideal of a form or something greater than ourselves and our senses, which is often referred to as the divine or as the creative muse. In the "world of the becoming," things are said to exist in our material world only because they take on forms with actual shapes and structures. And true insight into these forms occurs only when we recognize the ideal form that shapes the structure (Solomon, 1989) or the ideal as it is manifested in its symbolic form. Plato's ideas about beauty and aesthetics also inform psychological process and function; psychology and art are not physical sciences but bring an epistemological and phenomenological lens that provides understanding of the individual psyche and its relationship to symbolic function and form.

In the *Allegory of the Cave*, Plato explored ideas about forms, education, and enlightenment with respect to human nature by providing an example of a group of prisoners who had been chained to a wall all their lives. Across from them was another blank wall. Behind them was a raised walkway where people passed by carrying vessels, puppets, and other items. And beyond the people on the walkway was a fire. The shadows, cast by the objects of the people walking by, were accompanied by the echoes of their voices. The chained individuals came to know and understand their environment through the associations with the shadows and echoes, because they presumably knew no other. The shadows spoke the only kind of truth about the actual objects the prisoners could know. The shadows, cast by the light of the fire, mimicked the actual forms, including distortions and a mix of associations, but they were not the objects themselves, and thus the prisoners constructed a limited conception of them.

The understanding we can take from this illustration as it relates to art and psychological process is about what the dancing shadows represent and what we know about our own experience. Plato illustrated that we are all such prisoners, susceptible to distortions and associations and often unable to see beyond our own experiences. Because we must use our own eyes to see, we can never be fully outside of our experience; we are never truly objective about our own experiences. We understand the forms in our lives as they are cast though our perception, which is colored and distorted by experience, circumstance, and belief. They are mere copies, secondary reflections.

Plato went on to describe the experience of a freed individual, showing us what happened when he was dragged to the surface and the light of the sun. As his eyes adjusted, he was temporarily blinded by the brightness of the light. Eventually, he was able to look upon objects on the surface and was able to know them as substance or, in Latin, *materia*. Accordingly, the freed man would eventually be able to look directly at the sun and, thus, be able to reason about it. In the *Allegory*, Socrates' student Plato stated that the freed prisoner would believe his new perception to be superior to that of the still-chained prisoners, and thus, he would take pity on them and attempt to free them as well. But the prisoners, upon hearing about the journey of the freed man, would think he had been harmed and would most likely resist a similar fate. Plato even went so far as to predict that the chained prisoners would therefore kill anyone who attempted to drag them out of the cave and challenge their worldview.

The implications of this are profound as they relate to working with individuals who do not wish to see or are unable to see a worldview that may be different from their own. The unconscious process of resistance to or denial of another worldview might account for numerous feuds in couples and misunderstandings among coworkers. It may also contribute to political strife and countless skirmishes and devastating wars. It is really empathy for their perspectives that the prisoners needed because, from their vantage point, they believed real harm would befall them if they left the cave.

We can never fully see the fire or the light; our position as prisoners, bound by our earthly domain does not permit a direct gaze. This light is often compared to the divine or a source that is outside of our knowing. In psychological terms, the light blinds when looked upon directly. The divine is the source of the illumination or the muse of the creative process. It is a part of a transcendent experience, taking one outside of ordinary mundane experience into a greater awareness or experience, able to see from a different perspective. The interpretation of the ascension to the place of light can be viewed as the journey upward into the intellectual world (Goldblatt & Brown, 2011):

> . . . that in the world of knowledge the idea of good appears last of all, and is only seen with effort; and when seen, is also inferred to be the universal author of all things beautiful and right, parent of light and of the lord of the light this visible world, and the immediate source of reason and truth in the intellectual; and that this is the power upon which he who would act rationally either in public or private life must have his eye fixed [p. 91].

Further, "Images, Plato suggests, are like a 'drug' (a *pharmakon*) which may serve either as a remedy or a poison" (Kugler, 2008, p. 79). The image as a remedy provides a permanent record for posterity (Wadeson, 1980). An image may be seen as a poison when we are deceived and believe a copy, such as when an exacting painting like a *trompe l'oeil*, designed to fool the eye, is thought to be the original or when an image becomes an idol. For Plato, exterior reproductions of the external world are not first-principle or *a priori* archetypes or eternal images, but are all mere copies.

The present work provides scholars much material for philosophical and political debate regarding human ignorance about truth and those unwilling to see the truth and their ease of being manipulated. This discussion includes Plato's writings and a centuries-long debate about questions faced by philosophers of aesthetics, which are as challenging and intractable as the eternal questions faced by metaphysics, ethics, and epistemology.

Philosophy of Aesthetics

Two philosophical viewpoints that grapple with art and aesthetics are the epistemological and metaphysical standpoints. Epistemology is concerned with the origins of nature and the kinds and limits of human knowledge. It involves attempts to answer questions such as these (Stanford, 2005):

> How we are to understand the concept of justification? What makes justified beliefs justified? Is justification internal or external to one's own mind? Understood more broadly, epistemology is about issues having to do with the creation and dissemination of knowledge in particular areas of inquiry [n.p.].

Metaphysics is the branch of philosophy concerned with abstract thought or subjects, like existence, causality, or truth, and is incorporeal and thus immune from empirical testing. There are two types of inquiry in metaphysics. The first aims to be the most general investigation possible into the nature of reality: Are there principles applicable to everything that is real, to all that is? The second type of inquiry seeks to uncover what is ultimately real, frequently offering answers in sharp contrast to our everyday experience of the world. Understood in terms of these two questions, metaphysics is very closely related to ontology, which involves both "What is existence (being)?" and "What (fundamentally distinct) types of things exist?" (Craig, 1998). Metaphysics is now considered closely related to the philosophy of science because it is greatly concerned with the discovery of general laws and entities.

Plato

Plato minimized the arts and literature, even the work of Homer, because he considered the arts an imitation of life and not its real, divine nature, similar to Jung's conception of archetype. Something being pure in form means it is an exemplar of itself and not of anything else (Duignan, 2010). Plato was against the use of the arts and literature in education because they can be used to disseminate information and shape public opinion (Cooper, Lamarque, & Sartwell, 1997). The use of imagery can be a powerful tool to shape public opinion and change behaviors as seen in marketing and sales campaigns, and as Plato stated, "An image-maker, a representer, understands only appearance, while reality is beyond him" (Cooper et al., 1997, p. 19). Cooper, Lamarque, and Sartwell (1997) countered Plato's equating of illusory painting to sorcery and trickery: "Now, methods have evolved of combating this—measuring, counting, and weighing are the most elegant of them—and consequently of ending the reign within us of apparent size, number, and weight, and replacing them with something which calculates and measures, or even weighs" (p. 21). Plato's student Aristotle (384–322 BCE) argued against this Manichaeism dualism, a basic doctrine of conflict between light and dark and between reason and passion, and created his own doctrine called hylomorphism, where every physical object comprises two principles, an unchanging prime matter and a form deprived of actuality with every substantial change of the object. "Aristotle is the first philosopher on record to appreciate the distinctive functions of art, the manner in which encountered or experienced, and the value it can have independent of straightforwardly moral and political goals" (Cooper et al., 1997, p. 29). Aristotle's psychology, the study of soul, rejects Plato's idea that emotion is a distraction and states instead it would be "*ir*rational not to feel anger or shame. . . . Mature understanding and mature emotional sensitivity are inseparable ingredients in the good life of a person. And art can contribute to both" (Cooper et al., 1997, p. 30).

Aristotle

Aristotle was a Greek philosopher and scientist and is considered one of the greatest intellectual figures in Western history (Duignan, 2010). Art, for Aristotle, was not just a form of imitation but also a representation that provides understanding on several levels. Although Aristotle's system makes room for form as Plato described, his conception of form is significantly different. He viewed a particular thing as not separate from the thing itself because any form is a kind of form of itself (Duignan, 2010). Aristotle placed the value of a piece of art in our relationship with its associations of intellectual understanding and emotional resonance, and not in its construction, as described in his text *Poetics*.

As Kugler (2008) pointed out, for Aristotle, images are intermediaries, a bridge between inner and outer realties, between the inner world of the mind and the outer world of a material world that lies between sensation and reason. He stated that neither Plato nor Aristotle viewed psychic images as original sources of images but as secondhand reflections from processes, and that they saw them as imitation and reproduction and not of creation. The metaphysical order that has followed the duality of Plato and Aristotle contains "certain primordial dualities realities: inner/outer, mind/body, reason/sensation, and spirit/matter. Image is always located *between* the dualities" (Kugler, 2008, p. 80).

Medieval Period

The medieval view of aesthetics deepened the distrust of images. Fueled by the synthesis of Hellenic ontology and Biblical theology, the medieval philosophical view considered images as secondary copies and condemned them for undermining divine creation (Kugler, 2008). During the medieval period, from the 5th to the 15th century in Europe, after the fall of the Roman Empire, renewed interest in alchemical processes began to emerge. Alchemy was a mixture of science, philosophy, and mysticism, and it was very much considered an art.

The Arts and Alchemy

Due to their broad theoretical foundations, alchemists referred to themselves as philosophers and described their work as art. "Although the alchemical concept of art is derived from Aristotle's *téchne*, and refers generally to skill in both theoretical and practical matters, its similarity to the extended concepts in art of art in the modern age are unmistakable" (Roob, 2006, p. 14). Today, alchemy is considered by most as the attempt to transmute base metals into silver or gold by distilling impurities and altering their properties through various processes. As "the so-called *opus alchymicum*, besides being the founders of modern chemistry, the alchemists developed a symbolic kind of chemistry, aimed at producing the gold of mystical illumination" (Fabricius, 1976, back matter). It is believed the founding father was Theophrastus Bombastus von Hohenheim, known as Paracelsus (1493–1541), whose "empirical study of nature takes place against a visionary and mystical background" (Roob, 2006, p. 14). It was Paracelsus's belief that "medicine is not only a science; it is also an art. It does not consist of compounding pills and plasters; it deals with the very processes of life, which must be understood before they may be guided" (Paracelsus, n.d.). This idea continues to hold relevance today in psychotherapeutic contexts because often the belief is that treatment is best done with pills, instead of addressing psychological and social issues (Wampold, 2001).

According to Fabricius (1976), "This belief [to form mystical illumination] derives from the natural philosophy of the Hellenistic alchemists, basing their theory of nature on Aristotle, they assumed the material world was a *prima material*, or a prime, chaotic matter, which might only come into actual existence if impressed out of 'form' " (p. 8). The alchemist system of rigorous study consisted of symbols, rituals, doctrines, and procedures, which were undertaken even by the likes of Sir Isaac Newton and were kept with paramount secrecy until the practice fell out of favor in the 17th century. This methodology was believed to transform chaos into form, emerging from the four elements: fire, air, water, and earth. Blending these "simple bodies" of the prime matter in certain proportions, one would succeed in creating the limitless varieties of life. Thus transmutation would occur.

And while many of the prodigious writings included instructions about manufacturing pharmaceuticals and base metals, they also sought a spiritual pursuit of inner purification or spiritual gold. This spiritual gold is often confused with the idea that the *prima material* has a physical, tangible form. And thus, gold metal was deduced to be the optimum but elusive outcome. What is often overlooked about this alchemical process is the pursuit of spiritual gold, an attainment that would be larger than it parts because it relates to psychological function. This confusion is understandable due to the logical and possessive stance of the Western cultural view, which values matter over spirit. It is the spirit, or expression of the psyche, that may be found in image. Bruno, a 16th-century philosopher, revised the role of image as reproductive and instead suggested "that human imaging was the source of thought itself!" (Kugler, 2008, p. 81). His ideals shifted the creative force from the divine to within the human form, moving the source of knowing through images from an external to an inner process. These ideas were considered heresy at the time. Bruno was condemned for "placing imaging at the center of creativity and the human condition and was burned at the stake. Several more centuries would need to pass before it would be safe to introduce into mainstream Western thought the idea of imaging as central to creativity and the human condition" (Kugler, 2008, p. 82). And still, the idea that value may be found in the immaterial, spiritual, or psychic reality continues to be mostly relegated to a subordinate role within current culture. This is true even in psychological work in which external behaviors and functions are evaluated and given priority over internal awareness, intuitiveness, and process. The parallels between art and alchemy are undeniable. Often, the art product, the tangible form of a piece, is valued over the spiritual and transformative process.

Much of the influence of seeking tangible objectification of material has had to do with the available tools or measuring instruments and the prevailing ideals that have developed and become dominant over time. The idea that it is real only if it can be measured has plagued our thinking, discrediting other modes of experience and reality. Some of the famous early examples against this thinking were of Galileo and Copernicus and their discoveries of the universe. But because the tools did not exist to prove their theories about the forms and orbits of the universe, their views were met with much controversy, and many such thinkers were tried and even put to death for heresy. Only now can we confirm through new instrumentation and tools that the earlier observations of the movements of the celestial systems in the heavens were correct. Scientists are commonly artists, and they share the qualities of inquisitiveness, rigorous study, and the ability to express new ideals or paradigms. Faith, intuition, and the ability to suspend reality and currently accepted thought, coupled with rigorous study, guide these artist–scientists. In many ways, the skills of the artist–scientist are greatly needed for psychological processes because the tools and instrumentation to look at the inward constellations of the psyche do not yet exist, although the physical manifestation of the psyche can be seen in image and art.

The development of the neurological and psychological fields from the medical model met a similar fate. Before Cartesian measures or mechanized science for understanding the body and its functions, medicine was considered an integrated field. Physicians looked to realign the humors and believed there was integration among the bowels, the appearance of the tongue, the breath, and disease. Although practicing recalibration of the humors has fallen out of favor due to the preference for specific tools for specific systems, vestiges of the holistic approach remain in our modern psychological practices. This preference for specific tools is, in part, why we have specialties to treat our gastrointestinal, cardiac, and urological maladies, but rarely does a physician treat them by carefully considering the interconnectedness of the systems. Psychology, like medicine in many regards, has followed a path of separateness and treating the mind and body like objects rather than living processes. "One of the central concepts which has contributed largely to the existence of problems in contemporary medicine has been the continued acceptance of the Cartesian notion of mankind as a composite dualism: the separation of mind and body" (Gold, 1985, p. 664). The separation of cognitive or behavioral processes from other aspects of being human has skewed the priority in psychology from the whole to the parts. Psychological studies have not been immune to the pressure to view suffering as an object or mechanism of the mind, promoting patients as objects rather than complex beings who are "more realistically envisaged as multiphasic, experiential beings of finite freedom" (Gold, 1985, p. 664). Gold (1985) continues:

> It should now be clear that the predominantly phenomenological view of the "lived-body" is that it is not a passive, impersonal object either fit to be neglected or to be simply handed over to a health professional in times of functional impairment. It is, most essentially, the centre of one's experiences, moods, expressions and thoughts: the very nexus of intentionality. This intentionality represents a heightened awareness of the body in health. Thus prevention of ill health through increased personal (and even social) responsibility, together with an encouragement for self-help maintenance, can only be truly effective by recognizing the "lived-body" model [p. 665].

It is through the symbol and image that a living process, a lived-body model, is very much alive. The symbol takes on the contextual meanings of individual and cultural significance.

Symbol Formation

Perhaps the most notable aspect of a symbol is its ability to bridge the inner and outer experiences, representing a synthesis or emergent quality of the individual and the collective by providing a psychic bridge for expression and reflection. We are influenced by internal experiences and are affected by external events. This flux is constant. Artists have long played a role in traversing the terrain of individual and collective experiences, and in spiritual practice and function. The symbol may be seen as a manifestation of the soul presented as a kind of threshold leading to a new dimension of discovery (Ronnberg & Martin, 2010). A symbol opens a door, shedding light on and at times obscuring the view of a polyvalent perspective of self, culture, and history. As Paul Klee said, "Art doesn't reproduce the visible. It renders it visible" (as cited in Ronnberg & Martin, 2010, p. 6).

Through exploration of the symbol of the dragon, the following description may provide an understanding of how a symbol is manifested in its specificities. It may also illuminate how individual and cultural ideas have changed our relationship with our own creative forces as well as how powers reflect the ontological aspects of our nature of being and existence leading to assaults on humankind.

A Study of Dragons

The dragon is perhaps one of the most nebulous, complex, and ambivalent animals that inhabit the terrain of the imagination (Hargreaves, 2009). It is a symbol having different incarnations that I will refer to throughout this text, as it manifests in cultural ideas, drawing assessments, and children's art. It permeates our imagination, fables, and mythologies, and whether it is manifested in a work of art, a storybook, or cinema, the dragon lives on infamously. An explanation of its form is given in this section for later reference in subsequent chapters. The dragon makes significant appearances in the myths and the tales of travelers. From its iconic inclusion in tombs of Egyptian kings to its demarcation of unknown territories on explorer maps—*Here Be Dragons!*—its image is closely intertwined with that of the snake or serpent, appearing in religion, alchemy, heraldry, and medicine throughout cultures and histories, dating from the primitive, classical, and medieval periods, and present in both occidental and oriental mythologies. The dragon and its incarnations are associated with the powers of the earth, both good and bad. It carries a duality that is ever present, and it is an excellent example of how image and culture attribute different meanings and relationships, depending on time, place, and context.

The dragon derives its name from *drakon* and *draco* in the Greek and Roman Empires to describe a large snake. It "signifies aliveness, gleaming light and the eye that flashes fire and sees keenly, like the figurative 'eye' of the unconscious" (Ronnberg & Martin, 2010, p. 704). *Drakon* could also be used to describe a flying creature, and like many Chinese dragons, they did not need wings to achieve flight and transcend a terrestrial existence. In some cultures, the dragon had legs, whereas in others, it was legless; it sometimes shared bestial qualities with other animals, sprouted one or more heads of different creatures, and became the multi-headed Hydra or the semi-divine, semi-human Naga of Southeast Asia. The dragon has been associated with fertility and the feminine, such as in Egyptian hieroglyphics where the term *goddess* is expressed with the image of the cobra. The Egyptian fertility goddess, Isis, who had the face of a beautiful woman and the body of a serpent, has evolved over time and been appropriated into other cultures. Cultures that are subsumed into others either appropriate the early symbols or demonize them. In Christian cultures, in *The Garden of Eden*, discussed further in Chapter 3, the serpent can been seen wrapped around the Tree of Knowledge well into the Middle Ages. He and other mermaid-like creatures are known as draconiopides. Images and incarnations of the dragon include worms, the wyvern, the half-formed dragon, and the basilisk, to name only a few. The iconography is so prevalent that the dragon is considered archetypal.

Jung believed the archaic or primordial types of universal images have existed since the remotest times. They are part of the contents of the collective unconscious and known as archetypes (CW 9[1]:5; CW 9[1]:4). Their origin can be explained by assuming them to be deposits of the constantly repeated experiences of humanity (CW 7:109). One archetype refers to the *Imago Dei* (God-image) in man. Like an old watercourse along which the water of life has flowed for centuries, digging a deep channel for itself (CW 10:395) and switching back on itself across the landscape of time and humanity, leaving vestiges as the river changes course like a snake sheds its skin, the image reappears throughout cultures and times, emerging with a new but familiar cloak. An archetype is like the primordial river Heraclitus refers to when he says, "Just as the river where I step is not the same, and is, so I am as I am not" (Heraclitus, 2001, p. 51).

The most powerful ideas in history go back to archetypes. This is particularly true of religious ideas, but the central concepts of science, philosophy, and ethics are no exception to this rule. In their present form, they are conscious applications to variants of archetypal ideas. It is the function of consciousness not only to recognize and assimilate the external world through the gateway of the senses but also to translate into visible reality the world within us (CW 8:342). It is through the symbolic process that the inner world can be expressed and understood and likewise the external world assimilated. Art, like religion or spiritual practice, expresses both the divine and the mundane. It seeks to represent the invisible by means of the visible (Eliade, 1961). It is the carrier, or the vehicle, for both emergent and constant qualities, including the duality that exists in all, and has many examples, the mythology of the dragon being but one of them.

The staff of Hermes, intertwined with dual snakeheads, carries both poison and antidote. The winged staff, called the caduceus, is also the staff given to medicine as a symbol due to the great distances doctors had to travel to help their patients. The dragon's dually intertwined, cyclical powers are synonymous with the Ouroboros, shown in Figure 1.12, the ancient serpent who has both destructive and creative properties. The Ouroboros forms a mandala, a symbol of self and humanity. It symbolizes the ideals of the cyclic property of life and primordial unity. As it forms a circle, it devours its own tail, providing the fertility for

Figure 1.12 Michel Maier (17th century). *Alchemical Illustration from Atalante Fugitive: A Dragon Devouring Its Tail* (1618). Location: Bibliotheque de l'Arsenal, Paris, France. Credit: Snark/Art Resource, NY.

its growth process. It is associated with alchemical processes and psychological function in its ability to heat up and cool down or destroy and regenerate. And just as for the Ouroboros, this duality of good and evil, the creative and destructive powers, and the unity that this ebbing and flowing homeostasis forms are a constant in psychological wellness and in creative process. Unfortunately, the beneficial nature of the destructive aspect of creativity is often overlooked, marginalized, or even demonized. These are the result of cultural values at work that are sometimes polarizing. For example, the pagan dragon became demonized as Christianity rejected the serpent as a symbol for goddess, fertility, and earth, but it remains in Christian iconography. As I describe in greater detail in Chapter 3 when I discuss the serpent in *The Garden of Eden* as it relates to the Draw a Person Picking an Apple from a Tree (PPAT) assessment, the serpent is associated with Lucifer, the devil, or a demon.

In the infamous Medusa and Perseus myth, Medusa is an incarnation of a personified dragon, and her story is similar to those of a host of other dragon tamers and slayers who attempt to defeat or kill the dragon. Daimon is a projected aspect of the destructive force within all of us. Religion has been used to demonize and reject these aspects in ourselves and their projections onto the Other, as seen in the image of the imprisonment of St. Margaret of Antioch, shown in Figure 1.13.

Figure 1.13 Jean Bourdichon (c. 1457–1521). *Saint Margaret and the Dragon. Grandes Heures d'Anne de Bretagne. Horae ad usum romanum* (c. 1500–1508). Parchment. Location: Bibliothèque Nationale de France (BnF), Paris, France. Credit: © BnF, Dist. RMN-Grand Palais/Art Resource, NY.

During the Reformation and Counter-Reformation in the 16th and 17th centuries, two versions were told of how Christianity saved St. Margaret from a smitten and tortuous governor and would-be suitor. In one, due to her rejection of his advances, she was thrown in a tower and ordered tortured. While she was a prisoner, she prayed that the devouring dragon would be vanquished at the sign of the cross. In the other version of her story, the shape-shifting fiend (the governor) in the form of a frightful dragon swallowed her, but when she made the sign of the cross, his belly broke open and she emerged without harm. The image captures symbolically how she was able to overcome through Christianity. As represented in her image, her devotedness to the cross is conveyed in her placement of her dominant right foot on the dragon's neck, welding him into submission while simultaneously cracking him open through his belly (or being reborn though the dragon) without further consideration to his presence or meaning, other than being evil.

In some Eastern cultures, attributes of the dragon depict a converse meaning. "The Chinese dragon, for example, is connected with the ruler, whereas in the West the dragon often appears in battle with the hero" (Moon, 1997, p. xv). Perhaps the most frequently associated image with dragon slayers is that of St. George, who is tasked with slaying the mighty beast, usually while a damsel, hands clasped in supplication, looks on helplessly in the near background, as shown in Figure 1.14. This story is found in Jacobus de Voragine's medieval *Golden Legend*, which describes the saints and their deeds. The evolution of myths about dragons from lore to fairytales is a natural one. Laden with similar

Figure 1.14 Birket Foster. *St. George and the Dragon* (1930s). Credit: HIP/Art Resource, NY.

imagery, the idea of conquering or slaying the beast that resides in our environment, in another, or within ourselves is a captivating universal mythology. Whether the story told is of Prince Charming or other popular cultural stories where good over evil presides, it presents an archetypal image, in which context and culture are imbued with nuance. The dragon is further discussed in Chapter 8 as it pertains to a recurring motif a child used in the creation of a series of clay figures representing the many facets of her life, including representations of her tumultuous family situation in which she struggled with parental divorce and the death of a loved one, as well as grappling with wish fulfillment through fantasy.

As Kalshed (1996) described in his book *The Inner World of Trauma*, the demon or daimon relates to *diabolical* with the Greek roots *dia* (across) and *ballein* (to throw across or apart). And *Diabolos* means the Devil (i.e., he who crosses, thwarts, disintegrates, or dissociates). *Symbolic* comes from *Sym-ballein*, which means "to throw together." Diamond (1996) is clear in differentiating the *daimonic*, which holds the potential for creative as well as destructive pursuits, from the *demonic*, which holds only the negative destructive forces. Like the creative and destructive forces, the throwing apart and throwing together are essential to psychological life, and when optimally balanced though always in flux, they characterize the homeostatic processes of the psyche's self-regulation. These meditative processes are especially active at the transitional interface or threshold between the psyche and outer reality. It is here at the threshold or transitional space that defense is necessary and symbolic formation is possible (Winnicott, 1971). Significant to the study of creativity and psychological process, the idea of holding both the creative and destructive poles includes additional definitions for daimonic, such as befitting a demon, fiendish, motivated by a spiritual force or genius, and inspired. The unrest that exists in us all forces us into the unknown and leads us to self-destruction or self-discovery. It is also the journey and transition from innocence to experience. It is the place where light and dark meet—a threshold and an ability to traverse it.

The journey from innocence to experience is a part of the archetypal hero's journey and is a topic older than literature itself. The term *daimonic*, which originated with the Greeks, subsequently became the focus of the English Romantic movement in the 18th and 19th centuries. With this culturally significant tie, one can see how the dragon and the daimon have become coiled together but with serious ramifications for Western ideals, most notably in regards to psychological function, the role of women, and ecological ramifications. Shifting the prevailing associations of the serpent from a goddess, earth, mother framework to the misunderstood term of the daimon, replacing it with a demon in need of slaying and triumphing over, leads to some seismic shifts in cultural ideals. The hero's journey and the internalized daimon or evil forces proliferate some of our most cherished popular-culture art, literature, and film. The hero is most often a solitary, innocent character and many times arrogant, but under the mask of his mundane life, he harbors an unconscious desire toward corruption and destruction. He may be reluctantly chosen to achieve some feat or correct some wrong. An event, either external or internal, leads the character toward some type of isolation where he is forced to confront his daimons. These can readily be seen in such contemporary stories as *Star Wars* and *The Lord of the Rings* trilogy and also plays out in our lives and the lives of our patients. This isolation and destruction is not always perceptible. The arts allow us to more clearly focus on those daimons, which may lead to self-demise but hold the potential for regenerative creative forces as well.

Figure 1.15 John Singer Sargent (1856–1925). *Perseus on Pegasus Slaying Medusa* (1922–25). Oil on canvas. 137 × 125 in. Photograph © 2016 Museum of Fine Arts, Boston.

I will close this section with one more myth, which contains aspects of the vilified serpent and may be used to beautifully illuminate the role of art in psychological processes. It is the myth of the infamous Medusa and Perseus. Figure 1.15 shows John Singer Sargent's rendering of this epic tale. Medusa was the only one of the three Gorgons to be subject to mortality. Poseidon, enamored by Medusa, sought her favors in the Temple of Minerva. Minerva, upon learning of this profane deed, punished Medusa by turning her beautiful tresses into serpents, her appearance turning anyone who would gaze upon her to stone. Perseus, aided by Athena's gifts of a helmet, shield, and winged-sandals, set about to slay the dreaded Medusa, who in the myth held the aspects of the repulsive Other. It was only through the use of the shield as a mirror that Perseus succeeded in slaying Medusa by decapitating her. When her blood fell into the sea, it was said that the winged horse Pegasus and the love-child of Medusa and Poseidon, Chrysaor, were born.

In the same way that Perseus used Athena's shield as a mirror, reflecting Medusa's whereabouts in order to slay her (Edinger, 2008), so too does the imagery in art aid in seeing powerful and potentially dangerous psychic contents in a manner that makes them more palatable. Myths, like art, hold a mirror up to our external and internal nature in order to reconcile the waking consciousness and the *mysterium tremendum et fascinans*, the awe-inspiring mystery of the universe (Campbell, 1968). Those who look directly at the raw energy of the archetype are consumed by it or, like those who gaze upon Medusa, are turned to stone, frozen, and experience death—a physical or psychological death. In other words, they are likely to be drawn back into the space of the fantasizing, a dissociative state, or the *demonic*, and thus, show destructive symptoms only, such as addiction, in order to escape or numb its painful effects. Athena's shield not only possesses a reflective or imaging property, providing a seeing dimension to the otherwise unapproachable or unsavory, but also remains a shield, providing protection and a boundary. The shield, like the artwork in a therapy session, assists the patient in seeing the repulsive or unmetabolized aspects of self for which a direct gaze is not possible (discussed further in the chapters addressing trauma). As in the case of individuals struggling with addiction issues, so often there is a denial or a minimizing of the destructive effects the substances have not only on their health but also in their life and relationships. The slaying of the dragon, or eviscerating parts of oneself through dissociation, drugs, or other means, reenacts the archetypal mythology of the vilifying daimon, rejecting it as Other. This happens not only within individuals but also in the relations of families, communities, and nations. And therefore, great works of art and literature are riddled with representations of such conflict, such as the Montagues' and Capulets' feud in Shakespeare's *Romeo and Juliet*, where vilifying the daimon, with both its creative and destructive forces, is projected as the Other without consideration of the potent creative force that lies within all.

Conversely, by befriending aspects of self that have become demonized, individuals who have manifested symptomatic and destructive behaviors, thoughts, and conflicts may come to decrease self-hatred and thus integrate aspects of self that were formerly symbolized through symptoms: emotional, physical, and spiritual. By inviting these demonized and destructive aspects of self to present themselves as images through the engagement of art in a psychotherapeutic process, a voice is provided where there often was none. The art bridges; it provides a way of holding the duality and polarities, joining them on a continuum.

The dragon symbol is a way to reunite the earth, goddess, mother, and shapeshifting evil found in the serpent. It restores unity and creates the regulating powers found in the hermetically sealed vessel we call ourselves. This can be seen in Figure 1.16, which shows the *Splendor Solis* (*The Sun's Splendour*) of Salomon Trismosin, a 16th-century German alchemist. In this illustration, the putto figure in the hermetically sealed vessel heats up the serpent with the bellows while simultaneously cooling him with drops of water, or in some accounts blood from a flask. The dragon's wings produce vapor as it fires up the "primaterial" and feeds the universal spirit, the spirit of all things (Roob, 2006). This sealed vessel may be seen as representing the self, sealed within its own confines. It gives insight into the regulating and fluctuating process of heating up and cooling off necessary for psychological life—the creative and the destructive. The vessel is suspended in the mundane existence of life as depicted by the town's folk in the background. On the left is the portal of death through which the raw material of earth must pass (Roob, 2006). In this illustration, as in our own lives,

Figure 1.16 Artist attributed to the School of Nuremberg. *Saturn—Animation of the Dragon.* Illuminated page from *Splendor Solis: 7 Treatises on the Philosopher's Stone* (c. 1531–1532). Parchment. Inv. 78 D 3 fol. 21 recto. Photo: Jörg P. Anders/Art Resource, NY. Location: Kupferstichkabinett, Staatliche Museen, Berlin, Germany.

the inner world and outer world exist in tandem. The shared frame is significant and is not typical in current Western culture, where much focus is placed on the external and daily life events, and very little attention is given to the inner world, the world of the psyche, the Image, whether it comes to us by way of dreams or art. As art psychotherapists, patients, and culture, this means "cultivating new skills and enlarging our scientific horizons so that there is room for the creativity that is a part of our everyday experience of living" (Goodwin, 2007, p. 31). Cultivating scientific investigations that create room for the interior is essential. It may be said that Jung was interested in the image-rich world of alchemy and its chemical workings as a kind of scientific projection of psychological development (Roob, 2006).

Kant

Kant (1724–1804) was a German philosopher who is known as the father of modern aesthetics because of his belief that imaging was an indispensible precondition of all knowledge (Kugler, 2008). Kant's work dealt with aesthetics and teleology, and he felt there could not be a science of the beautiful. In *Critique of Aesthetic Judgment*, he asserts it is the combination of subjective status with the universality that makes judgments of taste what they are (Schaper, 1992). "To anyone who admits that in addition to cognitive judgments and moral appraisals, and over and above expressions of likes and dislikes about which no disputes can arise, there are also judgments which cannot be verified but which nevertheless lay claim to the agreement if other subjects of experience" (Schaper, 1992, p. 371). What was believed to separate taste from other kinds of judgment is the inseparable feeling of pleasure. Kant wrote about nature as a *beautiful thing* and the beauty of art as a *beautiful representation of a thing* (Schaper, 1992). Where he felt art had superior abilities was in its usefulness to depict things considered displeasing, disturbing, or ugly in nature, such as diseases, the devastations of war, and other undesirable events or experiences. This idea of the usefulness of depicting the *evils* of the world may relate to the usefulness of the arts for people who suffer from mental illnesses.

Freud and Jung: The Origins of Depth Psychology

The field of depth psychology originated with the work of Carl Jung and Sigmund Freud, who both cited the importance of the unconscious and what lies below everyday consciousness. Expressed through the arts and literature of different cultures and through individual and collective dreams, imagery, and symptoms, the psychic reality is revealed. Core to the belief is the importance of image, art, and metaphor as they are expressed in personal and cultural representations. Although both Freud and Jung postulated theories about the structure of image, including dreams and fantasies and their effects on the individual, there are significant differences in the theories they put forth. Freud dealt with the images of his patients, such as their fantasies, but he never embraced the idea of them depicting their fantasies through drawing their dreams. Jung "questioned the reductive and negative aspect of Freud's approach and chose a broader interpretation of the unconscious as being both collective and personal" (Naumberg, 1987, p. 21). Jung felt images were central because they manifested personal and collective meaning as seen through the archetype, a collective repository of knowing. To paint what we see before us is a different art from painting what we see within us (CW 16:106). Jung's foundational discovery was that basic symbols have a universal nature, and they recur in different epochs of human history and civilizations that are otherwise unrelated to each other; he said these arose from the collective unconscious (Bach, 1990), shared structures of the unconscious mind. The collective unconscious, with its mythic qualities, influence individuals through experience and symbolic expression, which are cloaked with meaning. Jung believed in the process of engaging images, the spontaneous manifestations of the collective unconscious, so he undertook his own examination, which resulted in the book now known as *The Red Book*. In it, he described, "The years, of which I have spoken to you when I pursued my inner images, were the most important times of my life" (as cited in Shamdasani, 2009, p. vii). Freud believed there are schemata, such as the Oedipus complex and its world of desire, whereas Jung described the structure of images as archetypes, and that it is within the Image that the world unfolds as experience, psyche, and psychic reality, not always as a thing but as "a world of image-as-such" (Kugler, 2008, p. 77).

Defining Art Psychotherapy

In order to clarify terms, a brief look at etymology may be helpful. *Psychology* derives from the Greek word *psych* meaning "soul" and *logos* meaning "logic," "word," or "speech." Thus the word *psychology* means the speech or manifestation of the soul (Dean, 2010b). "Soul work" is about the spiritual aspects of the individual and, as I discuss later, becomes problematic when generalized principles are applied to the individual, as I explain in the discussion of the PPAT. The speech of the individual is not defined to only words but includes other manifestations of expression, such as found in images and symbols. Art, psychology, and religion share a fluid symbolic nature (Dean, 2010b). Thus, the symbol is the lens through which we can see the world. It both consolidates and expands. And all symbols are relational, meaning they often lose their significance when taken out of context. Historically, psychology has had more to do with spirit than mind. Plato called it "giving a logos a psyche," and Lear (1999) stated an everyday rendering of the Greek is "working out the logic of the soul." The etymology of the word *art* comes from the Latin *ars*, which means "skill in scholarship and learning," "to fit together or join," or "to make." *Therapy* comes from the Greek *therapeuein* or *therapeia*, meaning "to minister, treat, attend, do service, or take care of, or healing." Thus, the practice of art psychotherapy may be loosely defined as the practice of fitting together or joining expressively while tending to the soul and the ability to give speech or expression of the soul in a symbolic artistic means. So if the work of art therapists is akin to that of spiritual guides, it would make sense that we too must possess some flexibility and creativity to see things anew and in relation as opposed to seeking separate parts or solutions. Although valuable work is being done in cognitive science, neuroscience, and statistical research, many psychology departments have little or nothing to do with learning about working with the soul (Lear, 1999). "Plato understood that . . . this thoughtful attempt to understand one's world is basically an erotic engagement" (Lear, 1999, p. 9)—a relational and, ultimately, creative process.

Symbolic content is always held in a relational context. Symbols are representations of content that can be expressed in no other way. They have a universality, a particularity, and an individuality. They possess universal formal properties (e.g., color, line quality, and form), are particular with respect to space and time (i.e., they occur in a particular time period and place), and are irreducibly individual because they embody a universal property in a particular context (e.g., no two artists can produce the same spontaneous works). These ideas are attributed to Hegel's concept-structure, including his theory of art. Signs, however, speak to universal truths or understandings and are unchangeable, such as those easily recognized in a red, octagonal stop sign. A symbol holds personal, idiosyncratic, familial, cultural, place, and time contexts. For example, the esteemed floral Dutch painters had a symbolic voice about the meaning of flowers and symbols included in their pictures. Political commentary was often expressed through these paintings when outward outcry was forbidden. Paintings that held the inclusion of flies, a symbol of mortality and impermanence, coupled with flowers representative of political parties or ruling families, gave voice to things that could not be expressed directly. Both collective expression and individual opinion could be expressed through the artistic media. And even today the most iconic of artistic works, whether painting, sculpture, or film, speak a truth that is larger than the individual and hold meaning for many complicated aspects of our human plight. Although much of the idiosyncratic meaning of creative works may be lost in societies of another era, art stands as an encapsulated reminder of the artists, the culture in which they lived, and the conscious and unconscious material expressed during that time. The cultural meaning of the time may be lost, but artwork continues to speak to new audiences not only through aesthetic appreciation of masterful works in their own right but also through use as a building block to project new meaning onto the imagery and form as it relates to the here and now. Metaphorically, it is a bit like rummaging through the attic of a deceased relative, unearthing objects that hold clues about the individual and the time in which they lived. This is not completely removed from the experience because there is always an overlap in lineage and a building of a personal and cultural foundation. Art holds the knowing and not-knowing elements of the time and continues to speak into the future, long after its creators have passed, creating relationships for viewers that may transcend immediate time boundaries. It is essential to note that all symbolic concepts must be viewed in relationship, and that changes in context may imply systemic changes to individual and collective definitions of symbols.

Some psychological symptoms may be viewed as symbolic expressions of a disordered context. Art therapy is very much about creating meaning, although too often meaning-making is confused with interpretation. Art therapy involves both the creative emergence of meaning and the revealing of existing but veiled meanings. At its best, art therapy is a co-created experience, one in which mutual admiration and respect are given to the art-making process and to the symbolic material of the individual, family, or group. It is a therapeutic experience in which art materials are used to facilitate insight and process, and integrate experiences. Much in the same way the physical manifestation of silver or gold was elusive to the alchemists, the physical manifestation of psychological process can be difficult to detect.

Mythology

Psychology and art are laden with mythology about the depiction of not only ancient myths but also current myths or stories that hold personal and cultural narratives, memories, and truths that we currently view as reality. Mythology is a psychological process. Myths function as a means to make sense of our world, and they are colored by and evolve or devolve over time. Memory is perhaps one of the clearest examples of myth making in that what we experience can only be seen through our own personal lens, and the lens is tainted by previous experiences, beliefs, and attitudes. For example, when working with survivors of trauma, with the exception of litigious cases, therapists render the facts of the traumatic event irrelevant to the emotional and subjective experience. Actual facts are considered secondary to the reverie required for a healing process that honors the emotional reality of the trauma. It is the narrative of the event, the individual's truth, or myth, that conveys the context of the situation, the emotions of the event, and the construct through which one sees herself in the world.

We construct myths about who we are, where we have come from, and who we are destined to become. We use mythic constructs, or archetypes, to inform us of similar journeys taken by those who have come before us and use them for inspiration and a loose guide as to how to proceed. Personally and culturally, myths help to define and transcend our current situations, which is why some historic myths have stayed with us and are retold again and again in multiple incarnations, including but not limited to religion, literature, cinema, and art. Myths are images, collective and culturally bound. "Image is a complexity of relationships, an inherence of tensions, juxtapositions, and interconnections. An image is neither pure meaning, nor pure relations, nor pure perception" (Berry, 2008, p. 93). One cannot say that an image is literally *this* and metaphorically *that*, these dualities—thing versus reflection, literal versus metaphorical—are not the images but rather ways of structuring images (Berry, 2008). And so, too, the images made in art are not always about *this* or *that*. Art is a structure, a bridging structure. The art and imagery create a bridge between the inner and outer experiences, connecting the manifest with the latent material, and linking the past with the present and ultimately the future.

In terms of relationships and the ability to bridge at least two terrains, the Greek Olympian god Hermes acts as a guiding patron saint for psychological work in general and art psychotherapy specifically (Dean, 2010a). Hermes's ability to traverse multiple terrains is akin to the necessary ability of the psychotherapists to nimbly traverse the psychic terrain of the patient as well as the combined therapeutic union. Hermes is most often associated with boundaries and the travelers who cross them. He was a communicator, translating and ferrying messages from the gods (the spiritual realm) to the humans (an earthly realm). As the messenger of the gods, Hermes in the myth of Persephone was the emissary to Zeus, demanding Hades, ruler of the underworld, to return Persephone to her grieving mother Demeter. Hermes's ability to enter Hades was unique to him. Hermes's role was vital in the negotiation of her return of Persephone for it set in motion the cyclical nature of Persephone's biannual habitation between Hades and Demeter and thus represents the changing seasons. The fluidity of the myth and of the ability to move between the upper and lower worlds of the psyche through the image of the story is imperative in psychological life.

Hermes was also a psychopomp, a conductor of the soul, and as such, his responsibilities included bringing newly dead souls to the underworld, which was credited with bringing the images of dreams to the living. In art psychotherapy, the work involves bringing one's images into consciousness, whether through narratives of one's life or recounting one's traumas, dreams, fantasies, or artwork. The work of art psychotherapy is to gain greater awareness by sometimes diving into the depth of the unconscious and preconscious material, which presents as image, and raising them to the surface where they may bubble into greater awareness and provide insight and enhance meaning. The rising up of an image is a transcendent, emergent, or birthing process. The art psychotherapist takes the role of a psychological doula, assisting in the birth of the image, which holds both a knowing and an unknowing in what can be seen and what is emerging. It is a fluid process of revealing. It is coupled with *hermeneutics*, the art of interpreting hidden meaning, a word that is derived from the name Hermes, and is a core aspect of art psychotherapy work.

The idea of traveling between the realms of the living and the dead is a common experience in therapeutic process, both metaphorically and psychologically. Many patients enter into treatment feeling depressed, paralyzed by anxiety, "dead in the water" or "dead inside," and stuck in their life. They may be struck down by illnesses and symbolic processes in response to personal conflict or cultural affliction. Our "dis-ease" with our situation and circumstances are spoken through symbolic function. Our cultural fabric and ruptures also rise up through the individual. Culture is the substance that we all live in, like a fish in water; it provides an environment and a steady diet of images, laws, customs, and beliefs that we are steeped in. The therapy process is a means of increasing awareness and consciousness by moving into the depth of despair, a dark underworld, or shadow world, and understanding what is there and what needs tending to in the soul. It is a process not about annihilation but about relatedness. Art psychotherapy is a kind of *soul spelunking* as it were, with the art psychotherapist's role being the guide. Or like the psychopomp in this process, as if dropping to the depth of the darkness in the psyche's cave to find illustrative pictographs that adorn the walls. The art psychotherapy process illuminates these images in order to better understand what is being communicated and how to best relate to these needs.

As I described earlier regarding the myth of *Perseus and Medusa*, Medusa was a once fair mortal maiden who took an oath of celibacy and was punished for her forbidden relationship with Poseidon. Athena turned each lock of Medusa's hair into a venomous serpent and gave her milky white skin a green hue. To deliver Medusa from the curse, Perseus was charged with the task of slaying her. This feat was not an easy one because looking upon her would turn him to stone. Cunning wit was needed to achieve this task. To look directly upon her face was death, just as to be consumed by the archetypal energy is a kind of death. Viewing the face of the horrible Medusa in the myth is like the overwhelming aspects that must be faced in the art psychotherapy process. In the same way that Perseus used Athena's shield as a mirror to aid in slaying Medusa (Edinger, 2008), the imagery in art aids in seeing powerful and potentially dangerous psychic content in a manner that makes it more palatable.

Brief History of Art Therapy

As discussed throughout this book, there are clusters of experiences, technological advances, and societal changes that give shape and shift to beliefs, and responses of individuals, culture, and ideas about art. Historical context is needed to best understand not only the events of the past but also our present. Art therapy is a profession that grew out of a long tradition of utilizing the arts for its transformative and healing aspects. Art therapy as a formal profession evolved from psychoanalytic practice in the 1940s, which was popularized by Margret Naumberg (1890–1983) and Edith Kramer (1916–2014) in the United States (Junge, 2010; Rubin, 2010). In the United Kingdom, artist Adrian Hill (1895–1977) is credited with discovering the beneficial effects of art while recovering from tuberculosis and was generally acknowledged as the first person to use the term *art therapy* (Hogan, 2001). His work with tuberculosis patients and injured soldiers was aided by support from The National Association for the Prevention of Tuberculosis and the British Red Cross. Additionally, Withymead (1942–1967), a therapeutic community dedicated to art therapy, was also flourishing at this time in Britain (Hogan, 2001). Subsequent to these developments, there had been a cluster of factors setting the stage for art therapy's emergence both in the United States and in Europe. These factors sprang from the rehabilitation of the Great War, World War I, coupled with new developments in education, such as the Progressive Education Movement, which focused on the needs and interests of the child rather than rote memorization, which was popular at the time. Shifts in power, politics, technology, and culture created seismic changes in the world and the people who inhabited it. Surrealism and abstract art erupted into the art world driven by expression of profound emotional and universal themes, which translated into visual form in the intense post-war wake of anxiety and trauma. Freud and Jung were developing, lecturing, and publishing their ideas about psychological process, which included consideration about images in dreams and artwork. Prinzhorn, a German psychiatrist and army surgeon during the war, published *Bildnerei der Geisteskranken (Artistry of the Mentally Ill)* in 1922, which was based on the paintings, drawings, and sculptures created by a group of patients who were schizophrenic. This collection of artwork, known as the Heidelberg Collection, featured the works of psychotic patients that was gathered from many asylums across Europe (Naumberg, 1987). It was one of the first attempts to analyze the work of psychiatric patients, focusing on the links between creativity, rationality, and illness (Black, 2011). Prinzhorn's descriptions of the work synthesized anthropology, psychoanalysis, and art theory, attracting the attention of artists and collectors alike (Black, 2011). However, his attempts to correlate characteristic forms and designs with specific mental illnesses was abandoned when he discovered "the fact that children and primitive peoples produce similar motifs, similar colours, etc." (Bach, 1990, p. 7). In the United States in the early 20th century, Freud's theories of the mind were confronted by the likes of Carl Rogers and others who focused on environmental factors. Part of this shift was due to the requirement for an advanced medical degree in order to practice psychoanalysis and the emergence of vocational counseling for returning servicemen. The term *counselor* was applied in many situations in order to reduce the stigma associated with non-medically trained mental health professionals. This shift contributed to the expansion of seeing individuals and groups not just as medical patients but also as people actualizing their developmental and career goals.

Art therapy in the United States and Britain was born out of the increasing awareness of psychological theory that Freud and Jung were putting forth in the early part of the 19th century, which included the idea that art was an expression of psychological process that holds both manifest and latent symbolic material. However, there was initially a divide between art psychotherapy and art as therapy. Art psychotherapy, as viewed by Naumberg (1987), had an analytic frame that the work was centered on the transformative elements of the unconscious projections that were key because they existed in the transference relationship. Naumberg believed that symbolic communication spoke through images. In contrast, Kramer's art as therapy, like Hill's rehabilitative work in the sanitariums, was rooted in the idea that art was therapeutic in and of itself and that the use of sublimation was transformative. Sublimation is considered a higher order, mature defense mechanism in which unacceptable, undesirable impulses are unconsciously transformed into more socially acceptable forms. It is similar to displacement in that it serves a cultural or societal purpose by providing a transmutative experience to the impulses. Although Kramer did not consider herself a psychoanalyst, she felt her work with children was akin to psychologically informed art education (Junge, 2010). Art education typically differs from art therapy in that it is concerned with teaching techniques and methods that expand the pupil's skill, and it is a planned, conscious process (Naumberg, 1987). These approaches to art therapy may not be seen as distinct today because teaching skills is sometimes necessary or helpful for the patient to reach the optimum potential of expressiveness, and thus the ability to engage in symbolic communication in a chosen medium is enhanced, especially if they lack artistic experience or self-confidence. Even if working from an analytic framework, sublimation may still be a part of this process. And like Bloom's taxonomy of learning, shown in Figure 1.11, the foundation is the exposure to skills in order to remember, understand, and apply them as necessary. Through these skills, higher order abilities of creating, analyzing, and evaluating may be possible. Personal preference and situational considerations, such as contextual considerations, appear to be important factors when deciding where on the continuum from rehabilitative to analytical is best when working with patients (Wampold, 2001). Nonetheless, art psychotherapy and art as therapy share the commonality that art is the release of spontaneous imagery and that the creative process is a psychological expression that can be expressive and transformative. These models share that image and art expression are core to their workings. However, changes over time in the field of psychology have broadened the understanding of the term *art therapy* to include issues that no longer pertain exclusively to the psyche, such as cognitive, behavioral, or medical issues, which are aspects of human function and are influenced by psychological process but may be seen as lenses of human function other than psychological.

This lens in mental health practice has changed markedly over the last century. There has been a shift from the psyche and the individual process to focus on evidence-based methods, apparently motivated by economic reasons, rather than clinical needs in the practice of psychotherapy. This shift has dramatically changed the paradigm, leading psychoanalytic process away from its roots and often replacing it with behavioral and pharmacological methods. The myth that evidence-based methods reign supreme is one that needs critical inspection because its roots in the medical model are not without bias or prejudices. In a landmark study, psychologist, mathematician, and statistician Bruce Wampold (2001) "reviewed decades worth of research and conducted analyses and meta-analysis of thousands of studies in an effort to clarify the determinants of therapeutic effectiveness" (Elkins, 2007, p. 483). In his text *The Great Psychotherapy Debate*, Wampold (2001) pointed out there are two sides to the debate of effectiveness. One employs the *medical model*, which states therapy works due to "specific ingredients" (i.e., techniques) and which arose out of a "biological psychiatry" in which certain elements were thought to be curative and needed to be proven. The other uses the *contextual model*, which views the common factors inherent in all therapeutic systems as playing an essential role in effectiveness, including therapists' faith in their theoretical orientation and providing a convincing rationale to patients (Elkins, 2007; Wampold, 2001). His results indicated that it was not the techniques that were responsible for therapeutic outcome, but certain other factors that are common in to all therapeutic systems, thus favoring the contextual model. Wampold (2001) stated,

> Therapists need to realize that the specific ingredients are necessary but active only in the sense that they are a component to the healing context. Slavish adherence to a theoretical protocol and maniacal promotions of a single theoretical approach are utterly in opposition to science. Therapists need to have a healthy sense of humility with regard to the techniques they use [p. 217–218].

According to Wampold, part of the preference for using certain techniques is that they may provide a sense of coherence of treatment. For nascent therapists, techniques may offer what sometimes appears to be a logical framework or structure to the therapeutic hour, but they can remove and buffer the therapist from the therapeutic alliance and experience. Additionally, "an eclectic therapist who randomly selects techniques from a bag of techniques or a therapist who fails to act strategically at all will be as ineffective as a therapist who slavishly adheres to protocol regardless of the client's belief in the rationale for the treatment" (Wampold, 2001, p. 219). These findings suggest the need for compatibility of approach with the patients and their attitudes, values, and cultures. Some of the most important considerations regarding attitudes include cultural, ethnic, racial, religious, and socioeconomic characteristics of the patient. The contextual model does not imply that psychotherapists can and should use any random treatment, but rather that they should be "well-grounded in psychological principles to be congenial and convincing" (Wampold, 2001, p. 223). In accordance with this rationale, art psychotherapists also need to be grounded in their own theories of image and art in order to take into consideration the contextual aspects of their work. It is my hope that the following chapters will add to this process for some.

CHAPTER 2

PRINTMAKING
Variations on a Theme

I address printmaking as the first method of this text because it provides the earliest traceable forms of art—prints made from human hands, permanent records of people who lived tens of thousands of years ago (Herzog, 2010; Hurwitz & Day, 2001). These handprints accompanying images of prehistoric ice-age animals are believed to be part of an enigmatic spiritual practice, which may have included an altered consciousness such as a trance-like state. The indelible imprint of a maternal figure is inexorably linked with the human lifespan as well as that of many mammals, fish, bird species, and even some insects. The imprint creates a lifetime pattern for attachment. This pattern is returned to again and again for reassurance, comfort, and guidance for social behaviors, including sexual behaviors (Hess, 1958). Many of these patterns can be seen in images and artwork, such as archetypes, that emulate the original forms. Manifestations of these early patterns have a profound effect on our lives, reaching far into adulthood, and are played out not only in art but also in technological advances, which relate to individual and societal processes. An impression is one of the first things that we make when we meet someone new. Printmaking is but one such process that holds the ability to imprint its significance through image-form on the individual and a society.

I explore the history of printmaking as a reflective process in this chapter because it is capable of expressing individual and societal identity, with its ability for repetition and multiplicity in its numerous iterations. Prints allow the communication of ideas to flow from an individual to the masses and for the masses to be heard by an individual. This has been made increasingly possible through technological advances such as the printing press and personal computers. Although printing methods can be found in China using wood blocks or carved bone pressed into clay or wax as early as the 2nd century (Ross & Romano, 1972), the most notable shift in the printing process came with the invention of the Gutenberg Press (Peterdi, 1959; White, 2002). The Gutenberg Press, with its movable type, revolutionized printmaking in the 13th century. This paved the way for artistic and technological advances that helped fuel seismic changes in cultural and societal beliefs, including the Protestant Reformation (1517–1521), moving the seat of authority of the Christian church from the Pope to the Bible, for some. This shift accelerated the need for the common individual to be literate and created great demand for reading materials. Soon, ideas were transmitted to the masses with relative ease in what became the beginning of industrialized, mass production. Linguistically, the printing press even changed our nomenclature; for example the word *uppercase* becoming interchangeable with the term *capital letter*. This usage evolved from the construction of the printer's cabinet that held the sets of type; capital letters were stored on the top shelf, the upper part of the cabinet, and the lowercase letters were in the drawers below. Thus, *capital*, commonly associated with the seat of power within a state, changed to a word regarding a commonplace piece of furniture. This shift mimics the shift in cultural and religious powers to the commoner. Such artistic and technological changes continue to build on earlier inventions, shifting and transforming their presentation according to cultural and societal values and ideals. Further changes reflect the ongoing linguistic terminologies and technological advances that have emanated from another print generating device, the ubiquitous personal computer, replacing parchment or paper with screens.

The qualities of reflection, multiplicity, and identity, coupled with ritualistic process, suspense, and chance described in this chapter expand on ideas put forth in the chapter "Printmaking: Reflective and Receptive Impressions in the Therapeutic Process" in the *Wiley Handbook of Art Therapy* (Gussak & Rosal, 2015). In expanding on these ideas, I give particular focus to some of the historical and psychological implications for printmaking in a psychotherapeutic process. Many of these printmaking processes may be used in the therapeutic context due to their potential to tap into both sophisticated intellectual abilities and spontaneous emerging primal process, connecting the conscious and unconscious aspects of self. Described methods include the rubbings, monoprints, marbleizing, transfers, and relief processes in printmaking, such as collagraphs and cardboard cutouts, created with additive and subtractive aspects.

The Psychological Aspects of the Reflective Process

Printmaking can be a source of fascination and challenge that requires an indirect way of working (Hurwitz & Day, 2001). To create a print is to weave the artist's experience and perception, insight, and differentiation into one (Neumann, 1974). In order to create a print, something must be done to one substance in order for another to emerge, like an alchemical process. There is a series of steps that must be undertaken that lend the process to ritualistic method. These steps also help to create distance from the final outcome, so many times, the self-consciousness of the accuracy of a shape is minimized during the process due to the seeming disconnect from the final picture. The details associated with shading, more appropriate to drawing, are not needed in the print making process, but in the place of this perceived limitation comes the power of strong-impact images made through simplification and contrast (Hurwitz & Day, 2001).

Reversals

Many printmaking processes employed in therapy result in reversed images. This reversal may change or distort one's original composition, intentionally or unintentionally. When one is printing letters and words, reversals can lead to illegibility or a kind of coding. The image is printed in reverse, "so *any handwriting has to be done backwards* and thus already feels *as if one were writing in secret code*" [italics original to source] (Nissen, 2008, p. 19). This secret code writing can be seen in many of Leonardo da Vinci's journals, which was meant to be both a challenging mind exercise and a protective measure to keep his inventions safe from potential theft (Chastel, 1961). The contents of reversed writing in a printmaking processes can be seen in a mirror, setting the writing into a legible form.

Reversal is also considered a defense mechanism; its primary purpose is to defend or hold emotional and cognitive dissonance. The dissonance arises when there are two or more conflicting beliefs. It results in a great deal of discomfort because there is often no way to reconcile these states of being. For example, in Aesop's fable *The Fox and the Grapes*, the fox rejects the grapes after being unsuccessful in obtaining them. In this retelling of the tale, one can see how the rejection of the unobtainable is illustrated:

> A fox, feeling very hungry, made his way to the vineyard, where he knew he would find a hearty bounty of grapes. In the vineyard, the glistening grapes cascaded in the sun and made him all the more hungry. Upon this sight, he was overwhelmed with joy as he licked his lips, although his elation was short lived. Try, try, try as he might, the grapes were just beyond his reach. At last exhausted by his efforts, he turned away in disgust remarking, "Anyone who wants them can have them; they are too sour for my taste."

It is easy to disregard, strongly dislike, or hate what one is unable to obtain, which is both the moral of this story and the protective function of the psychological process of reversal. The reversal expresses the opposite of what is desired, calling the grapes *too sour* even though they were very much desired.

Jung stated, "There can be no doubt, either, that realization of the opposite hidden in the unconscious—the process of 'reversal'—signifies reunion with the unconscious laws of our being, and the purpose of the reunion is attainment of conscious life or, expressed in Chinese terms, the realization of the Tao" (CW 13:30). Tao is considered the path or way of life and signifies the fundamental nature of the universe and its primordial essence. It is a part of traditional Chinese philosophy and religion and is a way of creating harmony with one's will or nature, coming into being or enlightenment, or experiencing an *aliveness*. This aliveness can also be experienced as the tension that is created and may be seen in many kinds of printmaking processes. This kind of tension sets up a situation in which it is necessary to hold polarities much in the same way the daimon holds the polarities of light and dark, as discussed in Chapter 1.

Holding the Opposites

Printmaking in regards to reductive work emerges in the process of holding opposites. This holding of opposites may be seen not only in the reversal of the form of an image but also in color. Taking a pliable substrate, the artist is able to remove part of it by carving it away. This is considered a reductive process. The recessed, carved portions become the negative space of the print or perhaps are better described as being devoid of pigment. If the paper is white, the carved portions are left white in the final print. The patient is removing the darkness of the substrate in order for the light to be seen in the final print. Much can be done with this analogy in treatment. It is the raised or original portion of the substrate that will receive the pigment, becoming dark. In relief printing, the artist is active in the removal of negative spaces as opposed to what is considered the positive, the mark-making portion. The opposite of this is true when working with additive methods such as the collagraph, where one is adding the raised portions to be printed.

Positive and Negative Spaces, and Black and White

A print created with a single plate is typically considered monochromatic: one color of pigment. In these types of prints, one may consider the play between the positive space (the pigment) and the negative space (the absence of color). Most commonly used is black pigment for the color, and the color of the negative space is the paper stock, typically white, but this can be different colors if desired or on previously printed papers, such as marbleized papers. The monochromatic image is striking and usually bold, as black printing ink is dense and has intense opacity. Printing ink is relatively slow to dry and has a denser viscosity than acrylic paint, which may be substituted if printmaking ink is unavailable. Creations that use this dichotomy of black and white can also lend themselves to expressions of the dichotomy of thought processes, like all-or-nothing thinking patterns or beliefs.

Multiplicity Building of a Society and Individual Participation

Prints allow the communication of ideas to flow from an individual to the masses and for the masses to be heard by an individual. Freed from the laborious process of hand scribing texts and images, described in Chapter 5 about book binding, printing brought the ability to create numerous copies of an image. Mechanized printing was exploited by rulers and political leaders who promoted and proliferated their images on everything from currency to propaganda materials. For example, Emperor Maximilian I of Austria (1450–1519) was elected Holy Roman Emperor in 1508, becoming a ruler, in name, of vast territories. In practice, he lacked the power and money to govern these lands, so with the aid of German artist Albrecht Dürer (1471–1528), he used woodcuts to project his image across his empire as a means to unite it under his image. His image was created not only on papers distributed widely but also on stained glass and other monuments, as shown in Figure 2.1. He portrayed his power, wealth, and ideals through the use of art. He was able to create prestige even when lacking the resources to merit such honor. These principles may be utilized in a therapeutic context as well.

Multiple prints reduce the preciousness of the art object. They can be shared or gifted, strengthening bonds among peers and group members. For example, utilizing an image printed on card stock, the individual or group members can be encouraged to write letters to their future selves, reminding them where they have been and what they intend to put forth as goals for themselves in the future. The group facilitator could then mail the letters after a specified length of time (e.g., one week, three months, or six months). A variation with more immediate results, but with the ability to carry a message well into the future, would be for the group members to create printed cards highlighting the other group members' positive attributes and gift them to one another (Dean, 2015).

Ritual and Preparation

Printmaking involves a series of steps before the final image is able to emerge. Some of the steps for most printmaking include the initial inception of the idea; the creation of the image whether drawn, carved, sculpted, or assembled; the inking; the pigment transfer; and then the final print or prints. This multiple-step

Figure 2.1 Prints made by German artist Albrecht Dürer (1471–1528) of Emperor Maximilian I of Austria (1450–1519) when he was elected Holy Roman Emperor helped to promote Maximilian's power and attempted to unite his vast territories under his image. His image was created not only on papers distributed widely but also on stained glass as seen here and in other monuments. © 2016 Michelle L. Dean.

process lends itself to ritual in the preparation process. The preparation in printmaking is as much a part of the art making as the act of drawing is for a picture. Understanding the multiple steps and the sequence of each method can become a ceremonial aspect of this art form that provides order, organization, foresight, structure, and patience (delay of gratification).

The Oracle: Printing from the Source

Chance is a part of life and occurs through biological predispositions (e.g., some illnesses), life events, losses, and traumas. Much of what happens is out of the control of those who experience it, but it is their response to the situations that determines their outlook and general sense of well-being (von Franz, 1980). In this way, art mirrors life. Even with the most well-conceived and thoughtfully executed designs, most prints still have an element of chance in them, just as many games do. "Most games are a mixture of chance and calculation. You can use your intelligence to a certain extent, but the chance factor always remains. Mah-jong, bridge, and so on are all based on such situations" (von Franz, 1980, p. 49). Once the plate has been carved and inked and the paper placed on top, its image is concealed. After a strong rub, like a wave of a hand over a magician's top hat, the climactic moment is when the print is pulled off the plate, revealing the magic of the image. Bagilhole (1983) agreed when she stated, "[Printmaking] will always have a magical quality" (p. 6). And as Neumann (1974) stated, "Artistic creation has magic power; it is experience and perception, insight and differentiation in one" (p. 86). Surrendering to this creative magic is like surrendering to the wisdom of the oracle of a higher power. It requires a receptivity in the wisdom of the process.

As a direct image-making process, printmaking provides ample opportunities for expression and can be an effective medium due to its ability to be modified for the particular needs of an individual or group. This chapter focuses on printmaking processes that would be best suited for most common therapeutic situations. As with any medium, it is best to let the context and the known entities of the therapist–patient relationship lead the therapist's choice of material rather than to apply the technique systematically.

Types of Printmaking Suitable for Therapeutic Settings

While all printmaking methods may be possible for particular individuals or groups, when working with printmaking materials, good common sense considerations and sound clinical judgment are imperative in regard to the setting and population in which one is working and in terms of the policies of the institution. Consideration should also be given to work that must fall within rigid time increments—commonly, a one-hour individual session or an hour-and-a-half-long group session. Of course, adaptations of the following suggestions are encouraged to best meet specific considerations of the situation. Hence, methods that commonly employ the use of hazardous materials (e.g., acids, toxic chemicals, sharp cutting instruments) have been purposely omitted because these methods typically do not lend themselves to general use in a therapeutic setting.

Printmaking Methods
Rubbings

Transferring an image from a ready-made surface onto a piece of paper is considered a rubbing. Using a leaf, branch, coin, or headstone and a thin piece of paper and a wax crayon, a transfer of image can be made. This is one time when the paper needs to be thin for a successful outcome. Creating multiple layers of rubbings of stone, brick, burlap, and wire mesh will yield a study of the *skin* of the environment. Textures inform our senses about touch and perception and about details that may be indistinguishable by the eye, like the delicate veins in plants and leaves. This way of "seeing" makes us more aware of our environment and our place within it, as the senses of touch and feeling are also employed. These images may be appreciated singularly or grouped together to create a larger piece, collaged, or bound into a book for an eloquent presentation. The nature of rubbings makes them suitable for abstract compositions where the subject matter is focused on size, shape, feel, and color rather than representational art.

Pulled Prints

Monoprints: A Painterly Process

The most painterly method of printmaking is the making of monoprints because they allow for a great range of fluid possibilities in an image. They are considered a "*natural* way of working due to the viscous quality of the ink and its glorious uncontrollability, which provides an experience of unequaled immediacy" (Nissen, 2008, p. 17). The juicy, vivid colors and thick viscosity of the ink may create a pleasurable kinesthetic experience as the ink is applied directly to a rigid surface or substrate, such as tempered glass or Plexiglas®. As shown in Figure 2.2, the pigments are applied directly to a substrate. In this example, acrylic paint is used with a drying retarder to slow the normally quick drying time of acrylics for a longer painting session. The direct painting allows for a degree of surrendering, or loss of control over the final picture, but also allows for a direct painterly experience. The images are considered one-off productions, as a second image from the same plate is typically compromised, faded, or ghostly. This aspect of the monoprint allows for truly individual artistic productions with an aspect of the mysterious for the creator.

The image is created by pulling off a piece of paper laid on top of the painted surface. Although traditionally oil-based paints or inks are used for this process, substituting water-based paints or inks for oil minimizes the inherent hazards associated with the chemicals in oil-based paint and inks. Successful monoprints can be created by using water-soluble inks and acrylic paints. Acrylic paint mixed with a commercial drying retarder or methocellelluous, a liquid adhesive commonly used in bookbinding and as an additive to create paste papers and finger paints, will increase the working time with acrylic paint. This type of printmaking does have an immediacy and spontaneity. It need not take more than a few minutes, and two to three images may be accomplished in an hour, depending on the detail and speed with which one works. The brevity of the painting session can provide a sense of play and even freedom for some.

Before pressing the image, it may be helpful to prepare the paper. Dampening the paper before pressing it to the substrate with a light misting from a water bottle sprayer will help draw additional color from the plate. Another variation of the monoprint is the *paper stop out* method. A stencil made from cut-out paper is created and then placed on the inked plate. The stencil will prevent the pigments from showing on the final piece, creating a *stop out* of white, or negative space, which may be left blank or worked into with another medium if desired once dry. In most cases, a hand-held roller such as a brayer, a spoon, a bone folder, or even one's hand, as shown in Figure 2.3, may be used to gently burnish the back of the paper. Any of these methods is typically sufficient to create adequate adhesion of the paint to the paper. The pulled image offers a surprise to the young boy shown in

Figure 2.2 The pigments of the monoprint are applied directly to a piece of tempered glass or plexiglass. The direct painting allows for a degree of surrender or loss of control over the final picture, but also allows for a direct painterly experience. © 2016 Michelle L. Dean.

Figure 2.4 because the vibrancy of the pulled print can range from a very intense thick color to a misty transfer. Like ink blots that are a result of placing paint in the crease of a paper and rubbing the sheet from the backside, this method allows for surprise images and associations. Typically, greater pressure and thicker paint result in darker and more striking image transfers. Because most monoprints yield only one successful image, they are unique in that they are singular works of art.

Figure 2.3 When creating a monoprint, in most cases, a hand-held roller such as a brayer, a spoon, a bone folder, or even one's hand may be used to gently burnish the back of the paper in order to transfer the image. © 2016 Michelle L. Dean.

Additionally, the print may be worked into a painting with brushes and other painting tools in order to bring details into greater clarity. This additional control of the art media may be beneficial, as well as telling, in terms of issues of control and willingness to surrender to the process both in the art media and in life. Experiencing this type of controlled unpredictability in a printmaking process may be helpful in rebuilding emotional resiliency and flexibility.

Figure 2.4 The pulled image offers a surprise to the young boy because the vibrancy of the pulled print can range from very intense thick color to a misty transfer. © 2016 Michelle L. Dean.

Inkblots

Inkblots are similar to monoprints, although the pigment is painted directly on one side of the page and then folded onto itself for a symmetrical image. This process can be rewarding in and of itself, but it can also be used in a kind of projective association process, similar to the Rorschach test developed in 1921 by Hermann Rorschach. In this process, the associations of the images are not standardized or rated but instead yield personal meaning and opportunities to use the image and its perceived content for associations, dialog, and storytelling, because it is sometimes easier to talk about an image than to describe oneself. It is a form of play in which sublimation may be incurred. Like daydreaming while looking at clouds, distinguishing shapes and objects, the prints may be admired for the images they portray, or they may be incorporated into other works such as collages, bookbinding, and visual journals, as discussed later in this text.

Marbleized Paper

Like monoprints, marbleized papers are pulled prints that can be made by suspending pigments on the surface of a liquid, such as water or another, thicker liquid medium made with carrageenan or methylcellolse. The earliest forms of marbleizing include Suminagashi, a Japanese form of marbleizing dating back to at least the 1100s (Maurer-Mathison, 1993). Sumi inks were floated on water, creating concentric circles mimicking patterns of waves and water. Suminagashi is one of the simplest forms of marbleizing, and its paler, softer-patterned papers create excellent backgrounds for writing and drawing papers or for incorporating into other projects.

The complex patterns and brilliantly colored sheets often associated with marbleized papers today were developed in the 15th century in Persia and called *ebru* (cloud art) by early artisans. By the 17th century, marbleizing spread to Europe but remained a tightly held trade secret, reserved mostly for end papers of books. Traditionally made with oil paints, acrylic, and even food dyes can be used in their place to reduce the hazards and potential mess.

To marbleize paper, a tray in which water or a thicker liquid medium can be poured is necessary. Although large trays (24 × 36 inches) are a lovely addition to the art psychotherapy setting, they are often unwieldy, and in their place, smaller aluminum or glass baking pans can be used, which need not be larger than 9 × 12 inches. In addition to a tray, brushes, and absorbent paper, pigments are needed. To create Suminagashi papers, fill the tray so the bottom is completely covered and, utilizing Suminagashi pigments (sold under the trade name Aitoh Boku-Undo Suminagashi Marbling Kit, which may be purchased from art vendors [see Appendix A]), dip the brush in the pigment and then onto the surface of the water. The dipping motion is repeated, usually inside of the previously made ink dot, expanding the circles of pigment outward, as shown in Figure 2.5. Some of the pigment may sink to the bottom, but it is the pigment that floats on the surface that will be used to create the pulled print. Once the liquid surface of the pan is filled with pigment, or is to one's liking, a piece of paper, smaller than the pan, may be gently rolled onto the surface, absorbing the floating pigments. Pretreating the paper with aluminum sulfate, a mordant, in order to increase the absorption of color can be recommended to give the paper or fabric more *tooth* and help set the pigments, but I have found this to be unnecessary in most cases. Experimenting with breezes that move the surface and double printing images can yield opportunities for experimentation, exploration, and patience. Because the pigments are floating on water, breezes and air currents can move the pigments rapidly and distort or change the image. Dragging a single strand of hair or thread through the pigment can also change the surface pattern.

With traditional marbleizing, the size or thickening medium used in the tray slows the process, creating images that are less susceptible to breezes or bumps of the table or work surface. This consideration may be important if marbleizing in a group, because the thickening agent slows the pigments and suspends them for longer pattern-making times. For the thickening medium, make the carrageenan

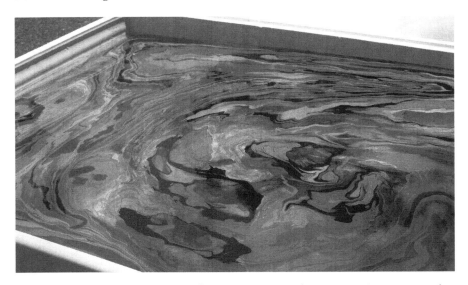

Figure 2.5 Suminagashi pigments floating in a tray of water creating patterns that closely resemble nature. © 2016 Michelle L. Dean.

or methylcellolse in advance and according to directions, usually the day before, or have some on hand; it can be stored for a week or more in an air-tight container (vendors for these products can be found in Appendix A). Like Suminagashi, traditional marbleized papers are created with acrylic pigments that are floated on the surface of the fluid. Using liquid acrylics instead of tube paints can be preferred. If tube acrylics are all that are available, they may be thinned with water to a creamy consistency. With a brush or eye-dropper, drip the pigment in whatever pattern is pleasing. Experiment with plastic combs, brushes, forks, or knives to comb the pattern and create designs, as shown in Figure 2.6. These papers are easy to create and yield high satisfaction. They produce a meditative quality in their creators as they contemplate the color, patterns, designs, and influence of the elements, such as breezes and direct surface disruption of combing tools. Metaphorically, the pans are like kaleidoscopes and mini-oceans that hold the potential for vibrancy and diversity influenced by the tides of their surroundings. The decorated papers may be appreciated as they are or may be drawn on, cut out for collages, or used in other projects such as bookbinding or as backgrounds for other printmaking methods, such as relief printing.

Relief Printing: A Reductive Method

Relief printing may conjure up images of detailed wood or linoleum block printing in which painstaking designs are carved into the surface, creating detailed and elaborate works of art. This method produces beautiful results, but the requirement of sharp tools may be impractical in many clinical settings. Fortunately, many alternatives exist to the traditional methods requiring sharp tools. Soft panels that can be carved with a wooden stylus, pencil, plastic spoon, or other blunt instrument exist as an alternative to wood or linoleum. Trade names for such products include E-Z-Cut printing blocks, Scratch-Art Scratch-Foam® Soft Surface Printing Boards, and Inovart® Printfoam, which may be purchased

Figure 2.6 A 10-year-old boy combs liquid acrylics across a carrageenan medium. Although this picture is taken outside and using a large pan, a smaller-scale process may be utilized in a therapy session. © 2016 Michelle L. Dean.

from some of the vendors listed in Appendix A. An example of a relief print created with an E-Z-Cut printing block can be seen in Figure 2.7 created by an undergraduate art therapy student. This image graced the cover of a letter that she wrote to herself as she contemplated her final year in college. Her letter was mailed to her at the time of her graduation, eight months after its creation.

Styrofoam trays that supermarkets sometimes use for holding fruit and vegetables may also be used to create printing surfaces (Weiss, 1976), as well as potatoes, broccoli, and apples. Plastic knives can be used with the Styrofoam, fruit, or

Figure 2.7 An example of a relief print created by an undergraduate art therapy student using an E-Z-Cut printing block. © 2016 Michelle L. Dean.

vegetables in order to create stamps that can be used to make singular patterned prints or combined with others for variation. Likewise, premade foam and rubber stamps may be used in traditional ways or in combination, creating patterns or used with mixed media such as drawing materials or collage.

Collagraph: An Additive Method

In addition to using a reductionist or subtractive method to create an imprint, additive constructions—assembled blocks—can be used to create the printing surface image by employing found objects and adhering them to the foundation. Clay, such as Model Magic®, can be sculpted and glued onto a board. The sculpted shapes can then be inked and printed, or rubbings can be made by placing a sheet of paper on the assembled block and by using wax crayons or an inked brayer, rubbing the raised areas to create an image on the covering paper. Additionally, found objects can be assembled in a similar fashion, such as gluing pieces of dry pasta, including alphabet noodles, doilies, bottle tops, string, rubber bands, hairpins, fabric, lace, and pieces of cardboard to a substrate board such as chipboard. This method can be particularly helpful with sight-impaired clients. The amount of time needed to create assembled prints can span two or more sessions to give adequate time for the glue to dry. Depending on the setting and population, a hot glue gun can be used to expedite the drying time, but under most conditions, this tool would not be recommended because of the potential for burns and other risks inherent with cords. Likewise, one may "draw" with liquid glue, such as Sobo® or Elmer's® White Glue (Polyvinyl acetate, aka PVA) onto a board and let it set and then use the board to ink or create rubbings, as with the methods mentioned above. Again, due to the drying time, this method may need to be spread over two or more sessions.

The use of found objects for prints need not be confined to paper. Pressing objects into a slab of clay to make a textured tile can create a detailed relief, which can be admired as it is or used as a printing block. The clay itself provides a tactile experience and adds another dimension to printmaking.

Printmaking is an art form that draws on reflective process allowing the communication of ideas to flow from an individual to the masses and for the masses to be heard by an individual. These qualities of reflection allow for psychological mirroring both within the individual and also with the larger society. Coupled with ritualistic process, suspense, and chance, issues of identity may be explored through this medium, lending it to be an adaptable and therapeutic art process ripe for psychological process.

CHAPTER 3

DRAWING
Engaging the Image

Drawing, in a general sense, encompasses all those representations in which an image is obtained by mark-making activity, whether simply or ornately. It has become associated with specific techniques by which marks show light and shadow by means of hatching, washes, highlights, and color notations (Grottanelli, 1961). Drawing is the expression of a boundary or a division of space. It defines object and ground. It can appear linear, or it can take a form to create illusionary planes. To draw is to make an intrinsic image extrinsic in its most basic form. Drawing is a process that signifies and reconstructs an environment, and it is much more than mere visual representations (Lowenfeld & Brittain, 1987). Drawings are typically held on a surface or plane, such as on a piece of paper or etched into a stone. For the purposes of this chapter, drawing includes the use of dry material applied by hand or by an instrument other than those used to apply paint or pigment, such as brushes.

Drawing materials can be thought of on a continuum of hardness to softness, or as Lusebrink (1990) describes, from resistive to fluid. These structural qualities are inherent in each material. Consideration of these properties is important when selecting materials to use because each material carries a particular potential for expressive ability. This is not to say that one is better than another, but matching them to the person and situation is key. An example that I believe may best illustrate this is the advent of digital painting and drawing programs. Although these programs may change a line to appear as if it were made by a pencil, charcoal, marker, or paint, the actual interface with the computer or electronic tablet changes the inherent potential for what it is able to express. Drawing with gritty charcoal on a large, rough piece of paper will not yield the same results as working with a computer program, such as Adobe Illustrator®, in the charcoal mode. While there are pros and cons to electronic media as there are with every material, the material itself has inherent properties that cannot be replaced by another. The materials elicit support and respond to internal expressiveness. Understanding these properties is imperative. Recent research findings support the use of art materials because they boost brain activity and assist with self-regulation, empathy, memory, visual processing, intelligence, creativity, and problem solving (Belkofer & Konopka, 2008; Belkofer, Vaughan Van Hecke, & Konopka, 2014; Buk, 2009; Franklin, 2010; Hass-Cohen & Carr, 2008; Kapitan, 2010; Lusebrink, 2004, 2010; Malchiodi, 2003). There is a relationship to the material that defines the terms, much like the people in the therapeutic relationship. The therapist and the patient define the relationship and its therapeutic potential, setting the stage for what it will be capable of manifesting. Replacing the therapist or the patient will not yield the same result because there is a relational quality dependent on the synergistic effects of the elements present at that time. So as a therapist, having an intimate relationship with art materials and understanding each of their properties, strengths, and limitations is essential in introducing an art aspect of relationship into sessions. Below, I describe some of the materials and their strengths, but a more thorough learning will come from familiarity through use and trial and error in a learning-by-doing approach.

The drawing utensil one is most likely to be familiar with is a graphite pencil. Its "lead" or graphite is a composite of various materials that can render darker or lighter marks. There is a feel to the pencil that corresponds to a hardness-to-softness scale—hard pencils make a lighter mark and feel scratchy and can even shred the surface of the paper while softer pencils surrender their point to darker and often thicker lines. Each material and manufacturer produces variations, and a scale of art materials from hard to soft that generally ranges from non-erasable rigid pens and pencils without erasers, to materials that allow for removal, to the soft pastels and chalks at the more fluid end of the scale due to their powdery nature. The resistive or fluid scale in art materials parallels their ability to provide more or less structure to a patient, as has been cited by several authors (Lusebrink, 1990; Rubin, 1984). Other structuring devices for drawing materials include complexity, space, surface materials, suggested art interventions, and time constraints.

The complexity of the drawing project varies in terms of the number of steps or processes that are employed. For example, drawing with a pencil is a relatively straightforward process. It is a universally familiar medium and, with only the exception of sharpening, it does not require multiple steps. In contrast, Pysanky egg dyeing is a Ukrainian folk tradition that uses a multiple-step process requiring fine drawing with a stylus. An example is shown in Figure 3.1. It

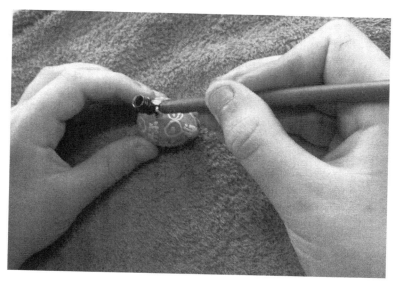

Figure 3.1 Pysanky egg dyeing is a Ukrainian folk tradition. This multiple-step process requires drawing with a stylus, as seen above, on a prepared egg in wax resist. This one is done on a quail egg by a 9-year-old boy. The eggs are decorated with incremental and elaborate designs with melted beeswax layered between each dye bath, sometimes using as many as eight to nine colors taking several hours or days to complete. © 2016 Michelle L. Dean.

Figure 3.2 Completed Pysanky eggs in nontraditional, free-form designs created by a 9-year-old child. Each egg is dyed through a multiple-step process using vibrant jewel colors. © 2016 Michelle L. Dean.

can be done on a prepared egg in wax resist. The eggs are decorated with incremental and elaborate designs with melted beeswax layered between each dye bath, sometimes using as many as eight to nine colors taking several hours or days to complete; see Figure 3.2.

Space is another consideration when it comes to structuring. Drawings are created on a plane or surface, typically a piece of paper. The size of the paper gives more or less structure or containment. Drawing on tiny surfaces typically requires more control than, say, mural painting, which usually requires more foresight into the final product but less fine motor skills. Reducing the size of the page may lead to tighter, more controlled responses, which may produce more or less anxiety or concern, depending on the needs of the creative expression and the individual producing it. Consideration may be given to utilizing a paper size that meets the objectives. A smaller drawing such as doodling with pens may be suitable on a 5 × 7 inch piece of paper, whereas group work may need a larger surface or a way to combine smaller pieces of individual pieces of paper to create a unified form.

Likewise, the type of surface material should be considered. Paper from a copier machine, which is usually flimsy and smooth or has little or no tooth, does not hold up well to some materials and mark making or erasures. Papers that have some tooth, such as drawing paper or charcoal or watercolor paper, have more heft and foster a sense of significance. They also may be archivally sound, such as acid-free papers, and will indeed hold up over time if stored properly to avoid moisture, which can result in mildew. Using poor quality and insubstantial materials can give patients the impression of insignificance for their works of art and, more importantly, may appear to diminish the importance of their psychological process expressed graphically. Conversely, using materials with more substance or a professional feel can produce pressure to create a piece that adheres to a perceived standard worthy of the materials. The perceptions and associations with materials can all be used in furthering understanding of psychological process and meaning.

Structuring may also be found within the suggested art interventions, such as those that are more or less complicated or that are considered nondirective as in a *free drawing*. Lusebrink (1990) suggests structure can be viewed as being on a continuum, and different situations call for one structure over another. For example, someone who would like to further engage in a dream sequence and for whom spontaneity is preferred could be encouraged to *Draw the dream or part of the dream*. When learning a new concept, people often need structure to increase comfort, familiarity, and confidence. Hence, it is common to give an overt directive like *Draw how you feel today*, *Draw your family as represented as animals*, or *Draw the events that have brought you to therapy at this time*. Such directives offer a wide range of responses, some of which may be very abstract and others more concrete. For example, when working as an intern at an inpatient psychiatric facility, I once gave a structured directive: *Draw what brought you to the hospital*. While most understood this to mean the conditions of their illness that precipitated their hospitalization, one person with very concrete thinking drew the ambulance that literally brought him to the hospital. As with any intervention or response, word choice is important, and most often, responses are reflective of psychological process.

A final structuring device common to art psychotherapy sessions is time. Constraints on time are constant. From the hour-long session to the seasons, everything is held within a time frame. However, when using art materials, the conventional hourly session sometimes feels too constrictive to reach flow capacity. In some settings and with some patients, psychotherapy groups may need to be adjusted to one-and-a-half- or two-hour groups to have time to engage in the actual process of art making as well as preparation and clean up. The responsibility to care for the materials and space is always part of the process, assisting with transition and ownership of the creative process.

Drawing materials most suitable to therapy include pencils—graphite and colored—and pens—ballpoint, felt, gel, nibs, and paint pens—as well as markers, oil pastels, colored chalks (also called chalk pastels), and charcoal, to name only the most commonly used. A list of online suppliers and vendors is provided in Appendix A of the book for easy reference and acquisition.

In a therapeutic context, drawing may be seen to enable a continuum of expressiveness supported by a continuum of drawing materials. Three types along this continuum are linear or contour drawings, expressive or dynamic drawings, and more picturesque or lyrical drawings. These terms describe expressive styles that arose in opposition to pure classical drawing and painting and may be seen in much of modern art after the later 1800s, when there were increasing rejections of the academic painting establishment known as salon art.

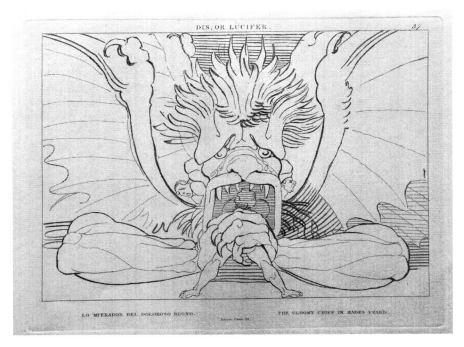

Figure 3.3 John Flaxman (1755–1826). *The Divine Comedy* by Dante Alighieri. Inferno (Hell), Canto 34, Dis, or Lucifer. Prints after the artist's neoclassical drawings, 1802 edition. Photo Credit: Alfredo Dagli Orti/Art Resource, NY.

Linear or contour drawings are concerned with the essence of the form. They are typically sparse outlines without indication of light or color. They have the appeal of Spartan simplicity with a hardness and heroic disdain for sensuous charm (Eitner, 1961). This type of image can be seen in illustrations of the works of Homer, Aeschylus, and Dante by John Flaxman (1755–1826) (Figure 3.3). Such illustrations influenced later artists, like those in the Nazarene movement, a group of German painters who aimed to revive simplicity in form and feeling of artwork. Their influential movement developed well into the 19th century, with the Pre-Raphaelites and the Art Nouveau movements. Line and contour drawings lend themselves to coloring books and textbooks. They are also ideal for comics, cell work (outline drawings that are colored in, like animation drawings prior to the advent of digital animation), and drawings that can be captured in a sequential process like flipbooks or recorded with stop animation software programs like Vine™ and Stopmotion Explosion Animation™. When using digital technology along with line drawings, each drawing is photographed and then played back in rapid succession to create the illusion of motion. The drawing sequences usually present with steady movement and usually appear to be done without erasures. They have crisp and solid line quality, which can be successfully rendered with pens or thin markers, and often exude an air of austerity and confidence. They also may be drawn in pencil to be inked over later, erasing the pencil markings if needed.

Expressive or dynamic drawing styles also incorporate contour drawing and can additionally use washes and highlights with gouache, an opaque watercolor, to bring out the forms. These drawings express impassioned intensity, as can be

Figure 3.4 Honoré Daumier (1808–1879). *The Divorcees* ("Sister citizens . . . we're spreading the news that divorce is on the verge of being refused to us . . . let's stick together permanently and declare that the homeland is in danger!"). Location: Bibliotheque Nationale, Paris, France. Photo Credit: Bridgeman-Giraudon/Art Resource, NY. Expressive or dynamic drawing styles also incorporate contour drawing but may use washes and highlight with gouache, a type of opaque watercolor, to bring out the forms. They express an impassioned intensity. Chalk, charcoal, and oil sticks are fluid and capture the immediacy and the aliveness to this line quality.

seen in Honoré Daumier's (1808–1879) *The Divorcees*, shown in Figure 3.4. The lines do not confine or appear as hard edges but as vibrant and vibrating strokes and dynamic movement. They leap and gesture with the ecstatic movements of the figures and their emotions. Chalk, charcoal, and oil sticks are fluid and capture the immediacy and aliveness in this line quality. Rapid movements can be made with dark and implied lines, and the softness of the material bends to show softness in the quick energetic movements needed to create such images and convey such ideas. These materials are ideal for expressing emotion, movement, and the immediacy of a situation, such as in drawing how one feels, a scene that was upsetting, or something that one wishes one could undo in one's life.

Figure 3.5 Jean-Baptiste-Camille Corot (1796–1875). *Stream in the Undergrowth Near Civita Castellana.* Graphite. Photo Credit: Thierry Le Mage. Location: Louvre, (Museum), Paris, France. Credit: © RMN-Grand Palais/Art Resource, NY. The picturesque style is particularly important when representing space and landscape. In the rendering of distance and atmosphere, light and color play significant roles in conveying feeling and mood. Corot working in hard pencils attends to the fine details focusing on the tangible of forms and shapes of nature.

The picturesque drawing style is particularly suitable when representing space and landscape. In the rendering of distance and atmosphere, light and color play significant roles in conveying feeling and mood. These drawings typically represent dramatic light, movement, and compositions rather than objective realism as can be seen in the works of Jean-Baptiste-Camille Corot and Jean Francois Millet, shown in Figures 3.5 and 3.6. Corot (1796–1875), working in hard pencils, attended to the fine details and focused on the tangible forms and shapes of nature. Millet (1814–1875) drew his simplified figures in sculptural style with crayon or charcoal, conveying dramatic arrangements. These artists went beyond mere observers and sought the truth beneath surface appearance (Eitner, 1961). In essence, the truth of an individual is what is told through their art and image. Truth is at the very core of psychological process and of a person's ability to express it in image form. It can be helpful to use the picture plane to think about things that are closest to the viewer (and the creator) and to depict future things by placing them further away or on the horizon when one is assessing perspective, both visually and psychologically. The materials used in the psychotherapy process also influence and in many ways dictate the amount and type of expressiveness that is possible. To create optimum conditions for expression, the materials ideally correspond with the situations and subject matter. Familiarity with a wide range of materials, not just drawing materials, is imperative in order to understand firsthand the potential each one holds and how to best apply it to individuals and their circumstances. The

Figure 3.6 Jean Francois Millet (1814–1875). *Study for "Summer, The Gleaners"* (before 1853). Black chalk. PD, 1906-2-13-1 Location: British Museum, London, Great Britain. Photo Credit: © The Trustees of the British Museum/Art Resource, NY. Millet drew his simplified figures in sculptural style with crayon or charcoal, conveying dramatic arrangements in the picturesque style, which is particularly important when representing space and landscape.

therapist's familiarity with materials can be used in guiding the patient (not presenting a pre-selected choice), helping them make their own choices and express their own agency. This is parallel to the subject matter in an art psychotherapy session.

For example, a rendering of an inanimate object can depict as much about the feeling state of a person as words used to describe it. As shown in Figure 3.7, Menzel's (1815–1905) depiction of the backyard of the Puhlmann House not only conveys place but also speaks to mood through the use of light, atmosphere, and attention to the details in this space. These ideas not only easily convey a

Figure 3.7 Adolf von Menzel (1815–1905). *Back Yard of the Puhlmann House Near Potsdam* (1844). Graphite, 12.5 × 20.5 cm. Inv. 1959–68. Photo: Christoph Irrgang. Location: Hamburger Kunsthalle, Hamburg, Germany. Photo Credit: bpk, Berlin/Art Resource, NY. The Puhlmann House not only conveys place but also speaks to mood, through the use of light, atmosphere, and attention to the details in this space.

description of place and time but also can be used for subjective representation of self. If a structured intervention is needed, the suggestion to *Draw a house that represents you* may be helpful to achieve a subjective representation of self. Different floors of a house (e.g., basements, attics, upstairs, downstairs) can imply a hierarchy and may hold certain secrets or treasures. Floors, rooms, and closets can represent the interior of a person's psyche while the structure and materials of the exterior walls, roof, and windows can represent the patient's outer appearance or represent what others may see or are be perceived to see. A house conveys the essence of containment and shelter—a place of belonging associated with our earliest experiences in the womb or nest; it may be a haven or a prison (Ronnberg & Martin, 2010). The house may represent the structural soundness of the personality (Ronnberg & Martin, 2010). Is it disjointed, out of balance, opulent, or run down? In contrast, a suggestion to *Draw a house of your dreams* may reveal not only how one feels about oneself but also what one longs for in terms of security, protection, and wealth. It may be a place of homecoming in life and in death, and it "is the goal of epic odysseys, spiritual quests and psychic transformations" (Ronnberg & Martin, 2010, p. 556).

What is most important in the drawing process in psychotherapy is not the intervention itself but the appropriateness and the connectedness the person feels with the experience. In the beginning, one may have much self-doubt about one's drawing abilities, but through encouragement and positive regard, confidence and skill will develop to communicate internal and external states of being through the use of imagery and art. The next section discusses examples of current tends of using art as an assessment tool, followed by examples of using art in clinical practice and supervision.

This Birth of Consciousness: The Garden of Eden and the PPAT

As in the sciences, empirical research has been sought in psychotherapeutic fields for its apparent ability to validate, including in art therapy assessments. And as evidence-based practice has been brought into the social sciences as its preferred "method," clinicians and researchers have struggled to situate the multifaceted and complex issues surrounding human function and relationships. While there are differences between therapeutic practices and research practices, there has been an emphasis on having research findings influence or even dictate practice. Establishing validity for the arts in a therapeutic context through art assessments has value but misses the larger picture of the image and its context of complexity and polyvalent natural strengths. As Cameron (1963) stated, "Not everything that can be counted counts. Not everything that counts can be counted" (p. 13). Art and psychological process simply do not lend themselves well to quantitative measure, but this does not lessen their significance.

Art conveys information that is unique to its mode of expression—a graphic form or an imagistic form. It expresses the whole of the individual's experience in that moment as he or she experiences it through the mode of creating art and images. The use of art for diagnosis is scientifically interesting, but this application is used by those who merely seek to validate the modality of image and graphic creation by limiting it to what can be gleaned via other means or modes. A reductionist process of a one-picture assessment appeals to our fact-finding nature but often oversimplifies results to the point where they become better as sound bites than as information that can inform practice and result in psychological change and transformation. This type of research lacks the depth and complexity of the symbolic function of the individual and recasts the work itself in terms that are actually opposed to its nature. Although quantitative empirical research of the arts attempts to cast a validating light on the work, it actually distorts the understanding of what the artwork achieves. Artwork is not a replicable thing. The meanings and significance of similar elements in different works are different by virtue of their being differently situated within the individual context. For example, three people may have the symptoms of depression, but all three of them may have come to have these symptoms through different experiences, and so, the three people may use the color green but with completely different associations. For example, one may associate green with a fond memory of a beautiful green field, another with money, a third, envy. Psychology is meant to be a study of a single soul, not a group of souls as in anthropology and sociology. It is a social science and originated out of analytic thought but in recent years has come to forsake it origins to the point of losing its essence. In many settings, the theoretical scaffolding has been discarded and standardization imported. This limits information to that found in large groups of people and attempts to generalize it to make statements about individuals. Moreover, research can include the projections and biases of the researcher. Although quantitative evidence-based practice continues to dominate the vernacular and color the execution of mental health practice, the qualitative research community now rejects claims of researcher neutrality as either possible or desirable (Leavy, 2013).

One such assessment, titled "Draw Yourself Picking an Apple from a Tree" (PPAT), used in the Formal Elements of Art Therapy Scale (FEATS) includes the attempt to solidify graphic elements, such as color, use of space, and rotations to name only a few, in an attempt to make it equivalent with the ever-changing and problematic diagnostic criteria listed in the *Diagnostic Statistical Manual of Mental Health Disorders* (DSM), now in its 5th edition (American Psychiatric Association, 2013; Gantt & Tabone, 1998). This assessment takes qualities of artwork and attributes them to psychiatric illness as defined in the DSM. The DSM attempts to define and categorize mental illnesses based on clusters of behavioral and cognitive symptoms. Often, symptoms for one diagnosis overlap with those of another, or an arbitrary number of criteria must be met; for example, a person must exhibit five out of nine symptoms listed in the criteria. The manual is a culturally bound document, reflecting various understandings and changes in ideals as well as biases, its changes with modifications to diagnoses and criteria over time.

The DSM lists dichotomous diagnoses (one has it or one does not) even though much of mental health is on a continuum. People are not either mentally ill or not; instead, the continuum of mental health presents in contexts including situational factors, stress, and trauma, factors that the DSM attempts to incorporate through its multi-axial system. While attempting to render psychological disturbances into workable and commonly understood entities, its emphasis is on the discrete, which tends to polarize mental health issues, contributing to stigmas and misunderstandings about the complex, multifactorial issues of mental health. Such a black-and-white paradigm is useful in studies that need neat criteria checklists to assign diagnoses, such as medication trials that investigate behavioral outcomes, but by looking at singular factors, they distort the psychological situation by suggesting it is more finite than it actually is. The phenomena that are measured are not as finite as the diagnostic criteria implies. And thus the quantitative studies outcomes tend to distort the phenomena as they are actually experienced. One of the limitations of utilizing quantitative research in the social sciences is the complexity of the subjects. In these studies, generalities are extracted and then applied in practice to the majority of patients. When working with individuals through symbolic imagery and symptom formation, as individual processes, the therapist is able to consider the influences on the patient of their unique personal, familial, and cultural factors. Applying techniques or methods that are generalized misses the importance of the individual in the psychotherapy process and the significance of the contextual patient–therapist relationship (Wampold, 2001). Although the studies may be useful and generate interesting truths, they do not hold the truth about the core of the work in regards to psychological process and artistic expression.

With respect to art assessment tools, specifically the PPAT, graphic indicators are used to match forms, colors, and usage with diagnostic criteria. And although graphic elements and aesthetics should be considered in the psychotherapeutic process, separating and reducing these elements into definable, reproducible parts, removes them from their context. Addressing validation of the benefits of the emergent field of art therapy, Ulman and Levy (1992) noted problems with the practice of art assessment and insisted that relating elements within paintings or drawings to psychopathological diagnoses was open to serious debate unless it could be empirically proven that even the crudest diagnosis—patient or normal—could be made with consistent precision on the basis of the artwork. Ulman and Levy's frequently cited article, "An Experimental Approach to the Judgment of Psychopathology from Paintings" (1992), spearheaded a call to create assessments that could be judged based on quantifiable graphic qualities, such as number of colors used, percentage of paper covered with color, and so on. Eventually, such concrete elements might be more precisely distinguished, and their associations with the subtler aspects of personality studied. These studies exclude content regarding the patient's strengths and health, verbal associations and qualifications, or multicultural socializations and influences, and are based singularly on subjective "judges" that are termed "objective" as to their ability to read drawn elements and qualities. The term *judges* in this article seems to reflect a time in which a clearly delineated hierarchy was present in patient–therapist relationships and may also have been what the authors felt: judged by the medical community in which they worked as not being valid due to the scarcity of empirical research. It may have also resulted from a need to distance themselves from the human aspect of the process by placing themselves in the superior role of the judger. Judgment, acceptance, and validation all have played out in the history of psychology, but they have become increasingly intense as the medical profession has moved toward Cartesian rationalism (Shorter, 1992). Similarly, art shows and competitions have a long history of judges, judging what is beautiful, what is high art, and what is worthy to be on display. This context cannot be ignored because it may contribute to an inferiority complex among professionals in the psychological field and in the arts because judging lends an air of superiority but is often pocked with subjectivity in the decision making. I mention this because we are not immune to complexes. Complexes that we are unaware of we project externally.

While the history of art therapy originated out of a field that has been largely impressionistic, psychoanalytically symbolic, and intuitive, it has sought increasing empirical validation as a means to prove worth to ourselves and others. Ulman and Levy's (1992) concluding remark seems to sum up this focus away from our roots and core values: "In the past we have been much concerned with *content* and its symbolic implications. Our present study suggests that research centered on *form* and its correlation with personal characteristics may point the way toward greater reliability in the use of paintings for diagnostic purposes" (p. 91).

> Gantt (1998) similarly pointed out that, although art therapists like to make claims about such things as how changes in art are related to changes in psychological state, or how certain features are indicative of neuroses or mental adjustment, those assertions can no longer be made without solid, scientific proof of their validity if arts therapists wish to maintain their reputability among other counseling professionals. That kind of proof cannot be established without empirical research techniques that obtain quantifiable data to support the claims [as cited in Rockwell & Dunham, 2006, p. 105].

Rockwell and Dunham (2006) called for research to "empirically quantify the connection between art and mental health assessment" (p. 111). However, their promotion of such research as a solution reflects two things: intrinsic confidence in the ability of quantitative studies to convey meaningful and clinically valuable material and belief in the usefulness of validation through empirical means. However, there is a logical error in viewing one mode as meaningfully reducible to another. Due to its polyvalent nature, art cannot be reduced to statistics. The true value of art in psychotherapy practice lies not in its ability to do what other modes do, but to do what it does that others do not. Specifically, art can convey the totality of the psychic situation in all of its complexity within the singularity of the image. Thus, "a purely empirical approach to evaluating art relying on features would be doomed to failure, because it would be arbitrary" (Bungay, 1987, p. 25). The departure from the symbolic puts the field at odds with its historic use and thus a departure from the essence of the core values and properties of image as a psychological carrier of emergent psychological material and transformation.

PPAT

Art therapists Gantt and Tabone (1998) used the directive "Draw yourself picking an apple from a tree" (PPAT) to assess diagnostic indicators in their Formal Elements of Art Therapy Scale (FEATS) screening, seemingly to take up Ulman and Levy's call for empirical study of form with amnesic regard to the archetypal and symbolic properties of the work. In their assessment, Gantt and Tabone (1998) proposed to evaluate patients' responses based on a set of elements that measure the way it is drawn, such as line quality, color, and rotation of figure, to name only a few of the fourteen elements. Looking at only the formal elements presents a disconnect with the underlying individual meaning that a response to the intervention elicits. A distinction between using art to assess global criteria and using it to elicit individual meaning is essential. As Wojtkowski (2009) stated, "The meaning arises from the context of associations that provide value, purpose and efficacy" (p. 8) rather than solely from "*the way in which it is drawn*," as cited in the Formal Elements of Art Therapy Scale (FEATS; Gantt & Tabone, 1998, p. 14).

The pursuit of knowledge and validation of the field of art therapy through formalized elements and quantitative research seem to leave gaps in its practice and historical origins and how these elements relate to this and other mythologies and ideologies. The dearth of information about art therapy and its symbolic origins creates a disconnect between some of its strengths and validity or value found through other means. This disconnection in the literature of art therapists seemed startling to me, even early in my career in the early 1990s. At that time, my work consisted of running group art and psychoeducational sessions on a locked psychiatric unit for acutely psychotic patients in a bankrupt, inner city facility. As a graduate student beginning my studies in art therapy, I cobbled together enough money to attend the American Art Therapy Conference in Las Vegas in the early 1990s. While there, I heard Gantt speak about the PPAT assessment and I, like many nascent art therapists, returned to my work excited to try out this and other new interventions with my clients. Armed with the information about the assessment, I was eager to try out this directive with the patients I was working with at the time, not as a standardized assessment, but as an intervention and means of expression.

On one of my first attempts to facilitate this directive with a group, a female patient whom I will call Mary was in my group. Mary was a young, child-like African American woman in her early twenties who wore her hair in platted pigtails, carried a blanket or stuffed animal with her, and continually sucked her thumb. Her teeth reflected a lifetime of thumb sucking and protruded from her mouth, and she was unable to care for some of her most basic hygiene needs. Suffering from severe neglect as a child, she had pronounced developmental delays. She grew up as a ward of the state, living in foster homes until she turned eighteen and then was bounced in and out of residential communities with periods of homelessness. She had profound mental health issues and had experienced significant trauma as well as nearly debilitating cognitive impairments, which had left her dissociative and oftentimes inarticulate. She, like many of the patients I worked with on this unit, suffered from schizophrenia with delusions. Her delusions were of a religious nature, and her most recent hospitalization was marked with psychotic features. It was also discovered upon her admission that she was pregnant, which she adamantly denied. It was later discovered she had been providing sexual favors for cigarettes and other items frequently bartered among the residents of the unit, and we had to assume she had been prostituting herself before her admission. For much of her time on the unit, the social workers and physicians struggled with the ethics of medicating her while pregnant or providing abortive services. The patient, who was deemed incompetent to give permission for sexual relations due to her psychosis and cognitive impairment, also was unable to consent to a medical procedure like an abortion, but it was something that was regularly discussed at team meeting, which included Mary. As Mary neared the end of the term in which she could legally have an abortion, her complex situation gave rise to increasingly contentious issues among the doctors and social workers responsible for her physical care.

The contentiousness did not remain in the team consulting room, however. In the group Mary was in, I suggested that the group members *Draw yourself picking an apple from a tree.* Mary refused to participate, objecting, "Drawing an apple is like participating in the original sin and I will have nothing to do with it." She was outraged at my suggestion! She looked at me distrustfully, as if I were Satan himself tempting her to participate in a forbidden activity. Although our relationship had been amicable and she had willingly participated in numerous groups in her protracted hospitalization, she just could not separate the activity of creating this picture from the image of the ideal it held for her. Art therapy is concerned with exactly this process and the moderation between the real and the imaginary, what is felt to be real and known to be, but with delusions, the boundary between the real and imaginary becomes indistinguishable (Springham, 2008).

In keeping with her religious delusions, Mary went on to cite passages of the Bible and protest that drawing an apple was the same as picking the apple and thus she believed it to be the equivalent to participating in the very same act for which Adam and Eve were ejected from the Garden of Eden. I listened empathically for several minutes and gave her other suggestions about ways she could participate without having to focus on the apple. But Mary was not receptive to my suggestions, and her fixed beliefs won out. It had struck a concealed nerve; she paced about and passionately preached some more in an attempt to coerce others in her rebellion to defect from group this day. The indifferent members of the group, who were dutifully drawing, were oblivious to her remarks, and thus, she walked out of the room murmuring biblical quotations. She would later fully participate in other groups again without further discussion or seeming memory of this incident, but there was something in this encounter with Mary and her delusional content, her current situation, and its interface with this art intervention that left an indelible impression on me: The connection between *Draw yourself picking and apple from a tree* and the expulsion from the Garden of Eden.

In 20 years of practice and asking hundreds, perhaps thousands, of patients to draw themselves picking an apple from a tree, I can recall a handful of patients making an association with the apple as an object of desire like the one plucked by Adam and Eve but have never again had a patient refuse to engage in the drawing due to religious convictions or delusions. It would have been easy to dismiss Mary's comments because of her delusional nature. Most would disregard them as being nonsense, ungrounded, and meaningless, but there was something very striking and important in her response that had me contemplate the connection between this directive and the biblical association, a story with archetypal imagery and incarnations in numerous religions and belief systems throughout the world and dating back to early antiquity. A place where, due to psychotic impairment, archetypal elements protruded into the psyche. Not wild psychoanalysis as Freud once accused (2010), but instead a thoughtful and very personal insight from the psychotic delusions of a woman who carried her "truth," which contained the intolerable incompatibility between her religiosity and her awareness of her actions (whether through corrosion, rape, or consent) that had led to her pregnancy. Her refusal to participate is also a symbolic expression of an archetypal image.

Mary's inability to participate was about the merger of story and reality, about the inability to separate real from fantasy or illusion from delusion, or a merger with the consuming archetypal force. Mary, due to her psychosis, was unable to separate the collective knowing and her own reality. She was one with her delusion, and so participating would be equivalent to being swallowed up in the archetypal image of the expulsion from the Garden of Eden. This individual symbolic process was important to Mary because it was her own personal unique response and contained her own psychic conflict.

Lowenfeld first wrote about the art directive "Draw yourself picking an apple from a tree" in 1939. This intervention with archetypal and mystical origins, although not discussed in his work, has great potential when exploring relational and symbolic qualities within a therapeutic context. Von Franz (1995) discussed how creation myths are seen in many religions. They are essential in teaching the ritual of initiation and refer to problems of the human condition and to the conditions related to our existence, not only for ourselves, but also for the whole cosmos. The story, even if one is not familiar with the all facets of the biblical reference, holds elements of human temptation, the forbidden, the rejected, and shame. The directive points to the moment when one is given over to temptation or to humanly desires, whether of food, love, lust, or other human feebleness. It is the moment when Eve is implicated for man's expulsion from the Garden of Eden and denied eternal life, in which one is inseparable from nature, and subjected to otherness, separation from nature, and the need to cover the body with cloth to cover shame. It is also at this moment that human consciousness may be said to be born.

Before digressing into the application of this directive, exploration of its origins and historical context is necessary. When a new religion conquers an earlier one, old customs and deities are either incorporated into the new beliefs or demonized (Hargreaves, 2009). The picking of an apple from a tree harks back to the story of the Garden of Eden in the Book of Genesis and may be found in the religious texts of Islam, Christianity, and Judaism, as seen in *The Garden* in the Qur'an. In the Garden, Adam and Eve, the first man and woman, lived naked in the paradise harmoniously among animals and luscious fruit-bearing trees. In this garden grew the Tree of Life as well as the Tree of Knowledge of Good and Evil, among many others. They were told they could live there forever and could freely eat all of the fruit except the one that God had prohibited, which grew on the Tree of Knowledge of Good and Evil. The identity of the forbidden fruit was not given in the religious scriptures, and it has been speculated that the fruit is an apple,

Figure 3.8 Albrecht Dürer (1471–1528). *Adam and Eve* (1504). Engraving, 9 7/8 × 7 7/8 in. (25.1 × 20.0 cm). Fletcher Fund, 1919 (19.73.1). Location: The Metropolitan Museum of Art, New York. Credit: Image copyright © The Metropolitan Museum of Art. Image source: Art Resource, NY.

pomegranate, or in some accounts, grapes, figs, or even a citron. Figure 3.8 shows a work by Albrecht Dürer. "The branch Adam holds is of the mountain ash, the Tree of Life, while the fig, of which Eve has broken off a branch, is the forbidden Tree of Knowledge. Four of the animals represent the medieval idea of the four temperaments—the cat is choleric, the rabbit sanguine, the ox phlegmatic, and the elk melancholic" (Boorsch & Orenstein, 1997, p. 31). Each element in the engraving is symbolic. The fruit is associated with Eve's love, and so eating fruit is a frequent euphemism for lovemaking, as in the Song of Solomon, a text that introduces human sexuality within a religious framework:

"Let my beloved come into his garden, and eat its choicest fruits" [Song 4:16].

"Oh, may your breasts be like clusters of the vine, and the scent of your breath like apples" [Song 7:8].

Among the animals that lived in Eden was a serpent, an incarnation of the dragon. While Christianity personified the Egyptian Osiris and the Greek Dionysus in the figure of Jesus, the ancient horned and fertility deities were combined into the horned and hooved Satan, and dragons of wisdom, flow, and fertility became envoys of negative destructive power (Hargreaves, 2009). Thus, the serpentine dragon Lilith, who was initially presented to Adam as his first wife in some texts, was rejected. The serpent persuaded Eve to eat the forbidden fruit, despite God's instructions that would allow them to live forever in the garden. Interestingly, "A Hebrew text reminds us '. . . for before Eve was Lilith.' She is described elsewhere as the first wife of Adam, who refused to lie beneath him (and obey his commands), so when Adam spurned Lilith and married Eve, . . . she revenged herself on Adam's wife" (Hargreaves, 2009, p. 26). And Mary, my patient, had been scorned numerous times by the people she believed loved her; they abandoned her as a child, left her pregnant at least three times while she was unable to care for her children, all of whom had been taken from her either at birth or shortly after and made wards of the state and with whom she had no contact or knowledge.

In the Garden of Eden, when Eve plucks the apple from the tree, she and Adam are not killed but exiled from the garden. At that very moment, they felt a sudden jolt of sorrowfulness, remorse, and shame (Wallace, 2004). "Then the eyes of both of them were opened, and they knew that they were naked; and they sewed fig leaves together and made themselves loin coverings" (Genesis 3:7). After eating from the Tree of Knowledge, the conventional way of understanding this gesture is to imagine that Adam and Eve are newly aware and ashamed of their nudity. In that instant, on one level, what they now know is not only their nakedness, but also knowledge of nakedness, which presumes a far deeper knowledge of which shame is only a symptom. It is the knowledge of oneself as a visual object, *seen as*, in the mind of another subject who looks upon you (Wallace, 2004). This has many connotations in terms of objective and subjective experiences. The ability to turn one's focus to the act of observing oneself and actions is parallel to depth-oriented psychotherapy processes to observe the intersection of the inner and outer experiences and to become aware or conscious of them in order to change.

It must be pointed out that often Eve, the woman, is implicated in "the fall of humanity," as this passage is often referred to in Christian texts. The woman and the snake are often cast in a negative light (Moon, 1997). But when viewing the couple as inextricable parts of the self, because Eve was taken from the rib of Adam to be his companion, it is the feminine that jolts both the masculine and feminine parts into consciousness, not blaming one another for their actions. As Jung recognized, "It is a frightening thought that man also has a shadow-side to him, consisting not just of little weaknesses and foibles, but of a positively demonic dynamism" (CW 7:35). This moment is a birth of consciousness, when man departs from his natural, unified state with nature, and his otherness from it leads to his ability to see himself and his actions separate from the nature he resides in. As George (2014) stated,

Marie-Louise von Franz (1995) explained that this is a natural result of our psyche experiencing its own ego-consciousness coming into being as "world-becoming." As far as our psyche is concerned, our becoming aware of the world and the world coming into existence are one and the same. This process occurred not only when humans first developed ego-consciousness but also occurs in any young child's development (as shown by developmental psychology) and in the life of adults, such as when we wake up in the morning from an unconscious state and order falls into place [n.p.].

As a consequence of this couple's disunity and strife, some consider the expulsion to be divine punishment. It is theorized that the Garden of Eden symbolizes humanity's original harmony, and that shame, guilt, and fear existed outside of the garden.

The PPAT is an assessment used to glean diagnostic information from drawings by focusing on global characteristics of form rather than subject matter. This removes the drawing from the context of a therapeutic process. Gantt cautioned that, as diagnosable symptoms abate, so too do drawings change, and she stated that one must reexamine the idea of projective drawings—that the constituent parts somehow reflect personality traits (Gantt, Tinnin, & Williams, 1993; Kaplan, 1998). The parts are only a piece of the experience and do not address the complex aspects of the context of the therapeutic experience. And like the creative process and life itself, it is a fluid, dynamic process.

When used as an intervention, like the myth, it offers an opportunity for reflection, awareness, and in some cases, awakening through image. In sessions, when asking patients to depict themselves picking an apple from a tree, an important caveat is to have them draw themselves as a whole and complete person. This yields material for reflection about their perception of their body image and provides information about images of self as well as relational issues that extend to the tree and the apple, a rich mixture for associations. It is easy to fall into a shorthand schema of drawing only a stick figure. Mentioning a whole and complete person minimizes the use of stick figures in responses made by adults. I will add that the patient may depict at minimum himself or herself, an apple, and a tree, but the person may draw a whole orchard of trees, other people, and objects in the picture if so desired. By offering this creative freedom, it is my intention that the artists depict the images that best suit them and their psychology, reducing the mechanicalness of the response.

Once the image has been completed to the patient's satisfaction, I will ask her to suspend the thought for a moment that the person in the image is herself, and to tell a story about the image, using the following suggestions to focus on key points in the story. Who is this person, how did she arrive here, is she successful in reaching the apple, what will she do with the apple, and what comes next in the story? These questions help guide a discussion about a potential journey of the figure in the drawing, creating room for exploration of themes, which may involve past, present, and future situations or actions. Turning the image from a still frame into part of an imagined storyboard or moving picture gives an opportunity to discuss time and placement. This intervention allows further exploration of the "how" of the imagery and story, rather than just the "what." Consideration of the image as an active and alive process that undergoes change depending on context is imperative. Much as the contained therapy appointment is a point in time, typically 60 minutes, the image and experience are also only at one point in a much longer continuum of life, with past and future inexorably attached to this moment.

The symbolism and rich content held in the image and the moment are immeasurable. Careful consideration of how the image is constructed yields additional opportunities for reflection. For example, observing the person create the image reveals the sequence in which the elements were placed in the picture frame. For example, was the tree drawn first? Was space for the person accommodated or was it provided as an afterthought? If the individual picking an apple from a tree was an afterthought, this may yield in discussion the significance that the agent of change did not take a forefront position in the scene. An example is the client who spends most of the time drawing intricate branches, leaves, and details in the tree without regard to the person, only to discover the tree may be too large or too small to adequately place a person beside it, or that the person who is supposed to be picking the apple will be unsuccessful. When this observation is reflected to the patient, a discussion about her ability to identify and complete goals may come into play.

In this drawing, there are four main elements: the tree, the person, the apple, and the relationships among them. Items may be added, such as ladders, baskets, other people, additional trees, and a drawn or implied baseline, but for the most part, addressing the four main elements will yield ample information for discussion. On the latent level, all elements within the image refer to the individual's psyche and interrelations among various components of psychic life. The apple may serve as a metaphor for reaching toward a goal, or issues around nutritional needs, and it may even carry biblical associations.

In my experience, most patients begin by drawing the tree. It is less anxiety-producing than drawing a person and gives a foundation for both the apple and the person to relate to. The tree is a central, natural element. In the Garden of Eden, Adam and Eve were as one with the environment before the expulsion and the awareness of otherness. According to Jung, the tree appears frequently among archetypal configurations of the unconscious, and when drawn, typically takes on a symmetrical pattern in the form of a mandala: the self depicted as a process of growth (CW 13:304). According to Jung, to best understand the individual association with trees, knowing about historical antecedents is helpful. Most commonly, the tree has been associated with the Tree of Life, the unfolding of a form in a physical and spiritual sense, and development and growth from above and below. It holds mythical relevance and is often portrayed in myths, fairytales, and poetry. The tree connects the earth and sky and has material aspects; as animals nestle in its branches or take shelter in its hollows, it provides protection, offers shade, and provides nourishing fruits (Ronnberg & Martin, 2010). It is a source of life, rooted to the spot, representing old age, death, and rebirth (CW 13:350). Through its regenerative seed; we come to appreciate that the mightiest trees come from the smallest of seeds, which reminds us that we can do the same.

Although apple trees are common in many parts of the temperate world, it is important to note whether the patient has ever seen such a tree in person. The representation of a tree may be distinctly culturally bound, which is important to acknowledge before implying an interpretation. If the patient is working off a general idea of a tree, or a tree that is distinctly different from an apple tree, it is important to understand the relevance of the tree portrayed. Relating to the tree that emerges as opposed to what a preconceived apple tree would look like is also important. Keep in mind, however, apple trees kept for their fruit are typically short due to heavy pruning, which give their branches a gnarled nubby appearance like arthritic fingers. A diminutive size is desired for easier fruit picking but does bring themes of man's attempt to control or alter nature, because an apple tree's natural state can be quite large when left to its own design. And if left to grow on their own, unshaped or abandoned in a feral orchard, they can make fruit picking an ominous task, but they never take on the size of a tall canopy tree like an oak.

Knotholes in trees have been associated with trauma, but it has not been shown conclusively that children who have experienced physical or sexual trauma draw more knotholes in trees during the House-Tree-Person Assessment (Zannis, 2003, as cited in Brooke, 2004). However, studies have found that witnesses of domestic violence tend to draw more knotholes in their trees. This information is interesting, but it does not necessarily further our understanding of the individual and psychological function. It comes from a scientific lens, not an imagistic lens that encompasses psychological experience and is able to take into consideration the whole of its subject and its multifactorial elements. Because the tree is a subjective representation of an aspect of self, it may be just as helpful to see knotholes in trees as related to a chakra system, as in Hinduism and Buddhism, which corresponds to energy sources and channels within the body. These energy sources may directly relate to the systems in the body that are affected by trauma. For example, the voids and holes often phenomenologically associated in the body image representations of persons with eating disordered behaviors may be indications of disruptions in the plexus chakra, the seat of personal power and place of ego, passions, impulses, anger, and strength. Religious beliefs, like art, share a psychological construct capable of holding ideals, beliefs, values, experience, and perceptions along with the historical bases and cultural nuances inherent in myth, narrative, and memory. A psychological construct creates a lens through which to understand the image, which is larger than its parts, whereas scientific investigation of the image reduces it to its parts and removes it from context, thus losing the individual's meaning and psychological significance.

Although one could look at the artwork and imagery of the individual and make general associations, the true meaning will be in the responses, amplification, and therapeutic relationship held in the specific context. For example, the person drawn in the PPAT could be considered an objective representation of self and the tree a subjective perspective, which I will explain further through the following examples. If the person is omitted completely in the drawing, this may indicate avoidance or overwhelming anxiety, and thus, the tree may be used singularly as a subjective representation of self. Through the representation of the body, details about how one sees oneself in terms of body image, proportion, and relationship to others are to be considered. The ability to plan ahead and problem solve also comes into play as the drawing is constructed. If, for example, the tree takes over the page and there is no room for the person, or if the scale of the tree in relation to person is such that there is no way for the person to pick an apple, this, too, would be problematic and worthy of discussion as to how this relates to the person's daily life.

The action of picking an apple may represent the ability to reach for something and obtain it, or to possess agency in one's life. It may also relate to reaching goals or to nurturance and self-care. If the apple is far removed from the figure, the person may feel helpless or defeated, again confirmed by discussion with the patient as to how this observation may relate to their life. If there is only one apple and it is depicted as rotten, this may reflect the person feeling hopeless because even if one were to reach the apple, it would be no good and of no use. The most important aspect in the discussion part of the image-making process is the associations and the unfolding of the connections between the image and its creator—the gentle revealing of meaning.

Charlotte: Bobbing for Apples

In Figure 3.9 is an image of *Draw yourself picking an apple from a tree* created by a woman whom I shall call Charlotte. She was of African American and Hispanic descent, in her early 30s, and had been hospitalized for depression, co-occurring binge drinking, and bulimia. Her stay was relatively brief due to limitations of her insurance and inability to self-pay. This linear PPAT drawing was created on the day of her discharge from the hospital after only a fortnight stay. Once she and the other group members finished their drawings, the images were hung on a bulletin board in the art therapy room for discussion. When Charlotte spoke, she discussed her optimism about returning home and being with her sons. Her older son was a young teenager, depicted on the right side of the page saying, "My turn." Charlotte's seven-year-old was identified in a swing on the tree on the left side of the page, saying, "Look, Mommy." A group member inquired as to who the other figure was between the person identified as herself, dressed in pink, facial features omitted, and leaning over the bucket of water bobbing for apples by the tree. Of note, Charlotte was compliant with the directive; her figure was the only one not drawn as a stick figure.

Charlotte responded, "The other stick figure is my boyfriend. He lives with me." The figure of the drawn boyfriend was placed between her and the tree. She said he was laughing at her bobbing for apples, as indicated by his "HA-HA!" remarks. The group inquired why he was laughing, when it seemed as if she was

Figure 3.9 This linear PPAT drawing was created on the day of Charlotte's discharge, describing her situation with her eating disorder and inability to look at the larger picture of the problematic family dynamics. © 2016 Michelle L. Dean.

preoccupied with the apples in the tub of water—unable to observe her children or her surroundings. One of the group members blurted out, "It looks like you are purging."

Charlotte considered the comments of the group members as she studied her picture. She had what is sometimes called an "aha" moment as she said, "You know, that does pretty well describe my situation. My eating disorder does make me check out and unable to see what is going on. I am so focused on getting the apple in the tub I fail to see the others that may be available to me on the tree." She continued by describing the tree as a cyclical spiraling vortex that could be spiraling inward or outward, she wasn't sure.

She said, "The spirals in the tree are very much like my disorder—both eating and drinking—pulling me in and making me go around in circles in my life." I pointed out a faint image of a face in the tree and asked her whether she felt it had significance, when another group member remarked, "I barely even saw that; it looks like it is there and not there."

Reflecting on the possibility that the knothole might be indicative of previous trauma, I asked, "Is there anything in your life that was present but may not be fully visible, either to yourself or others?"

She thought for a moment and said, "There are many secrets that I have to keep, especially secrets relating to the eating disorder and binge drinking. And there is something else . . ."

She went on to describe in detail her boyfriend who was emotionally manipulative and not supportive of her recovery. Charlotte reported how the boyfriend would purchase beer and wine and bring it to the home they shared, even though she had requested alcohol not be kept in the house due to her recovery efforts. It was later revealed that her welfare checks, once cashed, were then often used by him and not for food for her children. Because he benefited from using the money for his indulgences, he was not motivated or invested in her recovery, because while she was incapacitated by the negative effects of her drinking and purging she could not resist his actions. This dynamic jeopardized the family's ability to be properly cared for, and the fallout from it was apparent. Charlotte discussed how her older son had had episodes of truancy and bouts with drinking as well. He had come home drunk several times after being out with friends and was disrespectful to her when he taunted her for her drunkenness. His comment "My turn" seemed to hit a particularly harsh cord as she realized it was not just a turn at bobbing for apples he might be after, but his turn to struggle with addiction. In contrast, the younger son, tiny in comparison on the swing, pleads for attention with his comment, "Look, Mommy." The ropes that bind the swing and hold the seat he stands on are heavily drawn with dark black lines as if attempting to fortify the attachments or cords. Although only one drawing, it contained a visual treasure trove for reflection and a mirror of the way things were and could become in the future if alternative actions were not taken. With this information, Charlotte felt emboldened to throw the boyfriend out of the home as soon as she returned and to continue her outpatient treatment and 12-step program in order to maintain her sobriety.

A Perfect(ionist) Process

The immediate context in which the art is created is as much to be considered as what is actually drawn. Bearing witness to the art-making process is as important to the therapy as being in the same room with the client. So much can be gained about the feelings and expressions of the person as well as the overall feel of the tensions in the room. With the advent of online therapy and phone sessions, something often feels missing when the patient(s) and the therapist are not actually in the same room. Because a piece of art is created, some may consider allowing the art to represent the person. Although there is a record, the work of art, it is not the same as actually having a relationship with the patient and hearing about his or her associations to the work. In the art world this is done all the time; we look at a piece of art and feel about it. Although the artist's intention may be present, the context is lost and so most of what we feel is our own projections. We may stand before a famous work of art such as that of Leonardo da Vinci, but our experience of the art would be very different if we lived at the time he lived and were fortunate enough to have a conversation about what he drew and his associations and to watch his face and mannerisms as he created. Being present for the art-making process is significant. Although works may be created at home and brought into session, the container and relationship of the therapeutic alliance is essential. The importance of observing the art making could not be more clearly illustrated than by the picture shown in Figure 3.10, which was created by a young woman I will call Penny. Penny was hospitalized for a restrictive eating disorder, but what became evident from her art making was the anxiety around food was not the only issue that was haunting Penny and her ability to feed herself.

Penny was part of a group to which the *Draw yourself picking an apple from a tree* directive was given when there were several new group members in a revolving group at a women's eating disorders facility. Penny took a piece of paper and collected her markers, laying them out before her in an orderly way so all of the ends lined up in a straight row in front of her. Once she had one of each color, she proceeded to draw the outline of the tree followed by the string-like branches that radiated outward from the trunk. Once the branches were complete she set

Figure 3.10 Penny was hospitalized for a restrictive eating disorder but what became evident from her art was that anxiety around food was not the only issue interfering with her ability to feed herself. © 2016 Michelle L. Dean.

out the green, yellow, and orange markers. Each leaf was completed after removing the lid from each marker, creating the mark, snapping the lid of the marker back on the marker, and returning it to its place. This pattern repeated with the next colored marker—lid off, leaf mark made, lid snapped back on, and returned to place. One at a time, this went on for the better part of our drawing time, approximately 20–30 minutes, until I pointed out that our time to draw was nearly complete as our group time was coming to an end for the day. I reminded the group that if they needed to add anything else to the drawing to go ahead and do so as we would be hanging them up to discuss them, and group members could share if they wished to do so. Registering the time limitation, Penny colored in the tree trunk and returned to working carefully on her person and struggled over getting the correct proportions of her figure. She then moved on to drawing the basket and then the grass.

As Penny discussed her drawing, she was irritable and seemed guarded as she said, "My figure is sitting on the ground waiting for the apples to come my way. I really don't need to pick any because my basket is full, and I would not eat them anyway from the basket, off the ground, or from the tree."

What became apparent from her drawing were the two drawing styles, or energy uses. First, the obsessional linear drawing of the leaves, meticulously depicted one leaf at a time, consuming not only her time but her focus and energy. Each colored leaf falls in a consecutive order with the previous ones; order was imperative, as if possessing a magical control over something. Coupled with this was the passivity of the figure that, without the grassy area, looked as if it might be jumping toward the tree to grab the apple falling, but there was also her refusal to eat the apples, a source of nurturance or possibly symbolizing her goals she would like to reach toward. In contrast is the expressive or dynamic drawing style that conveys an agitated line quality as seen in the filling of the inner tree and grassy areas. The ground that the figure sits on is ragged and was created with quick, sharp gestures; it required a nervous energy and has much less control than the leaves as demonstrated by the slanting lines of a right-handed creator, overshooting onto the pants legs, and the marks that ran off the page onto the table. Penny remained guarded, but what became apparent in her drawing was the need to feel control over the nervous anxiety that she experienced as her base and in her core. She used her obsessional thoughts, her calculations of calories, and her controlling and potentially life-threatening restriction, as a means of keeping paralyzing anxiety at bay. Addressing the anxiety and obsessional thoughts became a significant part of her therapy as it was a primary contributor to her eating disordered symptoms.

Tree of (Pseudo) Success

As a part of an adult day program, I ran art therapy groups that often had adults with diverse difficulties who sought mental health services and utilized this program either as a step-down from inpatient or as an attempt to diffuse a condition or situation that could precipitate an inpatient hospitalization. Most of the patients were diagnosed with depression, anxiety, bipolar disorder, or schizophrenia, often with comorbid drug and alcohol issues. The individuals in the group had varying levels of acuity and a multitude of concerns. In one such group, a woman I will call Belinda entered into treatment for bipolar symptoms, including mania, risk-taking behaviors, grandiosity, poor insight and judgment, and a self-reported substance abuse history. She was loud and boisterous, often interrupting or cutting off other members of the group with direct advice and suggestions. On the day that the group chose to *Draw yourself picking an apple from a*

Figure 3.11 Tree to Success drawn by Belinda, who drew a linear, spiraling canopy in her tree, investing much energy in the upper part of the tree. © 2016 Michelle L. Dean.

tree, Belinda created the image shown in Figure 3.11. She described it as her "Tree to Success." Belinda, like Charlotte, drew a linear, spiraling canopy in her tree, investing much energy in the upper part of the tree. The large apples resembled hearts until she, observing the similarity, placed leaves on many of them. She hastily drew herself in one color and missing an arm. Her figure is not securely grounded and appears to be floating. What is most notable is the relationship she has with the apples and her need to label each of them with a fine-lined ball-point pen. As she discussed her picture, she boasted about her desire to leave the program, that she was all better and no longer in need of treatment. She was preachy and condescending to some of the other group members who appeared more disheveled than her. But discussion of her artwork allowed the group members to call her out on the thin veneer she seemed to be presenting to "fool" the staff and possibly herself so she could be discharged. But her art relayed a different message. As she read the labels in the tree: helping, family, marriage, friendship, parenting, success, money, God (listed twice), sobriety, patience, love, understanding, trust, humor, personality, and honesty, to name a few, she seemed to say all the right things that one may need to consider for recovery.

Belinda went on speaking about her relationship with God, 12-step programs, and the traits she admired most in herself, rejecting the things she felt led to her problems of power, control, and lust for money. Her rants about being better than everyone else seemed disingenuous as she protested about how the moment she could be released from the hospital, her life would be better. She asked me for my observations of the picture and I said that before I gave her my thoughts, I wanted to hear more about hers.

"Sobriety, God, friendship, faith, and helping others are all the most important to me," she said.

"That's interesting, because the two things closest to your reach are money and success, not sobriety, supports, or faith," I responded. As members of the group pointed out the inconsistencies between what she said and the image, she began to lose her aplomb.

I asked the group where the energy or investment in the image seemed to be, and they responded that the spiraling "craziness" in the tree canopy seemed to hold the most energy. The intense marks made it difficult to see her goals or apples placed inside of the tree, leaving only those on the outside to be obvious. In contrast, the figure was hastily done and was missing an arm—"It must be like going through life with a hand tied behind your back," said one group member.

"The ball-point words looked like an afterthought, not only because they were one of the last things placed on the page, but also like you were trying to get some control over the things in your head you wanted—you know, doing the talk, but not the walk of recovery," said another group member.

Belinda's reaction at first was anger and frustration, which softened as more group members and I assured her that it might be best to know where you are by taking a personal inventory. Knowing what you want could be helpful in placing the supports needed to prevent a relapse.

"What do you think your image is trying to tell you?" I asked Belinda.

She admitted that she felt deflated and, as much as she would like to be these things, she still was very much in her addiction, and her mania made it difficult to stay focused on doing the "sober" things in her life.

Belinda's image is a reminder that the image holds a truth, or a knowing, that often presents itself even when we are still grappling with it. This pre-emergent knowledge, needs skillful attending to as it can be experienced as a vulnerability. Much like a seedling of knowledge, harshness can drive the potential awareness back into itself or be experienced as cut off, as Other.

Bearing Fruit: The PPAT in Supervision

As a part of the professional supervision I provide to recent graduates and to new or established professionals, I encourage my supervisees to keep a personal journal of their experiences by documenting their responses in both written and graphic forms that reflect their experiences of the therapy session with their patients. My methods are similar to what Fish (2008) called *response art*:

> Art created by an art therapist to contain, explore, and express clinical work. It is the primary tool used in the practice of art-based supervision. Although the clarity that a therapist experiences as a result of response art ultimately benefits clients, it is fundamentally the therapist's work [p. 70].

Response art can be used for specific questions concerning a patient or their relationships, clarity about group dynamics, or personal reflection on clinical work. It also may be utilized to gain greater clarity on personal issues arising as a result of transference and counter-transference both with patients and between the supervisor and supervisee.

Supervision is a relationship full of complexities and ambiguities; one of its primary goals is to promote self-awareness (Carrigan, 1993). My supervisory model utilizing art in supervision promotes self-awareness through what Calisch called "eclectic blending." According to Calisch (1989), in eclectic blending, four clinical models of supervision are employed: psychodynamic, interpersonal, person centered, and behavioral. I would add imagistic because the image is able to simultaneously hold a multitude of modes of knowing, understanding, reflecting, and self-actualization.

Supervision can be an intense, personal experience because, according to Carrigan (1993), it "allocates most of the responsibilities and power to the supervisor" (p. 134). This may lead to the supervisee's feeling disempowered, activating previous traumas, relational dynamics, or other transference issues. These issues are often overlooked or dismissed as being outside the scope of supervision, but I disagree.

Transference and counter-transference in supervision can be as helpful as they are in therapy so long as the container and expectations of the supervisory relationship allow for it. The self-examination process can never fully be objective. We see ourselves with our own eyes, never as a fully separate observer; and as such, like our patients, we must work at insight through our senses and perceptions. Kielo (1991) stated,

> Unconscious reactions are unavoidable as the art therapist travels with his or her client into pre-verbal territory, no matter how much analysis or psychotherapy the therapist has undergone. The art therapist's effectiveness depends partially on an ability to gain insight into such personal reactions as the subtle interplay of projections, unconscious distancing, or undefined feelings so that they may be used to facilitate the treatment process [p. 14].

Avery was a recent graduate fulfilling her supervisory hours for her art therapy and counseling state licensure credentials. She sought supervision and support for her work as an art therapist working in the field of addictions. Avery was practicing in a high-acuity setting with patients addicted to multiple substances. Typically, Avery's clients had low compliance rates and limited resources and insight into their issues. Like many new graduates, Avery felt overwhelmed by the volume of her caseload of 35–50 clients per week and by a lack of organizational support and oversight within her agency, as well as by attempting to thrive in an environment with a high turnover of employees.

Upon our initial discussion about what she was seeking in supervision and the other customary items about work history, experience, and my supervisory philosophy, I asked how she came to want to work with me. Her response was, "I have attended multiple conferences and workshops as both a student and new professional and I had seen you present in the past." She added, "Additionally, I understand you work with clients with eating disorders, which is an interest of mine, and from then I knew I wanted to work with you."

Avery's insecurity and emotional volatility at her current place of work was compounded by being let go from her last job that she held right out of school, for less than 6 months, over interpersonal issues between herself and the agency supervisor. With every rupture or disagreement she had with her current onsite supervisor, she was convinced she would be fired again. She came to her off-site supervision and said, "I vacillate between being resentful, overly burdened, and feeling pissed off about how much I have to do, while also having intense feelings of insignificance. I am overwhelmed."

These feelings were particularly pronounced one day when reeling from the news that her site would undergo an inspection during the following week, and it was discovered that a large portion her charts were incomplete because her immediate supervisor failed to educate her about forms that needed to be completed. Because of this oversight, she and several of her colleagues whose charts were out of compliance were going to be mandated to work late nights and the weekend to complete the documentation. After affirming the injustices of the situation and how the idea of quitting this position out of spite would be unrealistic at that time, issues about inadequate guidance and nurturance arose.

In the beginning of our discussions we spoke of the relationship she had with her on-site supervisor and the dual relationship she was forming with her in terms of a friendship outside of work with phone calls, text messages, and social interactions. While having amicable relationships with one's boss is desirable, the increasing blur of boundaries between work and personal life became a challenge for Avery due to her isolation and desire for friendship. She had become isolated when she had moved, primarily for work, and knew few people in this new location. This was further complicated by her diminished ability and desire to see her on-site supervisor as a superior or leader. "I want her to be my friend or someone to help me both at work and outside of work. I want to have a special relationship with her—for her to be a kind of work-mother," Avery wept in our sessions about this unrealized desire.

What unfolded in our discussions was a history of inadequate caretaking, a tumultuous childhood, and much loss and separation from her parents after they divorced. Like many children of divorce, the effects reached far into adulthood, coloring relationships with peers and colleagues. For Avery, at the age of 12, her parents abdicated their parenting roles after they separated, making her understandably vulnerable to intense emotions when parental or authority figures were to provide guidance but were incompetent or absent. Mental health practitioners are not immune from childhood trauma, and this may actually lead many who experience childhood trauma to pursue a career as a therapist. Jung (1963) discussed the concept of the wounded healer, stating, "Only if the doctor knows how to cope with himself and his own problems will he be able to teach the patient to do the same" (p. 132).

The Wounded Healer

As Bardot (2008) described, recognition, acceptance, and healing are necessary in art therapy, and strong supervision with continual exploration of emotions utilizing art, journaling, and poetry is essential. It is imperative for therapists to seek support through their own therapy and supervision to help address woundedness, manage additional losses, maintain authentic empathy, and nurture the therapeutic bond (Bardot, 2008; Hardy, 2005; Waller, 2002).

Avery continued to struggle with feeling overwhelmed with her workload and some of the interpersonal issues that arose with her on-site supervisor. At one point, she had decided that she would rather have had her supervisor as her as friend than stay at the place she felt intolerable. Avery also began to share more about her personal struggles with binge eating. She used food as a means of comfort as well as punishment. The chaos at work was directly related to Avery's feelings of being out of control and vice versa. We spoke of the similar patterns inherent in addictions and eating disorders, including the tendency to seek approval outside of oneself. This is due in part to early childhood trauma that leaves one vulnerable to inadequately regulating affect while also externalizing one's locus of control by seeking events or people outside oneself to provide comfort or reassurance. Although this may be done by all in varying degrees, it becomes particularly challenging in the transition from adolescence to adulthood and in the processes of individuation that are ongoing into adulthood. Avery, as a new professional, was now in her new career faced with the great responsibility of not only negotiating the demands of her new job but also attempting to balance her own personal needs.

As we continued to discuss her patients' artwork and the conditions at work, she presented an image that she said she had done while in session with one of her patients, shown in Figure 3.12. Drawing in session with a patient is a practice that can support the use of the art therapist's artist-self as a participant in therapy and the development of empathy by means of an authentic, visible response (Rubin, 2001). The image of her drawing herself picking an apple from a tree was self-directed, and she said she had not provided associations

Figure 3.12 Continual attention to the therapist's wounds is imperative in both therapy sessions and in supervision. This PPAT was used in a supervisory situation in order to gain greater clarity about the situation. © 2016 Michelle L. Dean.

with it in relationship to her patient. Her expressive marks were made with much intensity, laying the oil pastels on the page with a thick sheen. She said she was not really thinking of her patient because she had been too consumed with frustration after a disappointing interaction with her supervisor followed by thoughts of leaving the agency. As we spoke about the image she laughed and said, "There is no way I am going to reach those apples," noticing the tree was too tall for the red figure to reach.

"What do you think the apple and the tree may be about for you?" I inquired.

"I am sure it is about my job and finding a place to work where I will be happy," she responded.

"It looks like you have lots of questions?" as I noted the question marks in the speech bubble.

"Yeah, I am not sure where I can work that will make me happy. I keep thinking that as soon as I have my credentials and license, I can move on to get a better job and not feel so stressed," she said.

We spoke more about the picture, noting the intense colors and the effort needed to fill the page with the oil pastels. She agreed it was very cathartic to put her pent up frustration into color. Our conversation turned to the figure when I asked what she thought of the person and if it had a story?

"I don't know, it's kinda weird with no face and being all red," she said.

"It reminded me of an apple itself. It is red like the apples in the tree and even has a reflective shine; I wonder if you are the goal here and that the answers to some of your frustrations are not totally outside of you but a part of you?" I said.

Avery smiled and agreed as we continued our discussion about how her vulnerability of wanting to have others, especially her supervisor, take care of her at work could be limiting her ability to change those things that she could do herself to increase her contentment in her workplace. Looking to others to create an orderly situation that was ideal for her left her feeling helpless, frustrated, and out of control. In this and subsequent meetings, we discussed actions she could put into place to help her develop a sense of increased control that best met her needs, including expanding her skills and connections as an art therapist through professional trainings and networking opportunities, negotiating her on-site supervision in a way that felt more professionally rewarding, taking on more leadership roles where she felt empowered to create the changes that would be helpful to her agency and patients, and enlisting the support of others, including her own personal therapist, while continuing with her off-site supervisory relationship.

Hayes, Yeh, and Eisenberg (2007) found that therapists who remain self-aware and effectively resolve their own issues of grief and loss are especially able to empathize with a client's loss. However, "to draw from one's suffering and use it in the service of the client requires the therapist's . . . continual attention to his or her own wounds" (Hayes et al., 2007, p. 351). This attending process is imperative in both therapy sessions and supervision. Using art and journaling creates an ongoing record of facing the issues, concerns, and experiences, contemporaneously, and then it can be brought to supervision or session to explore and understand further. Durkin, Perach, Ramseyer, and Sontag (1989) also encouraged art and journal writing as a means of communication throughout the supervisory process. Bringing "the tools of the trade into the supervisory relationship" (p. 391).

In Through the Backdoor

When working within an art-based intervention framework with patients, the emergent, individual content and cultural context becomes visible simultaneously through the art image and process of the art therapy. The psychotherapist is able to amplify associations with the created imagery in order to offer opportunities of awareness and meaning of the symptoms, which often lie beyond verbal recognition. The drawing intervention *In through the backdoor* (Dean 2006a, 2006b; Dean, 2013; Earley 1999a, 1999b) encourages the use of abstract imagery and time limitations in order to reveal latent content related to body image and the relationship between self and environment or others. The intervention encourages participants, either individually or in a group setting, to complete six abstract images utilizing prescribed times as a structuring device, which will more fully be described later in this chapter.

Often patients are self-conscious, doubtful, or even skeptical about their ability to create meaningful or acceptable works of art. In my opinion, much of the self-doubt is residual from early art education that stresses product and likeness rather than expression and process. Additionally, there have been misunderstanding, minimizations, and the subordination of creative processes, as expressed in von Franz's (1995) statement, "A number of artists and creative scientists avoid contact with us [psychoanalysts] because they believe that we, in a reductive analytic way, are going to destroy their creativity" (p. 18). She continues with the idea that the fear to enter into treatment is "justified to the extent that not enough analysts know about the creative process in the psyche and, misunderstanding it, use the reductive neurosis-cure methods when they would rather take the attitude of supporting a new birth of consciousness" (von Franz, 1995, p. 19). Art therapists and properly trained clinicians will be able to work with and ideally correct this view, assisting individuals to honor their creative process and birth of consciousness.

Although some individuals are inherently gifted with art, possessing the ability to see and render form, art expression can be accessible to most, if not all. Some may find it more pleasurable than others, especially those identified as talented or gifted in the arts, who naturally spend time honing their skills through formal training. The inclination to continue to pursue the arts or one's areas of strength, whether in music, science, or literature, tends to be heightened around the age of 9 and is consistent with the developmental issues of latency and the gang drawing stage described by Lowenfeld and Brittain (1987). Those who have been discouraged in the arts may abandon them or become self-conscious of ability around this time. Sometimes, this self-consciousness leads to shame about or resistance to utilizing the arts in a therapeutic setting, and this can be disarmed through various means.

Decreased Defenses

One means to reduce self-consciousness about creating art is an intervention I developed called *In through the backdoor* (Dean, 2006a, 2006b; Dean, 2013; Earley 1999a, 1999b). Employing abstract art methods has been shown to be effective in reducing defensiveness. It requires the patient to create six images using scribbles or other mark-making techniques, using page size and time restraints as a structuring device. The method embraces both the schooled and the unschooled when it comes to artistic abilities and skill. Because only one part of the suggested intervention is provided at a time, pre-planning is not needed nor is consideration to the final outcome. By asking participants to create an image using only scribbles, the defenses typically employed in art making are rendered useless, and thus, cognitive and intellectual processes are temporarily suspended. For some, this may be a welcome relief while for others who want to "figure things out" it may add some tolerable stress.

Out of the six images the patient is asked to create, only two will be utilized to create a new single image by ripping one into the shape of his or her body and adhering it to the second chosen image. It is nearly impossible to defend against latent imagery and also difficult to imply that skill is needed to participate in the creation of this intervention. So while the images are being created the patients are only given the directives to "fill the page with colors, marks or scribbles, attempting to avoid working in one small corner of the page."

The following provides detailed description and some examples for this intervention. It is applicable for individual or group work, and it requires six pieces of white 12″ × 18″ paper, a glue stick, and drawing materials of their preference (e.g., colored markers, oil pastels, and chalk pastels) per person. Having these materials ready in advance ensures a quick succession of drawing and execution. The participants are asked to fill the page as best as possible with lines, marks, textures, patterns, scribbles, or even imagery, which may or may not be pictorial in nature, with the requirement that they start and stop when instructed.

The therapist is responsible for keeping the time for each drawing and encouraging the patients to mark the back of each image with the corresponding number for each image in the series. The timed limits for each are as follows:

1. 1 minute
2. 1 minute
3. 30 seconds
4. 15 seconds
5. 2 minutes
6. 1 minute

The rationale behind the sequence is that starting and finishing with a minute sets a constant predictable amount of time in which to work. The predictable is familiar and can be reassuring. The second image is also one minute and is often used as a means of repeating the first one because participants may have just been "warming up" in the first one. The time then decreases to 30 seconds for the third drawing and then 15 seconds for the forth. There is usually an audible reaction in groups as some may feel greater pressure to complete the same amount of work in the shorter periods of time. The anxiety is usually raised and more frantic marks may be seen. This can be stressful for some who feel pressure to produce the same amount in less time or, conversely, liberating for others, who feel as if they do not have to accomplish as much if there is less time. The fifth image is 2 minutes and is often met with a sigh of relief. There is more time to spread out the imagery, create more marks, or fill the page more fully. Again, some will have the opposite reaction, preferring a shorter time or feeling they've completed the work before the 2 minutes have expired. Some may wish to stop working on their image before the time is over, which is fine. Again, the last image returns to the time of the first two, one minute, returning the patient to a kind of familiar homeostasis.

Once completed, all six images are spread out so all may be viewed simultaneously, if space allows. The participants are instructed to choose the drawing that is the most affectively charged, either positively or negatively for them. I like to say, "Choose the one that calls to you or the one that seems the most appealing or repulsing." And then, they are to choose their second most affectively charged image. Once both images have been identified, the other four are put aside.

With the two images in front of them, the participants are instructed to tear out the shape of their body using the first chosen image. Observation and discussion are sometimes needed at this point because there can be misgivings about ripping up the first or favorite image. The idea is to rip a whole and complete body from the scribbled paper. Even with this direction, it is not uncommon for only body parts to be depicted, which becomes significant in later discussions of the final piece. Once the body is formed, it is adhered to the second chosen drawing, creating a ground or environment for the body-shaped image. It may be attached horizontally, vertically, or diagonally. Likewise, some may choose to make their figure appear as if it is walking off the page or only partially adhered to the ground.

The rationale behind this directive is multifaceted, with many possibilities for discussion, associations, and amplifications. Without conscious intention, the emergent imagery carries underlying symbolic material. Some significant issues include the following: Is the first image chosen and used for the self-image one that had a longer time than the image used for the environment, or shorter, or the same amount of time? Does this resonate with the artist's self-directed energy when looking inward in a self-absorbed way or a reflective, self-aware way? Is there congruence between the foreground and background (i.e., do lines merge or overlap)? Visually, is there a pattern to the marks or forms? Surprisingly, lines or marks may cross or demarcate a significant part of the body. Inquiring about the feelings about these parts of the body may be helpful in generating dialog or understanding about one's body, feelings, and place in their world. Likewise, the colors in the background and in the foreground of the body may blend in or stand out. Asking about what it feels like to blend in or stand out can also be helpful as it yields opportunities to know more about your patient by using their image as a guide. Has the final piece created other interesting imagery, or does the body feature blend in or disappear into the background? How does this reflect the person's experiences in his or her daily life? These are just a few questions used to engage associations yielding diverse and individual responses.

Fortuitous Accidents

Due to the roundabout nature of this drawing intervention, surprise and *fortuitous accidents* may happen. I believe these *fortuitous accidents*, or mistakes, are akin to synchronistic events or unconscious manifestations of the psyche. For example, a middle-aged woman I will call Liz entered treatment in an adult day program due to depressive symptoms. A guarded, quiet woman who did not speak readily, she was willing to create some "scribbles" on the page for this group intervention. She created the image shown in Figure 3.13, and promptly hung it up.

She was at a loss for associations, stating, "I don't know what it feels like. It looks kinda swirly and a mess."

Then one of the group members gave her feedback about the lines, "The background and foreground seem to blend into one another. I can't tell where you end and the background begins."

Figure 3.13 In through the backdoor. Liz's image gave some unintended but valuable information about the voices she was hearing, indicating that her depression had psychotic elements to it. © 2016 Michelle L. Dean.

"Do you ever feel this way, that you are disappearing into the background, your environment, or home?" I asked noting the continuation of the marks that seemed to continue around in a circular pattern through the arms in different colored markers.

"I guess so. Sometimes I feel like I am invisible," Liz said.

"At first, I thought you were just the purple person and then I realized it was a person in your head. What's that guy doing in your head?" asked another group member in a jovial way.

Liz laughed and said, "You know, I didn't mean for him to show up there but that makes some sense to me. I always feel like I have someone in my head speaking to me—telling me what to do."

"Do you mean like you can hear someone's voice telling you things or hearing something?" I inquired.

"Yeah, always! It makes me feel tired. I try not to hear what he is saying, but he just won't be quiet. He never shuts up and I was afraid to tell anyone that I heard voices," Liz said.

"That's okay Liz. I am glad you shared this with us as some people hear voices when they become depressed. By knowing this, we will be able to help you better as I am sure the voices are indeed annoying," I said.

Liz's image, without conscious volition, gave some valuable clues about what was going on for her. Her quiet and guarded nature was a defense against the voices she was hearing, which indicated that her depression also had psychotic elements to it. Her shaky line quality reflected her uncertainty and fear as well as what might be considered a relatively primitive or developmentally regressed drawing style with possible signs of brain impairment due to the organic nature of the lines, which may be consistent with psychotic features. Her associations with the drawing and comfort in the group helped her speak about the underlying issues of the voices she heard.

Listening to the *Chaos*: Finding Beauty in the *Mess*

It is common for patients to seek the aid of professional mental health services when their lives have become disruptive, dysfunctional, or simply, a mess. As discussed earlier in this book, chaos, at times, is a natural part of living. Chaos and the dissolving of normal structures and routines, whether through a death, a divorce, or a depression, may make one feel like a snake shedding its skin. Chaos can create an opportunity to recalibrate one's life to a new normal. An accompanying descent into darkness and sadness can be like a period of hibernation, a time for inner reflection and growth. Introspective work can be done during periods of grief, even if energy levels are low. Artistic expression can be used to explore the complexity of the *chaos* or *mess* in a way that is both illuminating and respectful while providing opportunities to find a new homeostasis. Berry (2008) discussed the importance of experiencing this chaos not so much as a linear narrative but as an image, predisposed to embodying shapes and forms within the chaos. She went on to caution that one must not rid oneself too quickly of chaotic feelings (by abreacting or partaking of primal screams) because one would then also lose one's forms. It is better to contain the chaos and even nurture it so that all of its shapes can exist. Using art in a therapeutic context is certainly one way to contain and relate to the chaos, allowing it to develop through image and form. Through this graphic form, relatedness and understanding may occur.

One way to engage one's chaos or mess is by simply drawing it abstractly in a two-part process, I call *drawing the mess (or chaos)*. First, by using lines and colors, the patient may draw the chaos or mess that exists in one's life. It may appear abstractly or more pictorially, and ideally, the paper used to contain this mess is no smaller than 12″ × 18″—the image can be created with a variety of art materials, which can include colored pencils, oil pastels, markers, and chalk pastels. This drawing can illicit responses, such as anxiety, relaxing, cathartic processes, or a combination of all and perhaps many others. Confronting one's mess can be painful and a stark reminder of loss or the destruction one has experienced or even created. The patient may experience guilt or remember shame. There may be reminders of the pains inflicted on others. And it can be used as part of a 12-step recovery model, which frequently calls upon one to take a searching and fearless moral inventory of oneself (Step 4) and admit to God, to oneself, and another human being the exact nature of one's wrongs (Step 5). In the safety of a therapy session, admitting the chaos, whether in actions or feelings, can be helpful. The containment provided by the art materials allows us to work through what arises. It is my opinion that these chaotic elements are already present, carried around within us, and the art gives them a voice.

Second, once the *chaos* drawing is complete and there is some discussion of the image, especially in terms of thoughts and associations, noting what is of particular interest or significance about the chaos or mess image. For example, does the chaos look like the artist imagined it; is it larger or smaller than how it feels; are there surprises in the picture; does it remind you of anything or anyone? After discussing the image in its totality, I next have the participant move a viewfinder of approximately 1″ × 1″ square over the image to identify a piece that seems to really call to him or her. I have the participant rip out this identified square from their image, and using another piece of paper, adhere the square to the fresh page using a glue stick or white glue.

Third, I have participants focus on the marks in the inch-square piece and create another image on the fresh page that can be a free drawing. Sometimes, more specifically, I ask them to draw an image of what recovery might look like. Again, this image may be pictorial or more abstract. Creating a new image that incorporates the chaos serves to acknowledge the mess, as well as its remnants or effects that may still be palpable. A new image or situation can be created or built upon past experience. We never fully forget a loss nor do we become indifferent to it, but there are ways to move forward and take a piece of that loss or chaos with us while building a new life or image. The new image incorporates the old mess with the new emerging image. The new paper creates a new frame, or situation, on which to build again. Again, the image can be a free drawing or it can be more directive, depending on the structure needs of the individual. Examples of more directive suggestions include creating an image of hope or of the future or specifying the time (e.g., next week, next month, or next year), depending on the situation.

An example of this chaos work is shown in Figures 3.14 and 3.15. Nancy had entered into treatment for some relationship difficulties, including struggles with intimacy and food. She was in her late 20s with a successful but demanding job that kept her working late into the evenings and sometimes away from home with travel for a week or more at a time. She often felt ill. She and her husband sought therapy due to emotional distance that had arisen between them. Childless by choice, they wanted to ensure they would have the skills to negotiate their current conflicts as well as some past traumas that were becoming increasingly burdensome in their relationship. Nancy eventually revealed in our fifth session how she had been molested as a child and questioned whether it could have an effect on her current relationship with her husband. She believed she, along with other family members, had been abused over a period of time at the hands of a relative, but that it might not be "a big deal." She had told her mother, but nothing had been done to stop the abuse. Memories of her feelings of powerlessness and anger at her mother, who was brittle and in poor health, complicated her current relationship with her husband. Nancy discussed what a mess things had been growing up, when her father abruptly left home and moved to another state to be with another woman and had, now, almost fifteen years later, just as abruptly left that woman, returned home, and began dating her mother again. She questioned the sanctity of marriage and her mother's dignity, and she felt that if her parents were going to reconcile that all of her childhood suffering was due to the whim of her parents and their reckless and hurtful actions.

I suggested she might wish to draw the powerful mess that she had experienced as a child or was experiencing currently in her life, or both. She drew with oil pastels, creating geometric forms and shapes out of blues and pinks. Once she completed making both soft and aggressive lines, we briefly discussed the mess and she said, "Looks like a bunch of boxes, waves, and grids. It makes no sense at all."

I affirmed that the chaos did indeed look messy but there appeared to be an attempt to order it in some way. This was congruent to the way she attempted to order her own life through work and external achievements, rising out of and disconnecting from her home life. I asked her to pick out a piece of the chaos drawing, an approximate one-inch square of the work, and rip it out. I then asked her to take the torn slip of paper and place it onto another paper. Once the slip was adhered to the page, I asked her to create another drawing that incorporated the chaos but it could also be more pictorial or unrelated. She created the work shown in Figure 3.15, an image of herself climbing a ladder. The slip of paper from her

Figure 3.14 Drawing the mess (chaos). Berry (2008) discusses the importance of experiencing this chaos not so much as a linear narrative but as an image, predisposed to embodying shapes and forms within the chaos. © 2016 Michelle L. Dean.

Figure 3.15 Creating a new image that incorporates the chaos serves to acknowledge the previous mess and its remnants, which may still be palpable while the
emerging image or situation may be created, building on past experience. © 2016
Michelle L. Dean.

chaos drawing is near the bottom of the page and makes up her right foot and the bottom rungs of the ladder.

"I look like I am climbing up out of something, but what I am coming from and where I am going, I cannot see," said Nancy.

"I wonder if that is what it felt like for you as a child, having a foot in chaos (or made out of the mess) and being unsure of where you were headed," I said.

"I think so," Nancy said, "And I look like I am hanging on real tight, or that the ladder might fall over or fall apart."

I responded by saying, "I know that the chaos and traumas we experience in childhood don't ever leave us, but instead, they become a part of us, a part that doesn't have to engulf or overwhelm us, but experiences that we can overcome."

"I hope so. Sometimes I don't feel as if I have a firm grasp on life or my footing isn't sure, just like the feeling must be like holding onto the precariousness of the ladder," she said, continuing, "I had a lot of trouble with my waist when I was drawing it; I went over it again and again."

"It looks like you were trying to give yourself a boxy T-shirt to wear, but then had another thought to create a body that was more hour-glass shaped," I said.

"Yeah, sometimes I just can't decide what body shape I am really happy in; it feels like no matter how thin I become, it is never enough and that lines need to be redrawn," said Nancy.

"The line that defines you?" I asked.

"Yes, like my boundaries, my identity, and who I am. I know what I need to do to be a good worker, daughter, and wife, but sometimes, I just can't figure out who *I* am," responded Nancy.

Our discussion continued about her chaos and her ability to rise above the mess through her academic and career achievements. We discussed how, even though she has become successful in an outward way (i.e., career-wise and financially), there may be a part of her emotional self that she left behind that needs tending to because a part of her remains on unsteady ground. This affected her relationship with her husband, and as such he too came to therapy with Nancy to work on their martial concerns, which I discuss in this next section.

What Do You Do When Life Hands You Something You Did Not Ask For?

Another drawing intervention, which I find to be very effective in circumventing anxieties around drawing abilities, is a directive my art therapy colleague and friend Johanna Kane developed. She created this as a student more than a decade ago, when I oversaw one of her graduate internship experiences at an eating disorder facility where I was employed. We have since gone on to teach and lecture about this intervention because it can be effective in addressing issues that result from unintended circumstances (Dean, 2006a, 2006b; McCafferty, Kwak, Dean, & Kane, 2007). This intervention is versatile in both group and individual settings with some modifications. It supports people in making the most of a situation when life hands them something they did not ask for or from which there were unintended consequences. The intervention can be utilized in dealing with day-to-day frustrations of messed-up schedules, flat tires, or more grave experiences such as a trauma, serious illness, or loss. Clinical judgment is imperative about when to begin working with trauma experiences. The degree of trauma can often be triggered by seemingly innocuous frustrations of the day, which might unearth and reactivate years of abuse or neglect. Conversations about only the daily frustrations can be useful for unloading, but they often do not tap into developed patterns of responses that can make responding to change difficult or into a possibly learned pattern of response that has become conditioned and paralyzing.

This intervention may be done individually, with couples, or in groups. If facilitating it in a group, each group member begins with a piece of paper of at least 12″ × 18″ or up to 18″ × 24″ if space allows. Each group member is directed to draw a line across the page, horizontally, diagonally, or vertically, using a colored marker. This mark can be a straight line, a wavy line, or zigzagged—there is no correct way, as long as it moves from one side to the other, creating a split in the page. Once the mark has been made, participants pass the sheet of paper two or more seats to either side. I like moving more than one seat so there is no pressure from the neighbor who created the line in the second half of this intervention. Once the sheets of paper have been passed, the instructions are to examine the line, turning the page in whichever direction is desirable and then create an image on the page. Group members are told they can incorporate the line as in the scribble drawing, projecting an imagined shape and embellishing it, or they may draw over it, essentially annihilating it.

If working in a one-to-one session and group members are not available to draw the line, the therapist can do so or the patient themselves can, without the knowledge of what is to come next. If the therapist draws the line, be mindful to consider the potential transference and counter-transference implications, which can be immensely helpful and may deepen the rapport between the therapist and patient, but like all things good, it also has the potential to be experienced poorly. Similar to working in the group, the person who drew the line may become attached to it and not want to give it up or see it altered in any way, especially if the recipient of the line has a completely different idea for it, as its creator. I note this because it is often very surprising how attached group members can become to a line that has taken them less than two seconds to draw when they realize the next step is to surrender the line to another group member. When processing this reaction, it is helpful for it to be less about the drawing and more about the process of surrendering. It can be about previous experiences of having to give up something that is theirs or that they created or something they wanted but did not receive, and the loss associated with this, as discussed further in Chapter 9. All of this information is helpful in amplifying and understanding the relationships to objects, relationships outside of the therapy session as well as within it, and most often relates back to times when participants may have felt out of control or had to deal with something that they did not necessarily ask for. As always, sound clinical judgment is advised regarding timing and interpretive work.

Once the sheets with the lines on them have been exchanged and the recipients have concluded drawing their responses, a discussion regarding what it was like to surrender the line drawing and to receive someone else's is important. Discuss what has been created as well as the relationship or response to the line on the page, their feelings about it, whether they wanted it there, whether it provided a welcome structure or whether it felt as if it divided the page in a way that was experienced as divisive. Relate the associations back to other experiences of what it was like to receive something that was not necessarily asked for, and what was their reaction, how did they handle it, did they wish for a difference response? Was there something that someone else could have done to help in the situation, and if so, what would that have been, and is it important to pursue this discussion with that person now to create amends? Relinquishing control of one's creation and accepting someone else's work to finish, presents a whole host of potential issues, which may include loss, interpersonal relatedness, and control. It certainly can elicit reactions about receiving something that was not asked for and the resiliency to deal with those situations as they arise.

John and Nancy

As a part of couple's therapy, John and Nancy, the couple whose case I began to discuss previously, engaged in discussions over their struggles with getting their needs met in the relationship, as well as different relational patterns that sometimes made them feel as if they were not communicating effectively, which resulted in hurt feelings and disagreements. Because each expressed that they did not feel like they were not getting enough from the other partner in the relationship, I suggested they work on this dynamic in their art. Sitting around the table, I asked them each to create a line or mark across their page. Once this was compete, I asked them to switch papers, each receiving the line their spouse drew. They looked at each other surprised and slightly saddened or distrustful in relinquishing their picture.

"Are you concerned what your partner may do with your line?" I asked.

They smiled and passed their picture to the other.

"Create something out of what you have been given by your partner," I encouraged.

"In some ways it is like your relationship with each other: you fell in love with each other and that means all parts: good, bad, and indifferent parts. Sometimes parts of the other you are asked to deal with are not always immediately visible. You may not realize the complexity of the other person until it rears its head, or has a need, that must be met in the relationship," I said.

As they worked, I noticed the striking similarities between John and Nancy's lines. Both lines travelled in the same direction from the bottom left to the upper right hand corner of the page even though the orientation of the picture plane was inverted, John's paper was created in a vertical orientation while Nancy's was horizontal.

Nancy's wavy blue line was turned into a sea-horizon for a ship in John's picture, Figure 3.16. In John's picture, drawn around the ship were rings or circles. The circle, or mandala, is often referred to as a symbol for self and wholeness,

Figure 3.16 John, *What Do you Do When Life Hands you Something You Didn't Ask For?* Nancy's wavy blue line was turned into a sea-horizon for a ship in John's picture. © 2016 Michelle L. Dean.

"eternity, heaven, [and] perfection" (de Vries & de Vries, 2004, p. 125). Within John's picture, the circle appeared to be a threshold or passageway. In the arch over the ship were wedges that appeared to be bearing down on the ship like teeth, like shark's teeth or similar to the *vagina dentate*, closing in on his sailing vessel. As he sailed along, the intensity of the water in the circle is denser and more chaotic, as it was made with more aggressive marks.

The sea is often associated with the "remnant chaos-water, the mysterious immensity from which everything precedes and everything returns [as well as] the collective unconscious—housing the monsters of the deep, related to the emotions of human sexual desire, a general longing for (spiritual) experiment and adventures" (de Vries & de Vries, 2004, p. 494–495). The aggression turned inward is apparent in this image, and may have related to fears of weakness, impotence, or annihilation by incorporation connected to unconscious notions of returning to the womb like the myth of the vagina dentate. Ships, commonly referred to as feminine vessels, may be described as "a symbol of containment, the womb, fertility" (de Vries & de Vries , 2004, p. 511). Ships are also seen as living beings (e.g., Phygian ships, which turn into water-nymphs) and many are self moving, as in the associations John gave to his ship, "which know the minds of their masters."

This ship, seen from a perspective below the ship or from sea-level, is equipped with cannons, and carries the red cross emblem on one of the sails, which may symbolized "love and mercy: military and civil emergency service" (de Vries & de Vries , 2004, p. 149), a tactic in keeping with John's role in the relationship to "fix" the problems and keep the "spirit" or spark alive in his marriage. John spoke of the cannons as a means to attack or defend himself and made the connection between the duality if the cannons and the flag that symbolized love. As we spoke more about the image, John discussed the complicated relationship he had with his parents growing up. They divorced when he was a child, and he felt he needed to be the man of the house when his father left. To be a favorited child while also being parentified created internal and family conflict for John.

"My parents' divorce left me confused about how a married couple ought to be. I know I don't want the fighting my parents had. When Nancy and I fight or I experience her as distant, I feel like we are going to turn out like our divorced parents," John said.

"There's no road map as to how to traverse living life together in your marriage, only lots of examples of what you don't want. You and Nancy will have to create a map together of what you want," I responded.

Nancy then shared about her image.

"When I got John's original red line, I thought it resembled incoherent handwriting—I didn't know what he was saying. So I kind of ignored it. I went on to make a planet that had the things I like there," said Nancy.

"When you don't understand what John is talking about or where he is coming from do you typically ignore him?" I inquired.

"Only when we are fighting do I give him the cold treatment," she said reaching for his hand in an affectionate way.

Nancy's created Figure 3.17 represented music, a small sailing ship, mountains or dormant volcanoes (the three triangles), family (the stick figures), a book, city, and an Rx for medications.

"The items in the circle I feel are my passions," Nancy said.

"What is this on the edge of the circle?" I inquired.

"It is a very small person peering through a telescope at the stars," Nancy said.

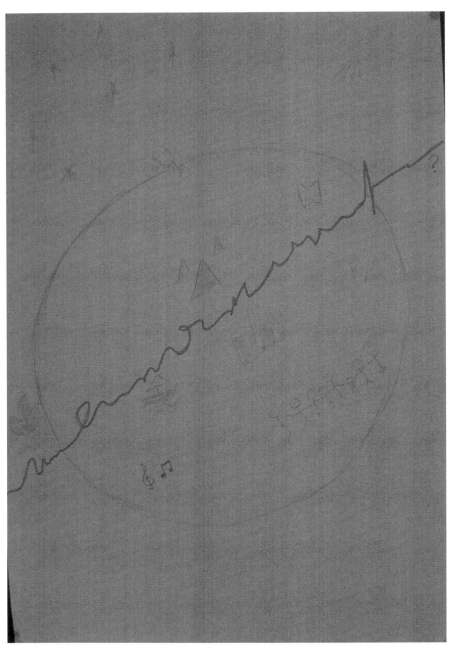

Figure 3.17 Nancy, *What Do You Do When Life Hands You Something You Didn't Ask For?* © 2016 Michelle L. Dean.

"Oh, I thought it was a wine glass," said John.

There is also a rocket ship, transcending the planet, and experiencing freedom from gravity.

"It looks as if it is about to enter into another planet's atmosphere and released from its earthly plane," she said.

This seemed significant considering her history of abuse and the increased likelihood of dissociation or perhaps her underlying desire to leave the relationship when things were difficult.

"I notice a campfire is outside of the circle," I said.

"Yeah, it reminds me of going camping and the warmth I felt when John and I traveled a lot," said Nancy.

"Is that something you miss?" I asked.

"Yes, I feel John and I have become so busy that we have difficulty getting on the same page with where we are going as a couple," Nancy said.

Through their drawings Nancy and John were able to hear each other in ways that talking on their own did not open up for them. They used their imagery to discuss both the positive and challenging aspects of their relationship. The images opened a personal and intimate space within each of them that they could then attend to as a couple. Our work together continued for a few more months, drawing on their creativity and expression to explore underlying dynamics and traumas that originally hindered their relationship but with understanding and attunement brought them closer.

Drawing offers a multitude of possibilities for expressiveness in the therapeutic session. Materials are easy to secure and employ with relatively few space requirements aside from a desk or table on which to work. A continuum of expressiveness and aesthetic response is possible when the structure of material is considered and closely matched to the needs of the patient. Attending to the patient through spontaneous drawings and drawing that taps into the historical, cultural, and contextual values of the individual is imperative.

CHAPTER 4

PAINTING
Fluidity of the Creative Unconscious

The term *painting* is from the Latin *pingere* and is related to the verb *fingere* (to feign); it conveys the idea of feigning reality or representing ideas. Its earliest manifestations are on the walls of caves, and its process has evolved into what is considered a high art. In Eastern cultures, painting is held in high regard, like poetry and historiography. During the Middle Ages, an almost "categorical distinction was maintained between the subject matter of mural painting and that of panel painting" (Argon, 1965, p. 906). Murals represented events that had an edifying or ideal meaning, such as topics related to religious and moral education, while panel paintings had iconic meaning and were considered objects of veneration. Around the 13th century, this distinction between panel and mural painting—that is, painting that produces an image and tells a story—began to dissolve (Argon, 1965, p. 906).

Painting and perception have a close relationship. The comparison relates to painting as a picture frame, like a window, portraying a kind of the depth. This kind of painting represents what is real, with the use of perspective and other drawing and painting devices. Another kind of painting is not concerned with reproducing reality or confined by visual experience but instead is concerned with creating images based on perception of experience. Such paintings are images about the divine, moral concepts, mythology, monsters, and in modern art, forms and colors unconnected to a visual reality. "These are, however, mental images, and whether mnemonic [from the memory or used to remember] or eidetic [especially vivid and detailed images], they are considered by psychologists as real, not ideal, perceptions, even though they are physically received by the retina only when manifest in painting" (Argon, 1965, p. 911).

Paint, with its fluidity and ability to create layers of color, hues, transparent light and building of depth, allows a meditative process, utilizing the liquid medium to transport one into the aqueous fluidity of unconsciousness. These qualities often lend themselves to a descent into the psyche's depth that is spontaneous and does not have to conform to the linear production often associated with line and drawing. Painting materials, like drawing materials, can be thought of on a continuum of resistive to fluid (Lusebrink, 1990). These structural qualities are inherent in each material; however, with paint, there are multiple ways to vary the fluidity and the viscosity of paint by adding more or less water or painting mediums and gels. Although the preferred paints of many Old Masters were usually oil-based paints, in this discussion I will be referring to only water-based paints such as watercolor and acrylic, due to their ease of clean up and the fact that they tend to be less hazardous. They are safer because they lack solvents and some pigments and additives that can be harmful if ingested or absorbed, or if working in a space without proper ventilation, can be hazardous if inhaled.

Working with paints offer visceral and kinetic movements that are generally pleasing to most. From the smearing of paints in finger painting to the meticulous fine-haired brush work on miniatures, the expressiveness and range of paint are vast. Coupled with this variety is the mercurial quality of the tinted and hued liquid. The paint is a medium for carrying shape-shifting imagery and holds the potential for working and reworking the image in the painting through painting and repainting, changing boundaries and forms. It is typically a layering process, building the medium in thick or thin layers. When paint is applied thinly, it can tint the previously applied color, shift the hue to have almost imperceptible nuances, or combine to create a new color. When applied thickly, it can defy the surface of the canvas, and sometimes, it can crack as the thin surface veneer dries faster than the interior. In many ways, painting mirrors the ever-changing and sometimes elusive qualities of a dream.

Dream Work

Disregarded by some skeptics as nighttime hallucinations that are created by irrelevant nocturnal synapses, dreams carry an enigmatic source of imagery and potentiality for engaging in imagery through dream-inspired artworks that hold the keys for greater awareness in the therapeutic process. Dreams have been thought of as sources of knowledge since the times of antiquity. Often, soothsayers, or dream prophets, were called in to make sense of a dream, which could offer a glimmer of edification about an impending prophecy. Dreams have fascinated us, inspired us, and terrified us. Out of seeming chaos and disconnected events, they captivate us as the imagery and dramas of our nocturnal soul are played out while we sleep. Jung applied the same method for understanding dreams as he did active imagination, using the imagery to amplify the symbols and expand knowledge (CW 9[1]:110). Jung described the dream as holding all of the personal resentments and affects of the waking individual while also holding collective aspects, vestiges of an earlier collective psyche. In contrast, "Freud . . . tried to reduce myths motifs to personal psychology, in defiance of his own insight that dreams contain archaic residues" (CW 13:347). Freud's *New Introductory Lectures* about dreams provided the pivotal point where "analysis took the step from being a psychotherapeutic procedure to being a depth-psychology" (Freud, 1933, p. 7), a study of unconscious processes.

Cartwright (2010), a sleep researcher, discussed the vital role dreams have in regulating emotions and memory. She examined the interconnection between sleep states and depression as well as memory. Memory is never a precise duplicate of what actually happened; instead, it is an act of creation, and dreams are similar products of creation. Artworks related to dreams and memories are natural productions in art psychotherapy because all are part of a creative process that utilize imagery and symbols in their language. As Moon (2007) explained,

> Artworks that are based on dream images offer the art therapist a unique portal through which to connect with the inner lives of clients. As clients work with dream imagery in the context of art therapy, they simultaneously create meaningful personal symbols and potentially intimate interactions with the art therapist [p. 128].

Dreams provide a glimpse into our hidden roots of self-awareness (Taylor, 1992).

Encouraging patients to keep a dream journal next to their bed can be helpful because the memory of a dream can be fleeting. Jotting down the dream and then returning to sleep if it is not the normal waking hour can be helpful for recalling the dream once awake for the day. The dream journal then can be transported to the psychotherapy session, where further discussion and processing are possible. It is seductive to want to subscribe interpretation to the dream, but it is best to allow the patient to assign meaning and relevance to the imagery. And like in a work of art, because the dreamer created the dream, all elements in the dream may be aspects of the self. So, for example, in a dream where one is being chased down a long corridor, the dreamer may find aspects of the self in not only the person being chased, but also the pursuer, the corridor, and the sensations associated with the experience.

Painted Dragon

One day, my 7-year-old son created a painting of a knight fending off a three-headed dragon, as shown in Figure 4.1. This painting was created shortly after he had seen me painting an illustration of a dragon for a story that I had written. He, too, wanted to create a dragon, imitating some of the drawing features and style of my own image. Though imitative in its genesis, his version ended up quite different, reflecting some of the themes pertinent to his developmental issues, his personal history, and his interests. At that age, he was involved in much play with figurines, including knights, castles, and dragons. This play often involved the theme of defending a castle while armies or beasts held it under siege. Having read to him many stories, fairytales, and myths, including ones involving St. George's dragon and King Arthur's court, he had a fairly rich fund of such imagery to draw upon for his imaginative world.

The drawing, while reflecting known themes, reflects not only what he knew, but also many of the issues he was facing. His imitation of my work suggests a desire to follow the lead of an adult, to be imitative of the adult, and this is commensurate with the theme of the image. The knight emerges from the castle, approaching the outer world rather than passively remaining behind its walls. Developmentally, this is in keeping with the developmental hurdle faced as the child begins to leave the pre-schematic worldview, a more ego-centric one, and emerges into the wider world. Developmentally, his artwork is also emerging as it moves into the schematic stage, with its objective use of color and fulfilling its developmental task of increasing autonomy. It is common for boys at this age to play predator and defender games, including cops and robbers, superheroes and villains, and other archetypal manifestation of good and evil. But if there is a personal history of trauma, the image may also represent a working out of these issues.

Between the ages of 2 and 4, our son went through several significant medical procedures and one life-threatening incident. Suffering from severe environmental allergies, he further developed life-threatening food allergies. He was hospitalized several times, once after a near-death experience when he stopped breathing due to a combination of asthma, virus, and allergic reactions. He was then subjected to a number of invasive breathing and medical procedures, including repeated needle injections, of which he was entirely terrified. This left him with an extreme fear of doctors and a series of ongoing night terrors. As if this were not enough, during one of his hospitalizations, it was discovered that he had three congenital

Figure 4.1 The Painted Dragon. Pencil, watercolor, and marker depict a knight fending off the three-headed dragon. © 2016 Michelle L. Dean.

hernias, two inguinal and one umbilical, as well as preauricular pits near his ears, all of which would require surgical intervention. The ensuing surgeries left him feeling anxious and often overwhelmed about his surroundings. He expressed these feelings through increased agitation, hypermotor activity, and anxiety.

My son's repetitively playing out the themes of the defense of the castle appeared to reflect his utilization of the themes available to him for working out his need to fend off the invasive and painful interventions to which he had been subjected. The theme of the dragon, a symbolic portrayal, mythically conveys the forces of nature that threaten to wipe out the developing ego structure, as seen in the man-made fortress and the knight. These gave form to the conflict and offered the opportunity for him to work through his need to reestablish himself as an inviolate being. The relative scale of the competing forces suggests the magnitude of the issues he faced, the scale of the problem, and the bravery of his emerging ego. The castle, surrounded by a moat, is dwarfed by the dragon. Its drawbridge is down, resembling a tongue protruding from a face, depicted so either in jest or agony. It is common to create buildings, trees, or other objects in our own image, either consciously or unconsciously. Images can present as physical or psychic projections, drawing from historic or archetypal elements. The dragon in this image has the ability to breath fire from its center head, spit flooding water from the head on the left, and blow dangerous winds from the head on the right. No doubt he was influenced by the stories we had read and images he had seen, including a popular cartoon television program we had discussed about avatars and airbenders. These qualities hark back to the classical elements of water, fire, and air. All of these stories and images create a framework, which may be repeated, with variances, indicating individual and idiosyncratic expressions.

In this image, the watercolor is applied in loose and expressive brush strokes with the most intense colors reserved for the background: the dark clouds and the grass, especially the ground around the knight, which was carefully painted to avoid contaminating the white knight and horse. The castle is also left white. It is as if there was a need to keep him free of the intensity he experienced as the elements in his environment moved in closer. In contrast, the sky begins to blur the boundary of the dragon's form. Repeating themes and motifs in the artwork and repetitive play contributed to establishing mastery and control for our son.

Many years later, we hung this painting in our office. Patients will often remark on it or provide their own associations with what they know about dragons and knights. Because we do not live in a vacuum, nor do our patients, imagery and narrative are ever present and ready to be employed for personal meaning and construct. Like the imitative qualities our son demonstrated, imitation is a viable means for building ego strength, problem-solving skills, and resiliency, serving as a framework for individual expression and variation as seen in a later chapter about utilizing three-dimensional work. As Einstein has been attributed with saying, "If you want your children to be intelligent, read them fairy tales. If you want them to be very intelligent, read them more fairy tales" (Winick, 2013). Fairytales are expressions of the human psyche that hold practical and the esoteric meaning ripe for cultural and personal articulation. The framework that fairytales provide is applicable to other art forms as well, including the visual arts.

El Duende

Miller (2012) described a painting method that she used in supervision that was inspired by *El Duende*, a Spanish term that connotes a mysterious power and spirit or soul and can be felt but not always seen. In this way, it is similar to the daimon previously described. In folklore, *duendes* are spirits, fairies, pixies, sprits, leprechauns, brownies, or goblins, some good-natured and others mischievous and possessing trickster qualities, depending on the culture and myth. They are like the elves who help the shoemaker and his wife in Grimm's fairytale.

The shoemaker and his wife, although poor and behind on their rent, still found it in their hearts to give away their last pair of shoes to a needy individual, leaving themselves destitute. Before retiring to bed for the night, the distressed shoemaker cuts the leather for a new pair of shoes he intends on making in the morning. Upon waking, he finds the shoes complete and of superb quality. He is able to sell these shoes for more than his normal asking price, allowing him to pay his rent and buy food and more leather for more shoes. The story proceeds as the shoemaker continues to do good deeds and the elves help him build new shoes each night. At last, spying the helpful elves late one night, the shoemaker creates clothes for them. Upon receiving this gift from the shoemaker, the elves have fulfilled their obligation and are not seen again. The elves in this story act like the creative muse or creative force that moves us to create: paint, sing, or break loose from our usual moorings. Often motivated by struggle, *el duende* is part of the usually unseen inspiration for creative and psychological work.

The *el duende* process as it applies to painting in a therapeutic setting can be utilized in multi-session format with patients or in the supervisory process. The process requires a canvas or sturdy board on which a protracted painting experience is engaged over a specified amount of time or until it has come to a successful fruition. The participants are encouraged to create reflective works as they ask themselves specific questions and reflect on their own life experiences, or as Miller (2012) points out for the supervisory process, through reflections of their clinical work. This process explores association, reactions, and responses in a graphic and painted manner. Each week, the individual is invited to paint over their earlier work, layering the questions and reflections from their life. These layers and their relationships with a single canvas invite archetypal images and knowing through emergent symbols. "The layered artistic expression of the student's authentic voice as it struggles to become visible in art forms is a central focus in this supervision model. The force of artistic struggle (el duende) brings forth needed emotional vibrancy" (Miller, 2012, p. 167). The development of the painting reflects psychological transformation and growth over a period of time. It reveals the development slowly, just as a child's growth over the years may be perceived only through measured tick marks along a doorframe. This process, which may span several weeks or months, is recorded with the aid of photography. A photograph of the painting is taken after each session to record the development of the day.

When utilizing this process in therapy, over a period of weeks, perhaps even months, painting on canvas or gessoed board is best because it will provide more durability than paper. Ideally, the canvas is set up in an office or studio space for work. The paint that seems to lend itself best to this application is acrylic because it has the ability to paint over previously painted areas with good opacity for most colors. If the paint does not have enough opacity, such as some of the lighter colors like yellow, white can be added to the color, or sections of the previously painted canvas may be gessoed to enable working over, adding, or embellishing. The canvas from week to week may be slightly or radically altered. Depending on the content that needs to be expressed on a particular day, the imagery that emerges is in response to questions posed for response painting or expression of free associations or capture a particular theme, topic, or concern. For example, living with chronic pain and its daily manifestations can be helpful for some to record. Documenting through visual images gives a voice to the internal struggles. Painting has a fluidity that is well suited for conveying the unseen landscape of pain. For Frida

Kahlo, painting through her pain became a cathartic outlet, which made her anguish visible, revealing and documenting her hidden dimensions of pain and suffering.

Frida Kahlo

Frida Kahlo (1907–1954) was an iconic Mexican painter who was celebrated for her uncompromising representation of the female experience, her depictions of her personal struggles, and her embracing of national and indigenous traditions in her work and life. She was plagued by chronic and, at times, debilitating health issues caused by exposure to polio at the age of 6 and a traffic accident in her teens in which she incurred multiple fractures to her spine, pelvis, leg, foot, ribs, and shoulder as well as irreparable internal injuries that resulted in ongoing gynecological complications. Over the span of her life, she underwent multiple surgeries, endured prolonged confinement to bed, and often was required to wear constrictive corsets. By 1944, her health had deteriorated to the point that she was forced to wear a corset made of steel. Her self-portraits and several of her paintings dealt with the subject matter of her experiences with emotional and physical pain. One such example is *La Columna Rota* (*The Broken Column*, 1944). In *The Broken Column*, shown in Figure 4.2, her body is split wide open to reveal a broken ionic column that replaces her spine. Her figure appears to be held together by the steel corset and draped in white cloth reminiscent of that of Christ's winding sheet (Kettenmann, 2000). Nails prick and pierce her body in ways that may be associated with martyrdom. The furrowed, fissured, and bleak landscape becomes a symbol of the artist's desolation, isolation, pain, and suffering (Kettenmann, 2000; Schaefer, 2009).

Creating self-portraits is a means for personal reflection. Most artists, as a part of their training, create self-portraits to hone their skills for representing the human form. They also can be used to record an artist's development over time, such as the feeling states and stages of the artist's life. In the case of London-based artist William Utermohlen, his series of self-portraits depicted his progression with Alzheimer's disease from 2000 until his death in 2007 (Zhang, 2014). With the aid of a looking glass, the model for a self-portrait is always available when the painter is ready to paint.

Portraiture painting throughout history has included symbolic representations, from jewelry that the sitter wears that represents authority, to clothes that convey status, to clues about the sitter's profession and accomplishments. A portrait can be used as a monument of one's lifetime work and, due to its relative permanence, can serve in portraying a legacy long beyond the life of the portrait's subject.

In Kahlo's work, her avant-garde approach creates an emotional expression that catapults the viewer into her world of pain and contemplation. Her work represents two therapeutic aspects of painting: the self-portrait and the visual documentation of emotional and physical pain as it is experienced in the body. Such a depiction of emotional and physical experience is sometimes called *body mapping*, as shown in Figure 4.3. The image in this figure was created by a patient who required inpatient treatment and struggled with eating disordered behaviors. Depicting her emotional pain, she used painterly water-miscible oil pastels on a pre-cut paper body form. These pastels offer vibrancy and the ability to blend, melting one color into another, and she portrays where she carries her stress and emotions by choosing colors and forms to represent each feeling or sensation. The black vacuous pit in her stomach directly links to the red spiraling "chaos," as she

Figure 4.2 Frida Kahlo. *Broken Column.* Image Credit: © 2014 Banco de México Diego Rivera Frida Kahlo Museums Trust, Mexico, D.F./Artists Rights Society (ARS), New York.

described it in her head. The jagged lines in the shoulders show where her stress resides, and the duality of what appear to be back-facing figures are depicted in the midsection. The back-facing figures "are having a standoff in my belly," she said, describing her conflicted feelings toward her recovery. The symbols that arise in the artwork have direct connections to the person, surroundings, and culture. In this way, many of the characteristics in Kahlo's work hark back to Christian iconography, which was prevalent in her community, including those of the ex-voto.

Figure 4.3 Body Mapping, created by a patient who struggled with eating disordered behaviors, depicts her emotional and physical pain. © 2016 Michelle L. Dean.

Ex-Votos

Ex-votos are devotional paintings made by an individual for a public place or shrine and serve a ritual purpose. Their creation spans numerous cultures, including European (not including England and Scandinavian countries), Latin American, and Japanese cultures. Devotional objects are universal to human art making. The word *ex-voto* comes from the Latin for *votive*, meaning vow, or *ex voto suscepto*, "from the vow made." Ex-votos are used as vows, prayers, or wishes. For example, one might express gratitude for safe passage on a sailing vessel during a dangerous journey or recovery from a serious illness. Ex-votos represent the moment of greatest need and not that of the cure. They were often commissioned by a supplicant, a person asking humbly or professing gratitude publicly. In this chapter, I will be referring to the ex-votos of the Italians and Mexicans, primarily, because they share many functions and structural similarities. They are usually painted as an offering of gratitude to a specific saint or the Virgin Mary, also known as Our Lady of Guadalupe in Mexico, in thanks for salvation from illness, accident, or other calamity (Kinsella, 2011). They can also take a three-dimensional form (an object ex-voto), as in the sculpting of a tangible object that demonstrates gratitude, like the symbolic immaculate heart, a devotional object representing the inner life of the Virgin Mary. The materials used to make the objects vary according to the class and economics of the individual wanting to make the offering. Often, ex-votos take the form of jewelry, photographs, crutches, or prostheses or even take the form of body parts, such as internal organs, representations of animals, or miniature reproductions of houses (Salvatori, 2015).

The practice of creating ex-votos dates to the early pagan Roman and Etruscan empires, and they can be found in Mesopotamia and Egypt, where objects were offered in temples to deities. These offerings or gifts were called *donaria* and were hung on the walls next to statues of divinities in temples; placed next to or hung in sacred trees, also called healing trees; and buried around sacrificial altars. Ex-votos are most commonly associated with Italian and Mexican cultures, which have been predominately Catholic since the 1st and the 16th centuries, respectively. The early history of the votive practice indicates that, originally, ex-votos were not unique to monotheism (della Barba, 2013; Salvatori, 2015). The tradition of painted ex-votos originated in Italy in the 15th century and migrated to Latin America during the Spanish conquest in the colonial period, reaching its height in Mexico during the middle of the 19th century (Salvatori, 2015). Paintings commissioned by patrons in return for favorable dispensations from the church were not new during these times, but the ex-voto's greatest hallmarks became its diminutive size, the use of inexpensive materials like tin and wood, and the detailed narrative of the miracle or gratitude it expressed. The commissioning of the painting was called a *pittori di pieta*, "painter of pity" (Italian), or *retablistas*, "painter of holy figures" (Mexican), from the word *retablo* (or *retablo santo* or *lámina*). The word *retablo* stems from the Latin *retro tabulum*, "behind the altar," indicating the original placement of such works. Relicarios share a similar history with the ex-voto painting (or other items), as they too were offered as a vow of gratitude. Although not a church-sanctioned profession of faith, the completed ex-votos are placed in the shrines of the church, which often accumulates hundreds of works of art, or visual prayers. They are ephemeral objects painted by artists called "miracles draftsmen" and sculptures produced by *santeiros*, "saint makers," who are now rarely found (Marques da Silva, Congdon, Salvatori, & Alves de Oliveira, 2010). Their paintings originally marked the status and wealth of the patron, but transformed into a more affordable practice as the artists shifted from being trained devotional painters to ones who were often self-taught and anonymous. The terms *retablo* and *ex-voto* often are used interchangeably for these two types of paintings because they share a similar structure.

The spatial structure of a painted ex-voto is fairly consistent and includes three main parts. Typically, in the top left corner is a painting of the saint to whom the vow is being made. The figure is often floating in luminous clouds and surrounded by a radiating sun or multiple layers of sunrays. The gaze is often turned toward the supplicant and the figure is frequently seen with arms stretched outward as if to comfort or embrace the situation or receive the devotion. The larger portion of the painting depicts the scene of need, which includes the people and the miraculous event. At the bottom, often taking up less than a third of the painting, is the inscription, a written letter or statement of thanks including the supplicant's name and a brief written account of the miracle, and occasionally the signature of the artist.

In an 18th-century ex-voto painted in Mexico by an anonymous artist, a woman undergoes a medical procedure with an enclave of onlookers: family and religious figures, praying and expressing concern for the patient as her left breast is surgically removed, as shown in Figure. 4.4. In addition to the act for which a successful outcome is desired, an altar has been set up in the room and is visible on the right side of the painting. It includes a statue of Mary and the baby Jesus, Jesus on the cross, another altar with offerings to Mary and Jesus, and portraits of saints hanging on the wall. The customary prayer or devotional is beautifully written in a decoratively illustrated panel at the bottom of the painting. Its brilliant hues of red coupled with meticulous details on the screen, wallpaper, bed skirt, and tablecloth attest to the painter's exquisite skill.

As in Italy, the Mexican tradition of commissioning ex-voto painters has become less common; however, ex-votos are increasingly being made by the supplicants themselves and now also include photography, collage, and assemblages of prayer cards, written notes, and embroidered pennants. Hanging these offerings, which may also include tying pieces of fabric in public view, begins as a private dialog between humans and the divine and ends up being stories of communal hope and inspiration to strangers (Marques da Silva, Congdon, Salvatori, & Alves de Oliveira, 2010). This practice provides the symbolic power to express multiple human dimensions from the illustrative individual story to the shared collective experience of humility and resilience united by sobering accounts of miraculous recoveries from illness, addictions, fires, accidents, family feuds, and other disasters. The medium combines human fears with material and divine needs as well as the dreams, desires, and life's dangers that are common to all, especially the

Figure 4.4 Anonymous Artist, 18th century. *Peres Maldonado Ex-voto*. Mexican. 18th century, after 1777. Oil on canvas. overall: 27 1/4 in. × 38 1/2 in. (69.2 cm × 97.8 cm). Credit: Davis Museum at Wellesley College/Art Resource, NY.

mostly underrepresented layperson in art. Much in the same way, art therapist Gussie Klorer's *Ribbons of Hope* project demonstrated as a contemporary public display that heightened awareness for the need for unity against violence in the wake of riots in the community of Ferguson, Missouri (Klorer, 2014).

Through the witnessing of art, being in its presence, and relating to the artist's work, the viewer is taken into this shared space and transformed, in the same way one feels changed by a work of literature or popular-culture movie. According to de Botton and Armstrong (2014), one of the unexpectedly significant contributions art can teach is the ability to suffer more successfully. The characters of some images or pictorial stories can be identified with, and the characters may hold archetypal aspects of self. The work of art and the artist can be viewed as the delivers of an image, which speaks to the viewer and tells a story that works on both manifest and latent levels. Like Hermes, who carried dream images, and like the dream, the art image resonates with the individual and his or her psyche. An interface between the creator and the viewer creates an active space to share in suffering and contributes to the overall experience by creating resonance and empathy. Even with its structured schema, the ex-voto may be helpful in reflecting on traumatic situations and gratuity over time.

Vision Boards

The ex-voto shares many aspects with vision boards. Vision boards, such as those created on bulletin boards or post boards, work by placing images or written statements about those things that one would like to manifest in one's life, typically focusing on the positive. Like a visual prayer, vision boards invite awareness of the desired changes or situations. The posted images may permeate into one's consciousness and provide a construct for imitation. For example, being exposed to a particular color or object in one's home or in a friend's home, say a beautiful blue vase, can attract feelings and associations with this object, or the color to the point, where one may desire owning the same one or a similar object or associate the color with this friendship and feelings of warmth or security. The idea of bringing this same colored object into one's home is like storing a condensed memory of place, people, and feelings, like a physical memory place-marker. For this reason, we can be susceptible to marketing images that make an impression on us to the point that we can feel the need acquire the advertized object, either knowingly or unknowingly. For a similar reason, some people who collect or hoard have difficulty letting go of objects; this is a similar process to collecting objects evoke nostalgia where the object is imbued with sacred meaning and memory, some of which may not even be comprehensible. English designer and author William Morris was notorious for stating, "Have nothing in your house that you do not know to be useful, or believe to be beautiful" (British Museum, n.d.). This would carry over to images one encounters daily, as well. Likewise, images can have negative associations and holding on to objects or images imbued with negative energy can be an emotional drain.

Prayer cards, like the ex-voto, are a centuries-old tradition of the Catholic faith; they bear a religious image, usually of a saint, along with a favorite prayer or verse. They can be used to commemorate special occasions and are commonly distributed at funerals along with the name of the deceased and their birth and death dates. They serve as ephemeral keepsakes. SoulCollage® cards, originated by Seena Frost, are reminiscent of prayer cards as they use collage pictures to create cards upon which meditation and reflection can be used. Each card represents an aspect of personality or soul. The works of C. G. Jung, James Hillman,

Roberto Assigioli, and others form the psychological and spiritual underpinnings of SoulCollage® cards. Originally, it was named the "neter card" process. Neters were, in ancient Egyptian lore, the gods and goddesses who came forth from the "one neter," or source, to help or challenge humans. The word *neter* continues to be used in SoulCollage® to indicate each of the many guides, allies, and challengers depicted in the cards. Using inner guides or calling on a divine source for knowing is not unlike calling on animal guides or religious or spiritual guides; the guides appear as images, much like the *el duende* or other creative forces and can manifest through painting as easily as they can through found, collected or assembled images.

Painting offers a range of expressiveness through pleasing visceral and kinetic movements that can range from the smearing of paints in finger painting to meticulous, fine-haired brushwork. Inherent in this variety of methods, are the mercurial qualities of the tinted and hued liquid primed for carrying shape-shifting imagery that holds the potential for working and reworking the image through painting and repainting, thus exercising elasticity of boundaries and forms. It is through a layering process, building medium in thick or thin layers that can seem to defy the surface of the canvas. The malleable nature of painting offers a medium akin to a primordial liquid substance that is able to tap into not only expression of our suffering but also our search for the divine. Utilizing various structuring devices such as the three-tiered ex-voto and other devotional art gives a specific form and function to this aqueous matter, engaging the intellect, the body, and the spirit.

CHAPTER 5

THERAPEUTIC ART BOOKS
Sacred Texts

Books have been deemed one of the most valuable kinds of art objects in the history of mankind due to their ability to contain some of our most cherished cultural and personal thoughts and ideas. Alcuin (ca. 735–804), an English scholar, poet, and teacher, is attributed as having said, "Writing books is better than planting vines, for he who plants a vine serves his belly, but he who writes a book serves his soul" (as cited in Cubberley, 1920, p. 134). The value of books has been evidenced by their ability to command extremely high prices at art auctions, including the c. 1180 *Gospels of Henry the Lion*, an elaborate work made for the Duke of Saxony and Bavaria, which sold in 1983 in a Sotheby's auction for a record £8,140,000 (approximately $15,000,000) to the German government. It held the world record for the highest price ever paid for an art object until 3 years later when Van Gogh's *Sunflowers* was sold. It was the *Leicester Codex*, a bound manuscript of Leonard da Vinci that fetched a record 30.8 million dollars, the highest price ever paid for a book, when it sold at auction to Bill Gates in 1994 (Baer, n.d). The value of books transcends their material worth and ability to command high prices at art auctions. Books are highly valued because they provide spaces for sacred texts, illuminated scriptures, transfers of knowledge, and recordings of personal and communal narratives across generations. They hold individual, community, and cultural legacies and create cultural bridges over time and people. In this chapter, I discuss the historical origins of the art form, its useful application in a variety of settings, and case examples from clinical practice. I also provide a hands-on approach to creating three kinds of folded therapeutic art journals.

Books originated in antiquity over 4,000 years ago with the tradition of coving sacred things, such as the clay tablets of Mesopotamia on which cuneiform writings are found (Finkelstein & McCleery, 2002, 2005). Later, wax tablets were shielded by wood and ivory frames, and Egyptian and Hebrew scrolls were protected by ceramic jars and cylindrical cases of leather and wood. Roman scrolls were once covered with fabric jackets, and in medieval Europe, parchment was preferred for codices that were laced with heavy wooden boards. By the 2nd century BCE, writing on bone, shells, wood, bamboo, and silk existed in China. At some point before 100 BCE, the Chinese developed the techniques to make paper from tree bark, hemp, and rags. Some authorities believe that Ts'ai Lun invented paper around the 1st century, and more than 6 centuries later, once the Chinese had perfected the process of making paper, captured papermakers who taught their Arab jailors how to make paper in Samarkand (now Uzbekistan in Central Asia) and spread the secret papermaking techniques to the West (Hakim, 2004). Papyrus was the writing material of the Mediterranean people and gave its name *ppr* to paper. Parchment made from animal skins, still considered a superior writing surface, was reserved for fine books and important documents and was not replaced by paper in Western Europe until much later. Paper was only one part of the book.

Before the advent of mechanical printing in the 1400s, most famously popularized by Guttenberg's modern printing press, books were written and copied by hand and made for the wealthy. Most commonly found were books pertaining to religious texts. Monks and other religious scholars who were among the few who could read and write transcribed the sacred texts for other nobles or religious scholars. Religious teachings were often read to the people from the pulpit because the layperson lacked the skills to read. According to Olmert (1992), Medieval scribes often wrote the word *Explicit* at the end of every book, meaning "It has been unfolded," surviving from the time of parchment and papyrus rolls, which then read *Explicitus est liber*, meaning "the book unrolled," not the modern association "the end." "The unrolling or unfolding of knowledge is a powerful act because it shifts responsibility from writer to reader" (Olmert, 1992, p. 299).

Divides were experienced between the people who wrote the script and those who illustrated the texts (Avrin, 1991) as they struggled to determine the superior value of the words versus the images. The images provided not only a graphic depiction of the characters of the text, as in one of the early editions of Chaucer's *Canterbury Tales*, but also vignettes of both elegant and simple lifestyles in this era, such as in the popular Flemish *Book of Hours* (c. 1500) and the intricate details depicted in the calendar of the "Très Riches Heures du Duc de Berry," which portrays the opulent lifestyle of the Dukes and their guests (Olmert, 1992), an early version of depictions of the lives of the rich and famous. Whether they were men and women of nobility or reflections of everyday individuals depicted overcoming the challenges of life in a book, their stories and images captivate the reader's mind much in the same way a work of fiction, a news article, or tabloid does today.

Wood block image-making, or xylography, has been practiced in the East for many centuries. The Chinese used blocks to print money, which fascinated Marco Polo when he visited the court of Kublai Khan in 1275 (Hakim, 2004). By the 11th century, a Chinese artisan named Bi Sheng developed a method for cutting some of the 30,000 word symbols called ideograms; he is credited for inventing movable type. European wood blocks were used in the printing of textiles and playing cards. Guttenberg revolutionized printing in part because he tackled the issues of suitable paper, ink, and design for movable letters as well as the matrix to hold the letters in place while pressing the print. One factor in his favor that led to his fame was that he was working with the Latin alphabet, which has only 23 letters (does not include k, w, and y), and when punctuation marks, capitals, and other symbols are considered, there are a manageable number of 150 characters. Guttenberg's press was able to convert the arduous task of transcribing books and images by hand into a process in which they could be quickly and inexpensively produced, encouraging a wide audience of readers and a great investment in the ability to read and write. Ideas and images from Greek and Latin scholars became accessible, fueling the great movements of the European Renaissance (14th–17th centuries), which contributed to not only advancements in art and literature but also mathematics, geography, science, government, and politics.

Today, books filled with images and text often bring to mind works for children, which were rare until the 17th and 18th centuries when spelling books, primers, ABC books, and books about morality, including tiny thumb Bibles, constituted the bulk of children's reading materials in England and America. One of the most beloved children's books is the classic *Tale of Peter Rabbit* series by Beatrix Potter. Originally written as a series of picture letters with watercolor illustrations, they told the story of a mischievous rabbit and his dealings with farmer Mr. McGregor. The books celebrate her love of nature and were published at her expense in 1901 after being declined by several publishing houses. The influence of fairytales and fantasy is apparent in her work. She combines image and storytelling in her enduring classic tales, which speak to a common need and capitalize on aspects of the function of myth.

Psychological Functions of Myths and Fables

Myths are collective stories; myths are our personal stories. Myths carry historical knowledge and personal details. The stories we tell about our lives, of the events and people, of the sensations and emotions, are the myths we create in order to tell us who we are. Narrative is how we understand the world as it is intertwined with emotion, context, and imagery. Memory is construed and recalled through a narrative framework and is plastic and flexible in the telling and retelling of a story. Emotion, memory, and story combine to create a truth, even if it is a fictional truth. Body sensations are empathically experienced when telling or listening to an experience, even if not as profoundly as originally experiencing the event. We have visceral reactions to the telling and the witnessing and re-witnessing of a story. We create internal images for the story as it is told. Author Siri Hustvedt (2011) said, "Writing fiction is like remembering what never happened." Memory and imagination partake of the same mental process as emotion and are central to storytelling in literature and psychoanalysis (Hustvedt, 2011). "For writers, literature is a carrier of history. In Chinese, the word remembrance, *jì yì*, is a pun that can be heard two ways, 记忆 (to recall, record) and 技艺 (art)" (Thien, 2015). Memory and art are inexorably entwined. Remembering is not the same as perceiving, because we need concepts, context, and language to name and to bring to mind images. These mental images are now popular in neuropsychological vernacular and are called neural representations. Like the previously described dreams, mental images can have a life of their own, a mythical life.

Within the image are mythical stories. Myths create balance, clarity, and adjustments, making events correspond to the inner necessities of things. The tension between dichotomies—good/evil, black/white, positive/negative, active/passive—gives ambivalent power. The psyche is often invisible without awareness of mythological images because without them we are unable to manifest the psyche's origins, structure, and transformations. The myth, or story, gives voice to the psyche; the book provides a vessel for the voice.

Definition of Book Arts

With respect to book arts, structure is almost always synonymous with technique. The word for the type of book also refers to the method used for binding, such as pamphlet, stab-bound, accordion, or codex. All types of handcrafted books, including blank books, rebinds, albums, journals, and artists' books, can be considered a form of book arts. Artists' books combine structure (format) with visual images and presentation; text is optional. Artists' books will be the main focus of the remainder of this chapter, with explanations of three types of book construction, followed by some suggestions for content. The ideas are further extended in the next chapter about therapeutic journals.

I selected these book constructions, a single pamphlet book, an accordion book, and a star book, for their relative ease of facilitation, limitless possibilities for adaptation in a variety of educational and therapeutic settings, and usefulness in promoting and respectfully revealing inner psychological processes in a range of populations. Bookbinding in therapy provides a multitude of possibilities, from its ability to contain, mediate, and express, to its fostering greater self-esteem and dexterity, for individuals and groups ranging in age from children to adults. The therapeutic factors and applications of bookbinding are highlighted and include working with collage, photos, and found objects with special considerations for working with persons who are chronically ill, patients in hospice and the bereaved, and persons struggling with trauma (Bechtel, 2009; Dean, 2009, 2011b). Additional suggestions for developing themes and content within the book will be provided in this and the following chapter about therapeutic journals. The book-binding skills here are provided so they can be incorporated into the larger context of art psychotherapy. Vendors for the book-binding supplies can be found in Appendix A.

One concern when creating books is the necessity of using sharps, such as utility knives, needles, and awls. These tools may preclude some from partaking in bookbinding, unless alterations are made in advance. One such accommodation is to provide pre-cut and pre-drilled materials so that participants will not have to cut or punch the books. For books that require sewing, plastic needles instead of metal ones can be used as an alternative. Again, best clinical judgment is advised.

One young woman I worked with wanted to attend a book-binding workshop I was facilitating. The woman struggled with severe cutting behaviors as well as binging and purging. She was a prolific writer, filling numerous store-bought books with poems, song lyrics, and pictures. Her desire to create her own book was sincere and came from a place of wanting to further personalize her journals by being able to select her preferred drawing paper for the interior as well as the final size of her book. We discussed in advance the necessity of sharps for this particular workshop and came to a mutual agreement that she was welcome to participate so long as she would seek out support if she experienced any harmful urges. She agreed, and at the end of the day-long workshop, she was beaming with elation. "I never had the urge to harm myself, and I really appreciate that you trusted me," she said.

She discussed how her prior history around X-atco© knives provoked old and familiar memories of cutting. "Now I have a new memory of working with knives that have nothing to do with self-harm, instead they lead to something really wonderful—my book! I can't wait to make more!" she exclaimed. And she did, creating several new books for herself and for her friends over the course of the several years we worked together.

Book Construction

Because the process of bookbinding requires knowledge so as to how to create a book, this section provides the lists of materials needed and the directions for the how-to part of constructing three types of books. It is the process of creating the book with all of its frustrations and delights that provides a medium for reflection and processing of psychological material.

Basic Book-Binding Tools

The following book-binding tools are used in making the three types of books described in this section:

- A threaded needle (ribbon, raffia, yarn, embroidery thread, book-binding thread)
- An awl or large needle
- A utility knife*
- A cutting surface
- A metal ruler
- A triangle (very helpful)
- 2-ply chipboard (as a cutting surface and for outer cover if hard bound)— 2-ply chipboard is the brown-grey board often found on the back of drawing tablets
- Interior pages: drawing-weight or charcoal-weight paper
- Cover paper(s): Make sure the paper chosen for the cover is heavy weight; wallpaper samples, fabric swatches, old calendar pages, and magazine covers all make great book covers.

You can add beads to the ribbon tails and mix up the interior pages or put together a collection of your artwork and photos, whatever suits the imagination.

* If working in a setting that precludes sharp objects like a utility knife, working with precut papers and cutting papers to size before the session are viable options.

A Single Signature Book

Materials

Cut your papers to size: 4″ × 8″ (4″ × 4″ when folded). The inside pages can be flush with the cover, or you can cut them smaller to create a border. Remember that your cover needs to be a bit longer, about 1/4 inch larger than the folded pages to cover the width of the fold if you want it to overhang the interior pages.

Directions

- Fold the inside pages and the cover separately. Use your finger or preferably a bone folder to make the crease sharp.
- Center the pages inside the cover, and use a clip or your fingers to hold them in place.
- Use your awl or heavy needle to punch three evenly spaced holes through the papers and cover.
- NB: To get your spacing even, it is easiest to start with the center hole. For taller books, you can use more than three holes (space them approximately every 1–2 inches). If you do not want to sew your book, you can also use a long-reach stapler to bind it together.

- With your threaded needle, go in the center hole from the outside of the book, and leave a tail at least 3–4 inches of thread or ribbon.
- Run the needle out through the bottom hole and back in through the top, pulling the thread or ribbon gently to make it snug. This creates a seam along the back.
- Sew back out through the center hole. Make sure the tail of the thread is on the bottom of the seam and that your needle goes out over the top. Gently tighten the ribbon or thread so it is snug on both sides of the book. Cut off the extra ribbon or thread near the needle. Tie a knot with the ends of the thread or ribbon, making sure your seam is in the center of the knot. Cut the tails to desired length, and you're done!

These are wonderful for self-expression, transitional objects between therapy appointments, gifts, or just a great way to make use of your extra papers.

Accordion Book

Figure 5.1 shows an example of a completed accordion book that was created as a part of a college art therapy class. The students created their own books and recorded their reflections, thoughts, and questions during each week of the semester.

Materials

- Inside paper stock cut to desired size
- Two pieces of card stock for covers the same size as the folded text block
- Bone folder
- Glue stick or white glue with pH-neutral methylcellulose

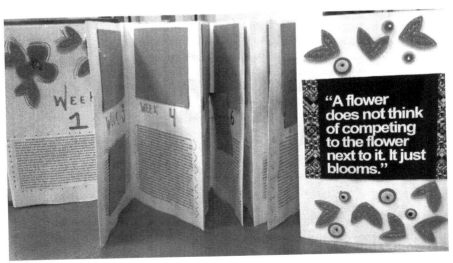

Figure 5.1 An accordion book created as a part of a college art therapy class. The students created their own books and recorded their reflections, thoughts, and questions during each week of the semester. The accordion folds create neat pages to paste the student's journal entries. Additionally she uses pockets and flaps to hold pictures that reminded her of each class. © 2016 Michelle L. Dean.

Directions

- Leaving a quarter-inch tab on one end of the sheet, fold the paper in half, and crease the edge using a bone folder.
- Fold one end to meet the center-fold, creasing the edge of the paper.
- Now reverse the direction of this fold.
- Fold the new fold up to meet the center-fold.
- Fold the end to the center-fold.
- Repeat with the other end-fold.
- Attach each folded page to one another by the quarter-inch tab in alternating directions. This will create the accordion effect of the interior pages when multiples are adhered to one another.
- Glue the card stock covers to the first and the last page of the text block.
- "Bone down" the edges of the glued cover to the text block, gently rubbing the glued text pages to the cover and making sure any air bubbles are removed.

Star Book

Figure 5.2 shows a semester-long book project by an art therapy student. She chose to make a star book as the container for her written thoughts and reflections of her participation in the class. In addition to pasting her typed journal entries, she used collage and drawings to express her understanding of the class topics. This book resembles an origami project more than a traditional book when completed. The book itself is easy to make in less than an hour, and it results in a simple but impressive book. Even though this book is a simple folded book that can be used with or without a hardback cover, its many folds give it a mysterious and complicated look.

Figure 5.2 This star book demonstrates the semester-long book project for an art therapy student. In addition to pasting her typed journal entries, she used collage and drawings to express her understanding of the class topics. © 2016 Michelle L. Dean.

Materials

- 12″ × 12″ paper—scrapbooking paper is often of this size and readily available at numerous retail arts and crafts stores. It comes in a wide variety of colors, prints, and textures, including embossed and flocked.
- Bone folder
- Glue stick or white glue with pH-neutral methylcellulose

Directions

- Fold one of the 12″ × 12″ sheets of paper in half and half again so as to have two creases dividing your paper into square quadrants.
- Flip the paper over and fold it diagonally.
- Repeat this process for as many pages as you would like in your book. (I suggest 3–9 pages)
- Open the square paper, having it in front of you in a diamond position, and place glue on one of the unfolded quadrants.
- With the next square's fold facing in the opposite direct as the first one, place the second square paper's unfolded quadrant onto the glued square.
- Repeat, alternating the direction of the folded square sheets, using care to only glue the unfolded quadrants. The quadrants with the diagonal fold will need to be kept free of glue and will not be used to adhere additional pages to because they will act like hinges for the interior of the book, allowing it to open and close like an accordion or an origami candy dish.

Therapeutic Applications for Books and Journals

"Great books endure because they help us interpret our lives" (Olmert, 1992, p. 299). They offer solace by our knowing so many have come before us and written down their experiences. They allow us to examine our lives and engage in the transcendental process of reading. Utilizing book making in therapy contributes perhaps many beneficial factors: It offers containment for painful affect, thoughts, or memories. It creates order and organization of its content due to its inherent structure, such as providing a chronological order. It has the ability to tell a story in the frames of its pages, similar to storyboarding. Books have the ability to promote myth-minded thinking and development. Like other forms of art, they provide a place for projection and objectification. Books provide a place for recollection, mirroring of life's events, and memories, as in their unwavering ability to concretely recall past events and provide a life's retrospection. Through creative narrative picture making and writing, a book can tell and retell a part of a life story. The value of a book that has endured the ages remains unfettered by time; it is a permanent record, an archival account, of aspects of the psyche that live on beyond the life of the individual. In addition, books offer containment. They have covers and pages that can be opened and closed as one desires. Contents can be revealed or concealed by a flip of the page. Additionally, books offer order and a built-in organizing device as most books move in a sequential fashion. Pages turn, one following after another. Complexity of order can be increased by adding pockets or additional foldout flaps and signatures to the book, but it still has an order.

Myth-minding refers to the ability to think freely, to know what we know, and to know what we do not yet know. Nietzsche discussed mythical processes, saying that "myth was not merely the bearer of ideas and concepts but that it was also a way of thinking, a glass that mirrors to us the universe and ourselves" (as cited in Travers, 2008, p. 3). A myth is a truth, a story, and a part of memory and history; it may not be fact, yet it is no less real. In telling our story in a book through images and words, we make the truth of our thoughts, our words, and our images known and seen by us. This is a way of recollecting and retelling our struggles and triumphs. It is a way of mirroring our life contemporaneously and a way to be nostalgic about memory that we recall from the past. Memory serves us in recalling our truth but also provides a life retrospective. If we do not take inventory of our life on a regular basis, it is easy to overlook how much we have accomplished and overcome, and reprioritize as needed. Our memories are fluid and change over time. Recreating a narrative from life's events serves us in rewriting our narrative so that we are no longer a victim or no longer all alone; it allows a panoramic view of the story arc of our lives rather than the myopic one that is easy to slip into when entrenched in the grind of daily tasks and obstacles. Books offer a medium for us to stand back from our lives and provide objectivity to our life myth. And if constructed with a few archival considerations, they provide a permanent record of our own life's journey, our personal myth.

Traditional Book Decoration Suggestions

The following are suggestions to supplement the book making with personal expressions. They can be considered art making in and of themselves or used in conjunction with other art processes. These are suggestions that I have found engaging and hold the potential for further exploration in a therapeutic context. More specific content suggestions are provided in the next chapter.

Paste Papers

For centuries, artisans have been decorating papers by drawing designs in colored paste (Maurer-Mathison, 1993), creating ornate patterns through very simple techniques. Paste papers are a lovely, easy way to create decorative papers, which may be admired on their own, incorporated into drawings, or utilized in a variety of contexts, such as collage, bookbinding, scrapbooking, or even wrapping paper, as shown in Figure 5.3. Much like clothes, jewelry, and body art, paste papers adorn the exterior of the book cover, enticing or preparing the reader for what lies inside. Paste papers lend themselves to a multitude of educational and therapeutic applications because the process for creating the paste colors is the same as for creating finger paints, substituting tempera paint for the acrylic paint suggested for books. Using these slick and flexible pigments can facilitate abstract and playful imagery as well as lessen anxiety and encourage creative flow (Chilton, 2013). The less structured, or sometimes referred to as regressive elements, inherent in working with paste pigments may lessen defensiveness and encourage spontaneous creation and play, as shown in Figure 5.4. Because of its regressive and fluid nature, it has the potential to be messy, so using protective covers on tables or placing paper in large trays to contain the spread of paint can be a helpful forethought when setting up your setting for a group or individual session.

Figure 5.3 Paste papers create lovely decorative papers, which may be admired on their own, incorporated into drawings or utilized in a variety of contexts such as collage, bookbinding, scrapbooking, or even wrapping paper. © 2016 Michelle L. Dean.

The patterning of the paper is made through the use of pigment and a paste agent, such as flour paste, cornstarch paste, or methylcellulose, my personal favorite, which is a clear viscous solution or gel product that is pH neutral and can be used in archival glue for bookbinding as well as an adhesive for paper repair and mounting. Methylcellulose can also be mixed with glue to create an economic decoupage and extend the life of many white PVA (polyvinyl acetates) glues such as Elmer's™ and Sobo™.

Poster paints, tube gouache, watercolor, and acrylic all may be mixed with the paste of your choosing to create the colors for paste papers. In my experience, acrylic mixed with methylcellulose is preferable due to its ease and availability. Patterning tools such as combs, hair picks, multiple line calligraphy pens, plastic forks, potter's tools, and wood-graining tools are also recommended because of the varied and interesting marks they make to create patterns. If wood-graining tools are not available, inexpensive homemade graining tools can be created with pinking shears, which are scissors with saw-toothed blades that create zigzag patterns and are often used in sewing. Use pinking shears to cut an edge from

Figure 5.4 Exuberant paste paper. The less structured, or sometimes referred to as regressive elements, inherent in working with paste pigments may lessen defensiveness and encourages spontaneous creation and play. Using a portion of this page for the bookend covers, Figure 5.5 "tames" the chaos of this exuberant paste paper. © 2016 Michelle L. Dean.

a plastic jug, or use a knife to create teeth of various widths from the side of a cardboard milk container. Additionally, stamping can be done on the paste papers with plastic or foam stamps, buttons, bottle caps, corks, lace, bubble wrap, and many other found materials.

The ideal paper is 70–80 lb offset printing paper or charcoal-weight paper. The paper must be strong enough to endure raking tools over its wet surface without falling apart. Highly absorbent papers should be avoided because they tend to shed or rip as you work with them. Wetting the papers first by soaking, sponging, or spraying with water allows the paper to relax and creates slower drying times, which may be helpful when creating intricate designs. Papers that are uneven in their moisture content will buckle and could create distortions in the patterns.

Brush the tinted paste of your choice over the moistened paper, and experiment with various pattern-making tools and mark directions. Many people first experiment with symmetrical patterns, which reflect historical designs (Maurer-Mathison, 1993). Be sure to experiment with asymmetrical designs and contemporary influences. Once completely dry, double and triple printing may be done by applying subsequent layers of colored paste on top of the first pattern. Recipes of flour paste and corn paste and directions for mixing methylcellulose are provided in Appendix B.

Working with larger pieces of paper, at minimum 18″ × 24″, is recommended because it encourages bilateral gestures, which are associated with restorative integration and improved cognitive processing. Once the pigments are dry, the paper can be pressed with a warm iron or placed under books to be restored to a flat sheet for drawing. If the paper is to be used in bookbinding or collage, pressing may not be necessary because the glue will assist in holding its new shape.

Bookbinding

In covering the outer pages of a book, one can select the parts of the paste paper that are most desirable. Figure 5.5 shows where a portion of the paste paper (shown in Figure 5.4) was used to create the book cover for a 7-year-old boy's

Figure 5.5 In covering the outer pages of the book, one may select only the parts of the paste paper that are most desirable. A portion of the paste paper in Figure 5.4 was applied to create the book covers for this 7-year-old boy's star book, allowing choice in the areas that will be used and seen. © 2016 Michelle L. Dean.

star book. The patient can choose the area that they most strongly connect with and place it in a way that it can be seen clearly. Along with choosing the cover of the book, patients can create blank journals in which to carry on their creative process outside of scheduled sessions. The book becomes a kind of transitional object, holding the emotional space to bridge time and connection between appointments. Journals may be filled with thoughts, reflections, and images. This process, referred to as visual journaling, art journaling, or creative journaling, creates individual time for personal reflection and can allow for experiences of underlying themes and increased familiarity with oneself. More suggestions are given in the next chapter about utilizing books and journals in therapy.

CHAPTER 6

THERAPEUTIC JOURNALS
What's Lost Is Found

This chapter about therapeutic journaling builds on the information from the previous chapter about therapeutic art books, which covered bookbinding and provided a discussion of construction, form, and function of books. In this chapter I now turn my focus to content and expression and the potentiality books hold. Books can hold sacred texts or illuminated scriptures, transfer knowledge, and record personal and communal narratives over generations. They hold individual, community, and cultural legacies and create cultural bridges over time, people, and places. They are vessels for recording memories and devices for memories to be told again into the future using imagery and words. Books hold the telling of personal, familial, and communal narrative and can literally be passed down generation to generation—creating a legacy or gifts for future generations. They are an archive, first-person accounting seen through an individual's eyes and recorded for prosperity.

Perhaps one of the best-known visual journals is C. G. Jung's *The Red Book*, which was a leather-bound folio that contained the imagery and written accounts of the Swiss analyst's experiences of the deep inner work of personal analysis. The parchment pages hold a record of the images and dialog of his active imagination, providing a visual record of his exploration of the depths of his own psyche. He practiced a willful engagement in *mythopoetic imagination* (Jung, 1963) by "deliberately evoking a fantasy in a waking dream state, and then entering into it as a drama. These fantasies may be understood as a type of dramatized thing in pictorial form" (Shamdasani, 2009, p. 200). *The Red Book*, created between 1915 and 1930, was held in the family estate vault until permission was given for its preparation and eventual publication in 2009. Jung's experiments on the unconscious and the pictorial elements that he engaged in laid the foundation for his theory on active imagination. Active imagination is engaging the images of one's mind's eye. Dialog between the images and their amplification is drawn upon to give a better understanding of unconscious processes and opposing elements. It can be thought of as standing on the threshold of consciousness while inviting the images of our dreams, daydreams, and fantasies to arrive as our guests. When images or figures arrive in awareness, an engagement through dialog by speaking about them to the psychotherapist, writing them down, or drawing them evokes greater awareness and understanding.

Schaverien (1992) speaks of this type of image and its ability to hold transformative powers, as in *embodied images*. Embodied images can express states of consciousness for which there are no words. By *alivening* these images through dialog or graphic depiction, they can become embodied, lived, and transformative. The image is recognized as a form of articulation of the soul, its whole greater than its parts. Experience with this type of process is akin to "aha" moments in learning and realization. And like these moments of profound insight and transformation, they do not happen each time art is engaged in, just as they are not common in every psychotherapy session. Instead, they build and break through awareness when ready.

In contrast to the embodied image is the *diagrammatic image* Schaverien (1992) describes, which is an image that is often rudimentary or linear and is made for the purpose of telling something to the psychotherapist. Although this type of image can be very important in regards to revealing previously spoken or unspoken thoughts and memories, this type of picture does not change the psyche of the artist. It can be a way of documenting daily life events like keeping a diary versus creating a work of literature. In my experience, diagrammatic images are most frequently seen early in therapy, and they can be more prevalent at times when one is physically or emotionally impoverished and experiencing a loss of self, or lack of development of an inner self, which is often cited as a factor contributing to eating disorders and other addictive processes (Dean, 2013).

A Selective Collection: Compiling and Limiting

Visual journals create an organized format. The thoughts, ideas, and dreams written in it fall within the confines of the pages of the book. When using the book to contain mementos and ephemeral materials, it can also take on a kind of ordering and containment. This containment can be especially helpful in limiting and organizing materials that are particularly charged with emotional affect. A scrapalbum, literally scraps of ephemera representing aspects of one's life and memories, can be pasted and held for prosperity. This process of distancing and holding can help buffer overwhelming affect, much like boxes made in therapy. This art media can even assist an individual in distilling a life of not having enough while being inundated with material possessions.

Artistic Materials and Methods

There are many artistic techniques and methods that can be employed in the art psychotherapeutic process, offering artists and art educators ample modes of expression. I offer here some of the artistic methods and applications that can be employed in psychological work that enlist the aid of art materials.

Collage

By combining images and found objects of interest, patients can overcome the anxiety associated with pressure to create a realistic image of their own as well as any general resistance to art therapy (Landgarten, 1994). Collage may offer relief to those who lack confidence in the quality of their work and allow for many different combinations to be tested before a final commitment is made. Increasing the patient's choices of imagery to be incorporated into a therapeutic artwork can also evoke an increase in dialog between patient and therapist about associations with the abstract and unconscious material. Found objects, photos, tickets, and pressed flowers can all be incorporated into a therapeutic journal. Selecting images and objects that are imbued with personal meaning and significance heighten the relevance and potential for storytelling and capturing a visual narrative. To place three-dimensional objects within a journal, it may be necessary to cut a pocket out of the pages to provide a chamber to set the object within the book. Chambers within a book also relate to the significance of utilizing boxes in therapy (Chapter 9). Additionally, envelopes and bags with different degrees of transparency can be used to obfuscate the contents, providing layers of secrecy or protection within the book itself. Pre-constructed or handmade bags made from paper, plastic, or velum can serve as pages of the book or be added to existing pages with glue or other adhesives.

Decoupage

Decoupage, meaning to cut from something, is similar to collage in that cut out images or shapes are glued into the journal. Its uses also extend to boxes and furniture. Tissue paper is commonly used in this process, building jewel-like hues. Tissue paper decoupage, when constructed on glass or wax paper, continues to have a transparent effect, which can be utilized when wanting to veil an object below. The act of layering, building a kind of flexible skin from sometimes hundreds of layers of delicate tissue paper and glue, mimics the reparative process of healing (Dean, 2008).

Stamping

Using stamps within the book can not only embellish the book but also offer much of the psychological significance of printmaking an image, as described in Chapter 2. Patterns for stamps can be made through pre-made rubber stamps or combining them with stamps that are individually made, as described previously. Stamps are able to not only carry patterns but also can be used for writing words, as shown in Figure 6.1. In Figure 6.1, "Pictures are like poetry" is stamped across part of an

Figure 6.1 Pictures are like poetry is stamped across part of an accordion book that expresses visual images from the author's active imagination work along with parts of a written poem. © 2016 Michelle L. Dean.

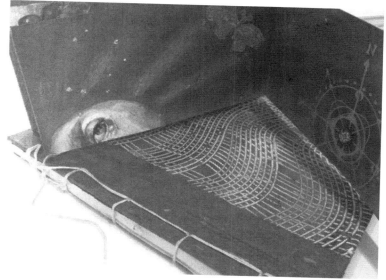

Figure 6.2 This image of the book utilized stamps, painting, colored pencils, found objects such as my grandmother's tadding, tape transfers (the butterfly) and dried flowers, gold leaf and glass buttons. It is sitting on top of another book, a stab binding that utilized paste papers also created by the author. © 2016 Michelle L. Dean.

accordion book that expresses visual images from active imagination sessions along with parts of written poetry. The book, also shown in Figure 6.2, utilizes stamps, painting, colored pencils, found objects such as my grandmother's tatting (hand-made lace), tape transfers (the butterfly), dried flowers, gold leaf, and glass buttons.

Stenciling

Stencils are the reverse of stamps in that the image is typically cut out of a sheet of paper or board, and paint is applied to the negative spaces. For example, if a heart shape is cut from a page and laid on another surface on which one intends to paint, an open heart is used to give form to the painted shape. When using found objects such as a piece of mesh, paint can be applied through the mesh to create colorful patterns and shapes.

Lettering

Lettering combines the written word with image. As in artist–poets books that are illustrated, lettering adds another layer of expression to images. Words or phrases can be created with rubber stamps, letter stickers, tape transfers, or collage. Of course, written passages can be hand-lettered with markers or calligraphy pens. They also may be printed in computer-generated type first and then applied later.

Tape Transfers

Tape transfers work with pre-printed images and words. They can be created from magazines or photographs. Utilizing clear packaging tape, place the tape strip on the right side of the image or words to be used. If the passage is larger than the width of one tape strip, several strips can be laid down to create a continuous sheet. Flip the taped image over and use moistened fingers or a brush to wet the paper backing. Once wet, the pulp of the magazine page will begin to fall apart and can be gently removed by rubbing fingers over the surface. The result will be a ghostly image in which some of the passages will be wiped away along with the pulp fiber of the page. Along with the tape, the semi-transparent transfer can be applied to a painting, collage or other application. This is particularly effective when a hint, faint presence, or ambivalence needs to be expressed. Likewise, when using them in a three-dimensional application, depth can be created by layering several tape transfers.

Abstract Drawings from Decorative Papers

Instead of beginning a work of art with a stark white page, use a paste paper, a marbleized paper, or an inked Suminagashi paper because it may take some of the anxiety out of starting a drawing or collage, as discussed in the chapter about printmaking, Chapter 2. For example, when working with the paper for a drawing, a design or pattern can inform the image because it may speak to the artist, and imagistic associations can be drawn or created on the page. This method is akin to the projective scribble drawing (Hones, 1995), except the scribble is provided by the pigment or ink. Additionally, these papers can be used to elicit a symbolic or metaphorical response to the question, "What do you do when life hands you something you did not ask for?" The graphic patterns of the decorative papers can stand in for the line created by another group member and can be used in a pass-a-picture intervention or by utilizing the pattern created by the pigments as the thing to be reckoned with (McCafferty, Kwak, Dean, & Kane, 2007), which is more fully described in Chapter 3. The patterned paper can represent an undesirable event and its sequela. For example, for a traumatic event, a graphic response—painted, drawn, or collaged—provides an opportunity to explore and work out various responses to an image and in turn to life's event(s) or situations.

Web Writing

Web writing starts with a word used as a theme or topic in a circle on a piece of paper or in a journal. On the outside of the circle, write down as many free associations that come to mind when thinking about the chosen theme or topic. If you like, group the words into smaller categories by placing circles or squares around the words that seem to go together. Write a paragraph or story using the words in the selected groups. For example, use all the words that were circled to create a paragraph or story while using the other groups of words for another paragraph or story. Themes for the center of a circle can include archetypal images, such as self, body, mother, father, survivor, child, and hero, or can include love, hate, depression, addiction, and illness. More suggestions for core themes and archetypal suggestions are given in Appendix C.

Once the written story is complete, illustrate it. The illustration can work around the writing or the initial web of ideas in a journal or be completely separate on another piece of paper. The image depicting the story along with the writing can be used to discuss underlying themes and associations that are either compatible with or dissimilar to the creator. I also find using web writing to solve a problem to be beneficial. For example, exploring an upcoming decision in pictorial form can provide insight because the images may speak to the weight of the factors through their use of space, line quality, and significance of placement. Whereas, words may express a concern, they alone do not convey a visual weight as it is related to significance as demonstrated in size, color or line energy.

Group Writing

Writing in a group decreases the isolation sometimes associated with writing alone. An intervention that may be used in a group is a collective group writing experience. Ask your group to write three (or five) words on a small slip of paper. Fold them and place them in a box or in the center of the table. Pull out a paper (not your own), and write a sentence or short paragraph using all of the words. Read it aloud. Repeat. Over time, themes or other collective experiences may become evident from the stories being generated in a particular group. These group writings can be done on separate pieces of paper and inserted into a journal for future reference. Or later in that or a separate session, illustrate the sentences or paragraphs, which can also be pleasurable and insightful as the image amplifies the words.

Writing in the Round

Each person starts by writing a sentence on a page and passes it to the person sitting to their left. Continue passing the paper until the pages return to the starting positions. Or if working in a larger group where time limitations prohibit a complete circle, select a designated number of times that each piece will be passed. Illustrate the returned story. In group discussion, share the stories and offer feedback and associations from other group members.

This method is similar to passing the picture, where instead of creating a story with a line from each person, each person contributes some visual form or object to a page. The shared image-making experience can reflect the group's ability to work together as well as dynamics among group members. For example, in one such group with members working in dyads, a woman who had difficulty fitting in due to her confrontational style took her group partner's image and scribbled out the original drawings of hearts and rainbows, replacing them with black boxes and smudge marks. This experience opened a door for discussion about self and other perceptions as well as fears of being rejected by others. The woman who scribbled out her partner's drawings realized that her projected fear that this was going to happen to her caused her to use this stance to guard against wounded feelings, engaging in the very behaviors she feared the most.

Engaging the Image

Engaging the image perhaps speaks most directly to the heart of art in psychotherapy in that, by engaging the image in dialog, there can be a greater knowing, or amplification, of elements that appear in pictorial or imagistic form. The image that one chooses for this method can be one that has come in a dream, is part of a visualized daydream, or has appeared in a drawing. It can also be an image found in a magazine or photograph. What is most important is for the image to carry a bit of charge. What I mean by *charge* is that the image speaks to the viewer: it can elicit a positive or negative reaction, it can be inviting or repulsive, or it can be an image that just won't go away, as in a reoccurring dream. Once the image has been selected, write a couple of sentences, poem, paragraph, or short story that describes the image. If there are two or more characters in the image, write a dialog they could be having with each other. If additional challenge is desired, reduce the control over the expression of the dialog by using left-hand–right-hand drawings and responses for dual characters. In this way, allow each character to speak by writing his or her dialog with a different hand. This process can be employed to record the thoughts, feelings, and responses of the drawn figures with each other.

Daily Writing

Julia Cameron (1992), in *The Artist's Way: A Spiritual Path to Higher Creativity*, popularized the method of "morning pages," promoting writing for 10 minutes per day as a way of freeing unwanted thoughts, images, and associations. The writing is meant to engage in personal process, not as a means of recording daily events but of inner symbolic process expression. A free association with one's inner world is meant to be captured in this free writing, including if the same word comes to you many times, write it again and again until something else appears in your mind's eye. Permitting a place for a verbal purge as it were can quiet the chatter and noise often associated with anxiousness and "dis-ease."

Acrostic

An acrostic poem is a form of writing in an alphabetic script in which the first letter, syllable, or word of each line, paragraph, or other recurring feature in the text spells out a word or a message. This type of spontaneous expression is often done by preadolescent girls. Girls use their name to describe personal attributes or characteristics. As an esteem-building exercise in a group setting, each individual writes his or her name vertically down the left side of the paper, and group members write descriptive lines or words describing the person that begin with these letters. Or participants can identify their own positive attributes, writing affirmative words for each letter of their names.

Found Poetry

Found poetry uses lines of previously published poetry to create a new poem. This type of poetry is created by taking words, phrases, and sometimes whole passages from other sources and reframing them as poetry by making changes in spacing or lines (and consequently meaning). The original source can be altered by adding or deleting passages, thus creating a new form and poem or writing that may or may not resemble the original form. This method can be used when creating an altered book.

Altered Book

To create an altered book, the artist takes a discarded book of their choice and begins to alter the cover and interior pages through the use of gesso (an opaque ground used in painting), the removal of pages, or the addition of other materials to the pages. Additionally, stamps, collage, and photographs can be adhered to the book. The original text can remain to varying degrees, depending on the artist's preference.

Symbolically, according to Chilton (2007), this method can be used to support rebellion in adolescents as they destroy and cover over the previous function and content of the book. Additionally, using a pre-printed book can represent neglected or forgotten knowledge, and an earlier chapter of one's life. As discussed in the previous chapter about books, the bound pages create order and have the ability to hold and contain expressed psychic contents. It is important to note that, when creating altered books, considerations of the cultural values and beliefs of the individual or group are imperative. For some, the book is sacred, and defacing it in any way would be considered sacrosanct. In these cases, creating a book from scratch and adding collage or pieces of works of found poetry may be a better choice consistent with honoring values and beliefs while still offering a potentially meaningful opportunity for expression.

Visual journals, the combination of words and pictures, provide opportunities for multiple benefits when working with patients in a therapeutic context because they allow a beautiful and expressive means of recording of personal expressions that may be utilized over a period of time. They hold individual, family, and cultural legacies creating bridges over time, people, and places. They are a vessel for recording memories, telling stories and expressing internal imagery. Imagery and words may be used for the retelling and become the repository for shape-shifting, personal narratives. These journals create a legacy or gift for future generations because they are an archive, a first-person account seen through an individual's eyes and recorded for prosperity to be passed down, generation to generation, whether the subject matter is as commonplace as an adolescent girl recording her challenges with budding sexuality or as traumatic as recording the horrors she has endured in a war-torn country. Books and visual journals are especially powerful to use in the context of working with individuals who are chronically ill, in hospice, and bereaved as they become a touchstone and a record of one's existence, importance, and meaning.

CHAPTER 7

MASK MAKING
Self-Concept and Its Illusive Nature

Masks, or "false faces," have a long history and numerous implications as they pertain to morality and sociology as well as expression of personas, aspects, or facades of self. Masks allow people to play or accentuate various roles, parts, or new characters. Most often seen in theater, they carry out life dramas and represent personas. Personas are aspects of self that one shares with others and the various roles that one may inhabit. They have a significant role in personality development and when dealing with traumatic experiences where the self becomes disrupted or shattered in response to overwhelming experiences. The mask as a therapeutic intervention can assist in reparative and integrative processes. If one has an underdeveloped sense of self, it may lead to vulnerability and reflect difficulties in psychological development (Ronnberg & Martin, 2010). The mask has a dual nature of both looking out and looking inward. It has the dual ability to reveal and conceal. The ability to put on and take off the mask can mitigate the shape-shifting nature of trauma and be used for its archetypal, transformative, and healing effects.

Historical Uses of Masks

Masks are often worn as part of costumes; they mold not only the wearer's personality but also elicit responses from viewers. A wearable art, masks share with their related cousin, the tattoo, the ability to perform defining, mediating, and boundary functions for personal, communal, archetypal, and spiritual purposes. Masks are used in religious ceremonies and offer assurances of social cohesion and hierarchy, respect for acceptable laws, and repression of unacceptable behaviors. Historically, masks have been worn in initiation rites as a means of establishing social rank for community and spiritual leaders. They are used for communion with nature and spiritual realms, as seen in shamanistic cultures such as that of Native Americans, where they have both anthropomorphic (human features) and theriomorphic (animal features) qualities. Shamanic masks have several purposes: to buffer against hostile spirits, to transform or evoke the assistance of beneficial spirits, to channel the shaman's focus, and to create distance between the shaman and the audience (Schulz-Weidner, 1967).

Masks are found in funerary and commemorative processes, such as in rituals of the ancient Egyptians and the Aztecs, who placed stylized masks on the faces of the deceased before burial; the Mezzo-Americans, who used effigy masks as a benediction; and the Americans and Europeans who used plaster death masks to commemorate the loss of a notable person, such as a political figure, by preserving the image of the dead and mitigating the traumatic effect of loss upon the bereaved. Additionally, masks are used for therapeutic and magico-religious purposes, such as to ward off illness, as seen in the herb-filled, beaked masks of the plague doctors, shown in Figure 7.1, doctors and medicine men who visited those who were ill with the Black Plague during the 14th century, and those that may be found among the Burmese, Chinese, and Sri Lankan during cholera and other epidemics. Masks have been used during times of war as a means of donning courage, strength, and intimidation of rivals, as well as in sports, where they are used for both intimidation and protection, such as in fencing or the brightly painted goalie masks of ice hockey and helmets associated with football, motor bikes, and car racing. And masks are used for festivals and celebrations, such as Halloween, Mardi Gras, masked balls, and the 1,500-year-old pagan ritual of Perchten festival (also known as *Krampus or Tuifl*) to disperse the ghosts of winter, found predominantly in Austria and parts of the United States. They are used

Figure 7.1 Chalk and pencil illustration of a plague doctor. Permission for its use given by author. © 2016 Michelle L. Dean.

in theatrical productions, such as those found in ancient Greece and even earlier in the East, as in the dramas of the Chinese and Japanese. Masks range from being realistic to abstractions and are made of materials innate to the culture and regions of the makers.

Some masks are unique and free formed by artist inspiration while others adhere to strict tradition requirements. For example, masks used to legitimize authority of certain families among the Temne people of Sierra Leone have a mask that represents the spirit responsible for protecting the reigning dynasty of power for each chief. The mask is only seen in public during the enthroning ceremony of a chief. It is not worn by him, but by the presiding dignitary to display the transmission of power from one chief to another. The same dignitary also acts as a mediator between the new chief and his people (Meyer, 1992). Figure 7.2 depicts a rare metal-appliquéd example of a Temne mask known as Ta-Bemba,

Figure 7.2 A rare metal-appliqued example of a Temne mask known as Ta-Bemba who calls at each house in the village to collect boys, leading them to the bush circumcision and initiation camp. Country of origin: Sierra Leone. Culture: Temne. Wood, metal. Credit: Werner Forman Archive/British Museum, London. Location: 38. Photo Credit: HIP/Art Resource, NY.

who calls at each house in the village to collect boys, leading them to the bush circumcision and initiation camp. The mask helps at the threshold between innocence and experience and between youth and manhood. Like the ex-voto (Chapter 4), which were traditionally painted by artists, the African artist who created the masks worked on commissions from a ruler, officiating priest, soothsayer, or member of a secret society. He was not permitted to follow an unfettered "inspiration": he worked within the framework of traditional norms and programs, but this framework allowed for a variety of important creations (Meyer, 1992).

Today, in Western culture, the best-known mask-wearing holiday is Halloween. Now considered a holiday for children, Halloween is a vestige of former darker customs and spiritual beliefs observed by adults because, like *Krampus*, the antithesis of Santa Claus, they are often considered too frightening for the young. Historically, Celts celebrated the New Year on November 1st, a day that marked the end of the summer and the beginning of the dark winter, a time associated with death. During this time, the boundary between the living and the dead was considered at its weakest, and thus, the celebration of Samhain was on October 31st, when it was believed the spirits returned to the Earth. During the celebration, Celts wore costumes and animal heads, and blackened their faces in an attempt to confuse and avoid the wandering spirits. By the time Christianity had spread to the Celts' lands in the 800s, there were attempts to replace the pagan holiday with the church-sanctioned solemnity of All Saints' Day or All Saints', also called All Hallowmas or All Hallows, the origin of the name Halloween.

Mardi Gras, another centuries-old tradition associated with mask wearing, has origins traceable to medieval Europe, spreading to Rome and Venice in the 17th and 18th centuries, then to France, and then carried to the New World by French-Canadian settlers. Mardi Gras is still observed in places originally settled by the French in the United States, like the famous annual celebration in New Orleans. This holiday, like Halloween, is also linked to pagan winter festivals and later became inexorably linked to the Christian calendar. Christians view Lent, beginning with Ash Wednesday, as the period of fasting and abstinence before Easter. In tandem with the beginning of this period of restriction is a climax of decadence, which culminates in Fat Tuesday, the literal translation of Mardi Gras. The masking during Mardi Gras permits the wearer to act with increased freedom, such as when he or she wanted to interact with other members of society who would be considered outside the bounds of identity and everyday convention. It was useful for a variety of purposes, some of them illicit or criminal, others personal, such as romantic encounters.

In performance art, Commedia dell'Arte was an exacting dramatic art involving pace, poise, and quick-wittedness. Shakespeare used it to convey his dramas. Commedia dell'Arte uses male archetype characters. These include the Harlequin, who was associated with the many sides to personality; he can be funny and stupid. Another is the Pantaloon, who is characteristically old, mean, and miserly, has long legs and wears red trousers. There are also the Pulcinella—better known as *Punch*—who has a hunchback and large nose and makes a sound like a chicken, and the Doctor, to name a few. Costumes, wigs, and the painting or powdering of faces are most often associated with performance arts and theatrical plays, but they can still be seen in use in Western cultures for civil duties such as justices. In some countries, powdered wigs and robes are worn for religious services. Other traditions include similar celebratory customs for holidays with religious and spiritual origins, as well as everyday beautification practices.

Tattoos

Tattoos, a permanent art form, are found worldwide dating back to antiquity. They have roots in tribal customs, serving purposes similar to those of masks. The word *tattoo* comes from the Polynesian word for knocking or striking, as a needle was dipped into ink and then struck into the skin. Like some masks, the facial tattoos of the Polynesian *Moko* showed status and ferocity. Many of the Pacific islanders had their own identifiable styles and techniques. Hawaiian women tattooed their tongues to mourn the death of a chief, and memorial tattoos, inscribing the names or images of the deceased, are common means of expressing in a palpable way the pains of loss of a loved one (Favazza, 1996). Favazza (1996) discussed the history and increased popularity of tattooing among young men and women as being akin to a search for connection—a connection not only to aspects of oneself but also to others. Like the *Moko*, tattoos are a worn image or corporal calling card.

Tattoos in this country were, in the not so distance past, once only associated with sailors, prisoners, and motorcycle gangs, who had them in part for the magical and tribal powers they possessed. For example, sailors believed that a tattoo of a pig on the left foot could prevent drowning, and motorcycle gang members displayed their defiance or nonconformity through their illustrated bodies. Tattooing, as a kind of branding, was commonly done to and by prisoners (Favazza, 1996). In the last 20 years, the popularity of tattoos has exploded in the United States, and the stigma and outlaw or rebel identity previously associated with them seems to have subsided. Although people come to the process of tattooing for many personal reasons, it is undoubtedly rooted in a tradition of identity, quest for belonging, mimicry of tribal art tattoos, expression of an archetypal process, and identification with an image or images. Identification with the archetypal experience (universal) is usually identification with something beyond the human realm. Identification with nonhuman needs and capacities often take a form such as addiction. It is an attempt to transcend the mundaneness of human existence, to be freed from the limits and suffering of humanness. If these needs are not well-mediated, one can become assimilated into the archetype and the individual can exceed human form (e.g., of the angels and identifying with something beyond the human). The skin is the boundary between self and other, and it can become a canvas of expression, but unlike the mask, it is unable to be removed, at least without the assistance of medical intervention, and becomes a way to merge with an image, idol, ideal, or archetype. People can also experience a physiological euphoria with the pain that accompanies the multiple needle pricks necessary for applying ink into the dermis layer of skin. This experience couples physical pain with image making as the image takes permanent residence on the very boundary or threshold that defines inner and outer experience.

Using Masks in Therapy

Oscar Wilde is attributed with saying, "Man is least himself when he talks in his own person. Give him a mask, and he will tell you the truth" (Ellmann, 1969, p. 389). The "truth" one can tell through a mask in therapy is polyvalent, and the possibilities for expression are endless. Creating one's own mask out of wire mesh or papier-mâché strips over a mask form or balloon is easy and is typically accessible for the young and old. An even easier method employs pre-made papier-mâché or poured plaster forms. Two examples of these are shown in Figures 7.3 and 7.4. The masks were created by young women in art therapy groups at an eating disorders facility.

Figure 7.3 Plaster mask cast in a mold. Painted and carved by a patient in an eating disorders treatment facility. © 2016 Michelle L. Dean.

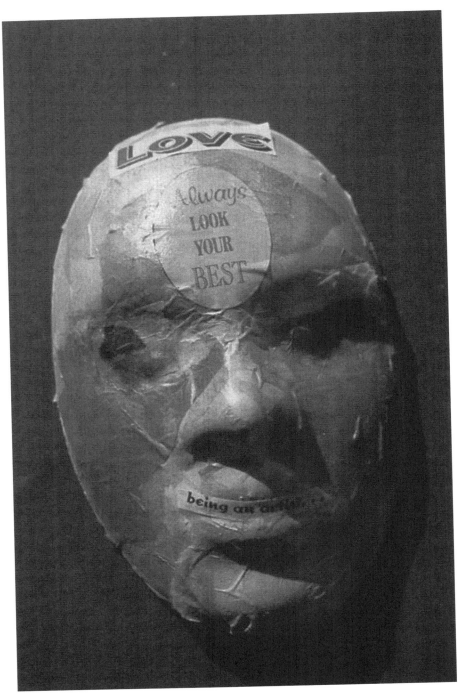

Figure 7.4 Collage and decoupage plaster mask covered in layers. © 2016 Michelle L. Dean.

The masks were either pre-made, papier-mâché masks or ones that I had created by pouring liquid plaster into molds and allowing them to set for a week. Due to their ease and relative lack of expense, I prefer these two types of masks to the plaster gauze strips that one drapes on the face or other substrates such as balloons or mask models. When working with a pre-made structure, the individual is supported to focus on content of the art intervention rather than on creating a life-like form, which can be anxiety-producing for some. Choosing a pre-made form that is durable and firm is helpful in order to hold up under the processes of adding and altering the mask for greatest artistic expression. And since most of my patients are trauma survivors, many of whom have dissociative symptoms, I prefer not to use the plaster strips directly on the patient's face because that can feel restrictive and limit mobility during the time needed for the plaster to harden, which can cause feelings of fear and discomfort. With these considerations, personal expression with masks can be limitless. I encourage participants to use the outside of the mask to show what she believes she shows others about herself or would like them to know about her. On the inside of the mask, I encourage her to depict aspects of herself that may be more personal or how she feels inside. The mask, due to its three-dimensional form, has a front and back, which promotes expression of the inside and outside duality that often exists with trauma survivors. The duality can encompass such feelings as wanting to put a beautiful or "painted" face forward that shows control or acceptable social standards while on the inside of the mask there are often feelings of incompetence, ugliness, fear, or secret-related items.

In the two examples shown here, both women struggled, for different reasons, with finding what was beautiful or redeeming within themselves. Figure 7.3 shows a poured plaster mask on which Ellie used paint to layer shades of blue and grey. Frustrated with the forms and images that were emerging for her, she wiped the paint away with her clenched fist and reapplied the paint. She proceeded to do this process of adding and wiping away the paint several more times while adding dabs of red to the muddy bluish-hue until she turned her paintbrush over and began scraping the paint way, eviscerating the surface of the mask and carving slashes and gouging stroke-marks into the surface of the form. Ellie struggled with the shame of sexual trauma. The doing and undoing in the artwork can be seen as a repetition compulsion and mirrors the intensity of Ellie's situation, spiraling in the raw reaction to trauma, just as in Shakespeare's *Macbeth*, as Lady Macbeth's guilt compelled her to compulsively wash her hands to remove the contaminating spot. Repetition compulsion is a common defense against trauma and may be seen as an attempt to protect as well as master a situation by reliving it with the unconscious hope of a different outcome, which is rarely actualized (Chu, 1991; Meshcheryakova, 2012; van der Kolk & Greenberg, 1987). When working with repetition compulsion, the art materials represent a "more durable attachment" (Phillips, 2003, p. 145) and as such can help to ground the individual and slow or cease the spiraling thoughts, tendencies to self-harm, and disassociation, as was the case with Ellie over time. An advantage can be seen in the pliability of the material as well as its ability to hold psychic content, feelings, emotions, and memories over a period of time without fading away as dialog does.

Benefits of Masks for Trauma Survivors

Two beneficial and inherent structures of using masks in a therapeutic setting include boundary and mediating functions, especially as they relate to working with individuals who have experienced trauma. Boundary functions relate to protective and defining functions that the mask, or wearable art, can provide. The mask acts like an auxiliary skin, infusing positive introjects as aspects of self are integrated and self-concept and self-esteem are reestablished or created. Masks also provide an opportunity to put on and remove any unwanted aspects of self through the removal of the mask or even, if not worn, the ability to view the unwanted aspects of self as a *part of* but separate quality or aspect of oneself.

When using decoupage or collage on a mask, the multiple layers act like thin sheets of skin, increasing flexibility and strength with each meditative application. The built-up tissue paper mirrors and provides a parallel process in the recreation of self after a traumatic event by building and healing, layer by layer. It is a meditative process where the method, the gentle application of glue and tissue, is a direct reflection and physical response of the healing process. The use of tissue paper and collage are shown in Figure 7.4.

For example, during a traumatic experience, one is overwhelmed with emotions when one is threatened, in harm's way, or experiencing assault. There is a physiological and neurological response to this trauma, which results in a shutting down of the brain areas responsible for language and speech, rendering it impossible to recall and express memories of a highly emotional nature (Greenberg & van der Kolk, 1987; Stone, 2015; van der Kolk, 1994). Psychologically, the trauma creates a breaking down of self, psychically, and parts of self become fragmented or split off. Kalshed (1996) described the psyche's normal reaction to trauma as to withdraw or, when withdrawing is not possible, to withdraw a part of oneself to preserve oneself. This results in a fragmentation, a split, and resulting dissociation. These split-off parts of self can be seen in some of the symptoms of trauma, such as flashbacks, and they also appear in a rigid and hypervigilent self, attempting to secure one's personal and environmental boundaries. Most commonly, aggressive and violent affect are what lead to the dissociative elements. In contrast, positive and soothing affect, often accompanied by adequate mediation of a caring figure, such as a mother figure or therapist, has the potential to restore and integrate these fragments. The art materials support these soothing acts by providing an additional means for nurturance.

Working with masks provides the opportunity to rebuild and try on various elements associated with protection. Whether creating a mask from a pre-made form, such as papier-mâché or a plaster mold, or actually creating the mask from wire mesh or plaster strips, the art effectively circumvents the verbal skills that become compromised when emotionally charged, allowing for expression and reintegration of fragmented aspects of the self and experiences (Greenberg & van der Kolk, 1987) in a nonthreatening way (Stone, 2015). The mask protects the individual from physical and psychic elements that can be experienced as threatening or overwhelming. Providing opportunities for protection through the image of the mask preserves the connectedness between the internal psyche reality and the collective, or outside world, by simultaneously withholding and shielding and thereby containing the traumatic element and energy. The mask also hides from others a view unique to the individual's internal content and can also conceal the contents within the individual psyche that are experienced as incompatible. The mediating functions of the mask permit the flow of psychic energy and content between the individual and others, or the collective, as well as integrating aspects of the individual disrupted by the traumatic experience.

With respect to the mediating function, the actual donning of the mask allows the wearer to internalize the properties of its symbolic content, and thus, the individual is transformed much in the same way a shaman is. For the trauma survivor, the mask is capable of presenting its polyvalent contents, including the traumatic experience, the self before and after the traumatic experience, and the transformative or healing process, to others and the collective by animating the symbolic, collecting the fragmented aspects of self, and simultaneously preserving aspects of self.

Bringing the aspects of self to consciousness is important for the traumatized in order for a kind of reparative psychic skin to evolve through use of the mask or a series of masks created over time. This role playing or trying on of different personas can be seen when the viewer looks upon the mask and its wearer, as in masks in dramas, ceremonies for acquiring new roles, or indicators of social rank. This becomes obvious when children don superhero masks and take to bounding about as if they have imbued with the super characteristics of the hero character. Although there may be more inhibition among traumatized children and more reserved adults, the masks still provide mediating and boundary functions. Out of these functions emerge three roles specific to the healing function of masks: containment of existing traumatic sequelae, mediation between the existing ego stance and the trauma effects, and mediation between individual experience and the collective.

First, containment of existing traumatic sequelae relates to the protection of the self from traumatic effects that may be split off or unmetabolized. *Sequelae* refers to all conditions and consequences that result from the disease or injury. With traumatic experiences, the sequelae can extend not only to physical injury but also to psychological and behavioral problems, as in nightmares, flashbacks, anxiety, depression, relationship issues, and isolation. When creating masks, the structure of the mask holds and contains painful affect; masks have the ability to express the fragmented, aggressive, and hostile residual effects of traumas. These aspects, often incompatible or incomprehensible, find a place of expression that can be free of judgment for the creator of the mask. The mask can also allow the preservation of particular persona representing the pre-trauma self, such as a loving mother or the type of person one believes one is, which includes qualities that have become tarnished or called into question by the effects of trauma. For example, war veterans may be suffering from moral trauma in addition to the psychological and physical trauma they may endure. Moral trauma has been defined as perpetrating, failing to prevent, bearing witness to, or learning about acts that transgress deeply held moral beliefs and expectations (Maguen & Litz, 2012). Betrayal, as in leadership failures, betrayal of peers and trusted persons, or not living up to one's own moral standards on a personal or organization level can also constitute a moral injury. The preservation of pre-trauma self or ego-stance mitigates overwhelming feelings of loss. Who the person was before the trauma can be expressed simultaneously with the after-trauma self, and through the mask the individual can acknowledge those aspects that are still available.

Second, the mediation between the existing ego stance and the trauma effects relates to the capacity of the individual to find representation of the traumatic event. Representation through art helps that which seeks to become integrated into the self-image. It gives a face to this capacity and ability. The mask both contains the effects of trauma and establishes a relatedness or mediation to the traumatic experience. The mask forms a bridge, both physically and symbolically, between conflicting internal elements that are the result of trauma and who the person once was before the trauma.

The third quality masks provide is the ability to mediate between the individual's experience and the collective. The mask permits distancing, buffering, and objectification. It again forms a bridge, this time between the traumatized self and the collective self. The collective self refers to the interpersonal relationships with loved ones as well as society. It incorporates the traumatic experience into social fabric and reality in order for a new persona to emerge that has integrated the wounds of trauma while also rebuilding and healing oneself. In my work with trauma survivors, the reintegration process is slow, not visible to the eye without the tick-marks of a ruler measuring growth. The artwork acts like a ruler, creating visible pieces to observe growth and integration. In physical scars, flesh heals stronger than the skin that was there before the injury. The metaphor of healing from injury providing depth and beauty is similar to the Japanese practice of Kintsukuroi, where an artist uses a gold lacquer to repair the broken pieces of a ceramic and restore its functionality, and thus, the pottery is made even more beautiful because of its wounds and its history.

Heather: *Initiation by Fire*

Heather, a visual artist and community advocate, was inspired and challenged by her work with individuals who had suffered serious burns due to the intensity of the work and the parallel circumstances of her own life's challenges. The burn survivors with whom she worked discussed their visual disfigurement, including facial cranial deformities and the stories of "the invisibly burned" also known as survivors of "the hidden burn." The clients who identified as invisibly burned had burns not on their faces but on parts of their bodies they could cover with clothing, like backs, legs, and arms.

"It was the story of an invisibly burned woman that really struck an emotional cord for me," said Heather.

One young woman spoke of feeling suicidal but refused to attempt it due to her intense sense of shame. Her hesitancy was brought on by the idea that she would be found by strangers who would judge her body, uncovering her "horrible secret" of the burns. Although her burns were not immediately visible, the pain and fear created life-altering consequences and reactions. She avoided swimming and dating as well as other situations in which she might be "found out." Upon hearing the desperation of this woman's story, Heather was confronted with her own story and an intense emotional response, so she turned to art to "work things out" and make her reactions "intelligible."

Heather entered life as an infant under circumstances that were less than ideal. Born with facial deformities caused by a bilateral cleft lip and palate, she endured seven surgeries before the age of 3 years. Two of the surgeries induced cardiac arrest. At the age of 12, she endured a skin graph under local anesthesia due to her high risk of cardiac arrest. Uninformed and unprepared that she would be awake during the procedure, she was terrified; the numerous Novocain™ shots were excruciating, adding to the intolerability of the situation. During the procedure, a square of skin was removed from her lower lip in order to repair her upper one. Although she recalled not being in pain after the Novocain shots, she experienced the pressure, pulling, and tugging of her lips and their eventual sewing shut for healing. Her tears on the operating table were met with the doctor's response, "Big girls don't cry."

This remark further silenced her need to express her fear, pain, and suffering in one of the few ways possible; her voice was not accessible through the use of her mouth, which was sewn shut. Her developing sense of self was further objectified as she became an example of successful advances in medicine. Heather was paraded into the medical lecture hall, where scores of male doctors viewed large projected images detailing her surgery, displaying in detail the cuts, stitches, and her eyes staring up, open and wild. Having to endure the surgery and then witness it again while doctors probed their fingers into her 12-year-old mouth for closer inspection left her feeling violated and traumatized.

As a teenager and as a young adult, questions about body image and beauty were many. Struggling with her *face value* and attempting to reconcile this with her body, she recalled a time in college when she was selling clothes in a department store in downtown Boston and a man walked up behind her and called, "Nice ass!" When he caught up with her and made eye contact, his face fell into disgust and anger, and he blurted out, "What a waste," implying the scars and disfigurement on her face made her damaged and unworthy.

These and many other of her memories were stirred up as she worked with the victims of burns. She turned her journey of pain, misunderstanding, and struggle into one of beauty with the aid of her art and, specifically, her encounter with mask making.

One of her first masks was created after turning 30, 18 years after her last surgery. Due to medical advances, she now had the option for a bone graph, connecting the bone between the two sides of her mouth. Without a bone connection, her expensive dental bridges were prone to breaking as the two sides of her mouth moved independently when eating. This procedure not only would unite the two sides of her mouth but also alter her appearance by changing the underlying structure of her mouth and nose. During the night after the bone graph surgery she encountered heavy and at times uncontrollable, frightening bleeding. The bloodied gauze and other medical waste that was used to help control the bleeding was later incorporated into the first mask she made. She buried the mask in a ritualistic way and continued to make masks out of other materials, repeating the work that explored issues of identity, power, self-worth, and transformation.

She began working on *Initiation by Fire,* shown in Figure 7.5, some months after returning to work. *Initiation by Fire* was created using wire mesh and plaster of Paris and painted with fiery reds fading into ember blues and greys and highlighted with gold. Crumpled rags like those of the bloody gauze were used, and found objects like seeds, glass, and earth were embedded into the plaster.

"The hidden objects in the masks are like secrets, sometimes alive secrets, like seeds, buried there waiting for the right time to germinate—like ideas and experiences, they need the right time to come forth," said Heather about her mask work.

Cutting pieces apart and then stitching pieces back together played an important theme in her work, much like her early childhood experiences of being cut apart and put back together. The layers of plaster gauze mimicked the reparative aspects of the skin and bone graphs. Over the mouth is a butterfly, a symbol of psyche, physical metamorphoses, and transmutations of the soul that navigates by using the sun (Ronnberg & Martin, 2010). The butterfly with its many lifetime skins has sewn the mouth shut in what may be a reflection of a stage where the gossamer cocoon hides the internal growth, like Heather's surgically sewn lips once concealed their healing. The butterfly is perhaps one of the most poetic images of psyche's self-renewal, conveying fragility and transience even in the face of traumatic events (Ronnberg & Martin, 2010). Found in numerous legends and lore, butterflies may represent the heroic sacrifice. The opening in the mask one may consider the mouth displaced in the throat. The fiery hands/antlers/wings rise up out of the head, framing a golden sun-like object while the cool cubist shapes ring the lower part of the mask, creating a dichotomy in colors and shapes. Much like the phoenix, rising from the flames, Heather's mask, initially inspired by the

Figure 7.5 Using wire mesh, Plaster of Paris, and crumpled rags, like those of the bloody gauze, *Initiation by Fire* was inspired by Heather's work with individuals who had suffered serious burns and disfigurement and her own facial cranial surgeries.

stories of the clients who experienced burns, is as much about her own journey as theirs. She described how inspired she felt, "It's like they grow from the cauldron of fire and transform their experience with disfigurement into triumph."

Heather's mask, in keeping with many shamanic traditions, has both anthropomorphic (human) and theriomorphic (animal) features, which buffer against hostile individuals, beliefs, and cultural values. Her mask, like others made in the context of art psychotherapy, assists in reparative and integrative processes. Through the incorporation of found objects and personal imagery, there is communion with nature and spiritual realms. And like masks that define, mediate, and provide boundaries for personal, communal, archetypal, and spiritual purposes, they offer a means for expression of those things that may feel incompatible or offensive. They create cohesion of those aspects of self that may have been split off.

CHAPTER 8

SPATIAL RELATIONSHIPS
Three-Dimensional Work

Three-dimensional artwork spans from amulet to monument and, despite the range in scale, these pieces have a similar essence: those of a material spirit. The amulet is a small portable charm worn as protection against evil or insurance of fertility. The monument is also a structure permeated with spirit. Some of the earliest monuments were phallic shaped: columns, pillars, or obelisks, jutting toward the sky, forming an axis linking heaven and earth. Originally, towers had the singular aim of the sculpture, but over time it became customary to make openings and hollow chambers within and deposit images of the divine, like a shell enclosing a seed (Read, 1977), creating a container for those things essential and precious. Aspects of the monument are like the sarcophagus, "a flesh-consuming" stone deriving its name from *arx*, meaning "flesh," and *phagein*, meaning "to eat." Tombs, natural caves, grave mounds, pyramids, and stupas, hemispherical structures containing Buddhist relics, often recorded the events of the deceased life through murals or relief carvings on their interiors. Doorways serve as passageways, a transition into the interior, while pediments, supported by pillars, turn our gaze upward upon entering. With each development, or utilization of a form, each element began to take on a significance well beyond the mundane. As Read (1977) described,

> As the art develops, in history or in sensuous experience of the individual, we may begin to associate with each shape an idea; we inhabit the shape with our spirit; and finally, if we are artists, we try to realize ideas as specific shapes, to create symbols for our indeterminate feelings—to become conscious, in the forms of art, of the dimensions of reality [p. 4–5].

Through time, the temple and the tomb were merged, and the spatial relationships transformed in multiple ways—enlarging spaces to enter, like Gothic cathedrals, or scaling the divine into carried devotionals or transportable sacred spaces like alters and devotionals, as discussed in greater length in Chapter 9.

As Read (1977) pointed out in *The Art of Sculpture*, more than nine-tenths of the sculptures found in museums are devoted to the human form. There is a convention between the human form and sculpture. Unlike landscape or still life, which are the typical subjects of painting, the third dimension requires a difference in our mental approach. To sculpt a form, a three-dimensional memory is necessary, one which visual perception alone does not provide. To clearly see a form in its entirety, memory coupled with sensation and imagination is necessary.

These abilities, gradually acquired through a phylogenetic, developmental history, both at the personal and collective level, are laden with psychological and cultural attributes. The image we possess of ourselves is not one that is inherited at birth, but instead is constructed through growing awareness of our internal and external worlds. Immediate sensations, both seen and felt, contribute to this image, as do the observation of others, cultural ideals, and external feedback. By conceiving an *image* of our body, we can place an *idea* of ourselves in the external world. This image is considered our body image. But our "vision is *colored*, as we say. It is distorted by memories, associations, and above all desires, and to a considerable extent we see what we want to see" (Read, 1977, p. 31). We look at others and see ourselves, often as a projection of our desires.

In the Greek myth of Echo, a verbose nymph who was cursed by Hera to repeat only the last words of others, and Narcissus, a handsome youth with whom Echo fell in love while he was ensnaring a deer in the forest, the two manifested aspects of a colored reality in which desire had grave effects. Narcissus called out to inquire who was in the woods with him and was met by Echo's mimicking response. Narcissus cruelly rejected her for she lacked the ability to express the substance of her true self. Thus she retreated to a cave where she pined and withered away, leaving only her echoing voice for others to hear. As counterpoint justice, Nemesis, upon witnessing Narcissus's cruelty, cursed him to fall in love with his own reflection. While attempting to embrace the noncorporeality of his reflection, he succumbed to the spring waters, leaving in his place the pale flower, narcissus. Both were lost because Echo, lacking a voice, was hindered. She lost her ability to be embodied and speak about who she was, and Narcissus was unable to be desirous of anything other than himself. Echo and Narcissus carried the potentiality that all possess—to be destroyed by desire, unable to speak or see the reflected gaze of another while compulsively pursuing the projected desire.

The inversion of this negative outcome of desire is the creation story of the artist Pygmalion, who fell in love with one of his sculptures and asked the goddess Aphrodite to give her life. His wish was granted, and upon marrying her, he named her Galatea. In some legends, Galatea was Aphrodite, goddess of love and procreation. Pygmalion is an excellent example of how artwork like the amulet and monument become imbued with the love or spirit of the artist. These stories have captured the imagination for centuries, and as can been seen in modern adaptations such as *My Fair Lady* and *Pinocchio*, which portray giving physical form to a mental projection of one's desire and self. Utilizing three-dimensional work in therapy possesses the same enlivening processes.

Unlike painting, the tactile values of sculpture are typically not an illusion. "Sculpture is an art of *palpation*—an art that gives satisfaction in the touching and handling of objects" (Read, 1977, p. 49). We engage our physical sensations in order to perceive the nuances of form, shape, and texture. With sculpture, our touch can transfer the heat of our hands into the object itself or we can feel the warmth of the radiated heat of the sun. The sculptor passes over the creation numerous times and creates a familiarity to the form by shaping it by hand. Sculpture is dependent on the sun for its light, unlike paintings or drawings, which supply their own light sources in the images. Light and shade are inexorable to sculpture, and the sculptor is aided by nature to illuminate the relief.

The word *sculpture* comes from the Latin verb *sculpere* and implies the idea of carving with sharp tools. The word *plastic*, when speaking about sculpture, relates to the malleability of materials by hand that can be assisted with tools to create objects, representations, or reliefs. The term *sculpture* will apply to both methods in this text. Because marble, metal, and wood are often prohibitive art materials in therapy settings due to their dependence on sharp tools to wield a form, I will discuss only those sculptural materials that may be more typically available and practical in art therapy settings, such as malleable or easily worked materials like clay and found objects. A discussion of shadow boxes and reliefs, also sculptural in nature, will be reserved for the following chapter.

There are a plethora of choices for malleable sculptural materials: air-dry clay; wax; plasticine, an oil-based modeling clay that does not harden but can crack and seep oil onto the surface it is placed on; oven-baked polymer clays such Sculptey™ and Fimo™; and the soft, marshmallow-like Crayola® Model Magic®. As with the two-dimensional materials described in Chapter 2, tridimensional materials also present with inherent qualities that hold the potentiality of the expressive idea. Each material has its own plastic and elastic properties, some being more resistive or fluid than others. Some can be varied in their resistive properties, depending on the addition of water or oil. For example, soft air-dry clay, which can resemble the consistency of mud when water is added, will yield soft forms and create gooey, slick piles, and materials can be added or subtracted as needed. In these cases, such expressive variability also influences the dynamic occurring between the artist and the medium itself. With the addition of water, the clay may clump onto hands and create stimulating tactile responses. As the clay dries, the residue on the hands may feel powdery and dry and give a sensation of cracking. For some, this may create a sensation of being irritated, much like plaster of Paris mask making does when applied directly to the face. Alertness to these qualities and what they may evoke in patients is essential. In addition to the tactile stimulation of the materials, such variations in resistance affect the degree of control of the media. With more fluid clays, forms may not be as pronounced as is the case when the clay is drier. One may end up with the materials leading to a sensuous journey or a regressed and undifferentiated mess depending on the application and the context of the work. Clay that is too dry, however, becomes brittle. The addition of ornamentation in this case will not adhere sufficiently. One begins to see that a balance may be struck that is both literal and potentially symbolic. As shown in Figure 8.1, the clay sculpture of a body did

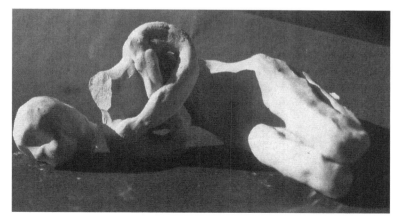

Figure 8.1 This fortuitous accident, occurred when the head of the clay sculpture did not properly adhere, thus resulting in a profitable discussion of "not feeling glued well enough together" for her impending discharge. © 2016 Michelle L. Dean.

not adhere properly when it dried because the clay was too dry, and a proper slip was not prepared to stick the two pieces together. With air-dry clay, when adhering two pieces together, a slip is made, which is a thin and watery mixture of clay, and the two sides of the pieces that are to stick together are scored. This creates enough surface roughness, coupled with the gluing effects of the slip, to withstand the shrinking that the air-dry clay will naturally go though. Even when there was a malfunction, shown in Figure 8.1, all was not lost. I like to refer to these experiences as fortuitous mistakes. While this may not be applicable in all cases, the woman who created the self-representation, upon discovering her broken piece, reflected on how she felt that she was not "glued together well enough" for her impending discharge. This piece led to discussions about how she felt she had the tendency to separate her thoughts (head) from her feelings (body). This separation was reflected in her ability to express and meet her physical needs while negotiating her tangle of thoughts that exacerbated her eating disorder. Although it was not originally intended, the mishap served as a means for further reflection in the therapeutic dialog. It is through repeated experiences that mastery and familiarity will arise, as well as preference. Again, like the two-dimensional materials, none are inherently good or bad, but rather it is important to match the potentiality of the materials to the person and their needs for expression as well as to observe the interaction between the individual and the expressive medium and understand such interactions are themselves expressive aspects of the therapeutic encounter.

Fantasy and Animals

The next most common form depicted in sculpture after the human form is that of animals. Animals in art have long been a symbol of human psyche and culture, permeating many of our legends and lore, from fairy tales to cinema to specific animal phobias to their adoption as our pets. They receive our projections and become our companions, protectors, and mystic guides. They share their ability to be receptive and mirror emotional response. Animals are often social and reflect values of family and community and connect us to our origins in nature. They are easy to identify with, and their characteristics hold special charms for us. Scholars have surmised that the sculpting of animals, particularly during the ice age, may have been about survival because the sculptures of animals from that time period were "most likely efforts at magic: making a picture of a mammoth or a bear would 'create' it in actually, just as hitting the picture with the spear would 'kill' the animal even before the hunt began" (Elder, 1996, p. 4). These practices are not unlike voodoo dolls, where magical spells are cast onto dolls that represent another person and are acted upon in a wish fulfillment manner, and the mental imaging done by elite athletes before a big event to *prepare* for physical activity by *seeing* it first. Beyond that, each animal possesses a set of unique qualities that renders it suitable as a projective device, carrying forward the expression of personal, but potentially less well acknowledged, attributes. A common use of animal sculptures is that of creating one's own favorite animal or an animal representing oneself, not unlike the way that such animal spirit images became associated with the individual in some Native American cultures, as seen in carved stone fetishes. Such processes provide a means for the individual to discuss their varying attributes, strengths, and vulnerabilities. Such an expressive process is suitable for both group and individual work or may arise spontaneously as described later in this chapter in the case of Cynthia.

Grounding Stones

The creation of grounding stones, a talisman object carried with one to protect or remind the bearer of the present and fortify one's connection to the earth, can be helpful when used as a transitional object. For example, grounding stones can literally be stones, preferably round and smooth, possibly polished or painted. The smoothness feels good in the hand and it should be small enough to fit in one's pocket unobtrusively. Touch, as much or more than sight, is an important factor in determining the correct choice for a grounding stone. When used at a treatment facility in a group as a part of a graduation ritual, each person graduating chooses a stone that is then passed around the group circle, with each person sharing their fondest memory of the departing (discharging) person and their blessings or wishes for them for the future. When the stone is returned to the graduating person, it is not only warm from the grasp of the group members but also imbued with the warm associations. Just as important, it remains a physical and enduring reminder of the connectivity to the group whose existence exceeds the limits of the group in terms of time. More individualized grounding stones can be made with clay or ceramic pieces. These too may be utilized in a similar fashion but with the added dimension that, due to the sculpted nature, the form may possess more originality and uniqueness, reflecting the unique personality of the creator.

Such small, portable sculptures have a long history. Sculpted grounding stones are reminiscent of the stone Venus figurines, such as the limestone Venus of Willendorf, estimated to have been created between 28,000 and 25,000 BCE. Although the actual purpose of such figurines may never fully be known, researchers speculate that they have a similar talisman purpose, perhaps used as a guardian for childbirth or safe passage or, because of their common cone-like legs, used as an object that is literally placed into the ground and used for prayer or other spiritual and religious practices.

Although carving stone is prohibitive in most psychotherapeutic settings, and creating sculpted deities may not have the same cultural appeal today for many, motifs favorable for sculpting into grounding stones includes animal forms. Most people can identify animals that they have an affinity for, like guide or spirit animals, or totems, as seen in many shamanic traditions. The roots of shamanism go back to the oldest forms of social organization, as seen in many hunting cultures, and have an animistic framework of reality. Shamanism is most commonly found among the hunting tribes of Siberia, the Native North American people of the Old and New Worlds, and the Lapps of Northern Europe (Schulz-Weidner, 1967).

When creating sculptural works in therapy, it is often easier to sculpt an animal than a person, especially if creative license is given to the sculptural product by saying to sculpt a fantasy animal. If needed, further encouragement or suggestion can be given to sculpt an animal that the individual identifies with or admires certain characteristics of, presenting a singular animal or an animal that is a composite of all of their favorite attributes. Allowing fantasy elements or a combination of animal attributes gives more choice in the representation of characteristics and also offers the freedom to not feel constrained by aspects of creating a realistic looking animal.

Divorce, Death, and the Family Dynamics of Dragons

Cynthia was a shy and quiet young girl who was brought to me by her mother seeking support for her in the face of a number of challenges. Her parents' marriage was dissolving and the fabric of her home life was crumbling. In addition to this, Cynthia had previously been diagnosed with an expressive disorder that affected her learning at school and impeded her ability to express herself verbally, something that she was also, by disposition, reluctant to do anyway. In addition to her own difficulties with the situation with her parents' divorce, she also needed to contend with the adjustment difficulties of an older sister who was given to bouts of frustration and rage.

Cynthia entered treatment with me at the age of 9 and worked with me for several years with a varying degree of consistency. She would develop periods of stability, drift away from treatment, but then return when things became more difficult. Early in our work together, Cynthia made the piece shown in Figure 8.2,

Figure 8.2 Birds on Branches reflects the fragility of the home environment and impending changes brought on by death, divorce, and much discord. © 2016 Michelle L. Dean.

Birds on Branches. Using a base of Model Magic® clay, twigs, and clay birds she created a shelter in which her blue birds could rest. On the twiggy fortress, she dripped white glue onto the twigs and base, creating what appeared to be a fresh covering of snow. The snow appeared to be blanketing the still life, as if to be "insulating the senses from the distractions of the outer world" (Ronnberg & Martin, 2010, p. 78), until the white glue dried, transforming it into a hardened shell of suspended clear liquid.

This glistening, washed-out look of rain froze the branches and birds in time. I thought of the distance between the parents, the loss of the sanctuary of home, and she and her sister left to emotionally fend for themselves. She needed refuge. Without a nest, or parents to watch over them, the diminutive birds were caught in a brittle coldness, a sudden chill in her emotional weather. They braced themselves for what's coming, the departure of warmth and security, the fragility of her home situation, along with the growing uncertainty in the face of parental divorce and discord.

Cynthia spontaneously developed and utilized the theme of "animal friends" repeatedly for approximately two years, creating a series of creatures, typically dragons, made from Model Magic® clay, her preferred media. Figure 8.3 represents one such set of creations in this series. These creatures dealt with nuances of character, internal experiences, and relationships. Her animal friends seemed to help her deal with changing relationships within her family and provided a pathway for the expression of her thoughts and feelings surrounding frequent changes, upheavals, and conflicts.

Cynthia's creatures became a constant companion, a motif that she returned to during our sessions. Each creature or set of creatures expressed its own set of

Figure 8.3 Engaging in a series of creatures over time, helped Cynthia deal with the nuances of character, internal experiences, and relationships. Her animal friends seemed to help her deal with changing relationships within her family and provided a pathway for the expression of her thoughts and feelings around such upheavals. © 2016 Michelle L. Dean.

special attributes, abilities, and adaptations as if holding and expressing qualitative aspects of herself as these emerged through her unfolding life experiences. After creating each figure, or sets of creatures, she would tell a story about how it came to be in the world, a mini-creation myth of its genesis, what it was doing in the world now, and what may come next in its unfolding of its life's journey. As such, each figure marked the emergence into life of an internal set of impulses and qualities generated by the unfolding of her own life's narrative.

During this period, while she was creating friend and family groups of dragons, her grandmother moved in with Cynthia and her family. This move was precipitated by the grandmother developing terminal cancer. Although Cynthia appreciated having another loving adult in the house, as her grandmother's illness progressed, the cognitive and physical decline became difficult for her and her other family members to endure. Her mother's attention was increasingly needed by the grandmother as her health deteriorated. The progressive illness and the stress took an emotional toll on everyone in the family. Cynthia's father had relocated to the other side of the country and began a new life with a girlfriend and her son, making visits with Cynthia and her sibling infrequent and stressful. The parents' divorce was contentious with many court proceedings and arguments about financial issues, which were made worse by the loss of jobs for both of the parents at different times. The father exerted his need for power and control by refusing to pay child support and for medical treatment, and he had difficulty abiding by the terms of their custody agreements. These breaches in the custody agreement resulted in more heated court hearings, the emotional results spilling over to the children. As her father's visits became less frequent and phone calls became few, Cynthia became more despondent and unable to speak about her visible pain.

Our work with dragons continued, and their attributes and characteristics morphed as the conditions in the home and relationships with family members changed. Cynthia's grandmother subsequently died, leaving a void and much emotional upheaval followed shortly by the death of their family pet dog that Cynthia had known since infancy. In the face of all of these changes, full of sadness, anxiety, and uncertainty and without adequate modes of expression to mediate against profound loss and sadness, she became increasingly depressed. Through her art and the creation of her dragons, she created and re-created multiple family groups, narratives about them that represented both her actual and wished for home lives. Each creature was meticulously crafted and had its own special powers and became her "friend."

The motif of the dragon was a comfortable repetition of a familiar schema. It provided constancy, a constancy drawing forth from her inner world when her outer world had none. The familiarity of the dragon, which was spontaneously created without direct suggestion from me, became an inner language through which variations could be enacted and reworked until a kind of mastery was sensed. Each dragon was carefully transported home and displayed on a shelf, joining the other members of her dragon family. She was drawing forth elements of her inner world, our sessions birthing places for that process, so that she could then bring those contents back to the outer world of her family life. Like the fierce nature of dragons, guarding over their treasures, Cynthia's dragons were a means of protecting and fortifying her precious, developing inner world.

As may be observed, the dragon motif that I have alluded to in a number of ways, like many other archetypal images, has many facets and many functions. The ones created by Cynthia present their own unique usage and performed their own role within the highly complex nature of her individual psyche and in the context of her individual situation. No single assumption may be made regarding such usage but a clear function may be discerned when one understands the role of the image in terms of its relationship to the life of a particular patient.

Art Psychotherapy Groups

Groups are important to our survival and well-being. Isolation and aloneness not only can bring on symptoms of emotional anguish but also are often symptoms of mental and physical despair. Understandably, group psychotherapy is a natural evolution to combat isolation and examine patterns of relatedness. Group psychotherapy has been considered a cost-effective alternative to individual psychotherapy in many settings and populations since its inception in the 1940s (Burlingame, Fuhriman, & Mosier, 2003; Yalom, 1985). Group art therapy has been used with individuals as a means of addressing anxiety (Chambala, 2008), depression (Chandraiah, Anand, & Avent, 2012; Ponteri, 2001), eating disorders (Rehavia-Hanauer, 2003), grief (Schut, de Keijser, van den Bout, & Stroebe, 1996), low-self-esteem (Green, Wehling, & Talsky, 1987), physical and sexual trauma, and sexual abuse (Brooke, 1995; Pifalo, 2002). Utilizing art within the group therapy context is a natural progression. Yalom (1983) stressed the importance of form and structure in the group psychotherapy process in order to best meet the needs of patients.

This form and structure can be seen in an art psychotherapy groups through the use of clay figures and group work. Such form and structure can be observed in art psychotherapy groups as being mediated through the use of diverse media, including that of clay figures. Joining a group often stimulates anxiety, as the possibility of inclusion also invites the fear of exclusion. Group members may be observed feeling out the reactions of other group members, assessing the receptiveness of other members to them, and trying to find a meaningful place within the group structure, so as to find a place of belonging and understanding. As a means of demonstrating the beneficial aspects of group work and group dynamics, I will encourage members to create a figure that they feel represents them. Often, this figure is an animal or fantasy animal. Working with the clay individually allows for control of the media and personal representation, like a talisman. Once completed, the figures are placed on a piece of paper in the center of the table on which a large circle or oval has been drawn. The circle creates a type of interior and exterior, or reflection of the containment of the group. As can be seen in the Figure 8.4, a teaching exercise for pre-art therapy students, I utilize this intervention for a hands-on learning experience about the group dynamics present within the classroom. The exercise, like an intervention in therapy, can foster many of the therapeutic factors as described by Yalom (1985) in his seminal text, *The Theory and Practice of Group Psychotherapy*. These factors are applicable and often visible when art media is incorporated. Yalom outlines eleven therapeutic factors in group psychotherapy. Like in group psychotherapy, groups that incorporate art into their practice share many of these underlying therapeutic factors and they, along with personal factors, may be made visible through the art and its process. Not all factors may be noticeable to the same degree in each group, just as it is so in group psychotherapy. However, their presence is often distinguishable when it occurs.

Figure 8.4 Art therapy students create animal representations of themselves and are then asked to describe their figures and contemplate where they are in relation to the circle and each other. © 2016 Michelle L. Dean.

Yalom described the corrective recapitulation of the primary family group as one of the therapeutic factors of group process. Its premise is that we bring patterns of learned behaviors and dynamics from our families to new experiences and groups. These roles may be conscious or unconscious. The idea of the psychotherapy process is to bring greater awareness of our roles enabling change when needed or helpful. When teaching group dynamics to art therapy students, the use of clay figures is helpful in order to identify relational patterns that may be evident not only in class but also in their work with other groups. As seen in Figure 8.4, students create an animal representation of themselves and place it on a piece of paper that has a circle or ellipse drawn on it. They are then asked to describe their figures and contemplate where they are in relation to the circle and to each other. The circle often will take on meaning for group members of either being in or out of the group. Hesitant or ambivalent group members may place themselves on the edge or directly on the line of the circle. After each group member has described their creation as well as their placement on the page, they are asked if they are pleased with where they are in the group representation. If not, they are given the opportunity to move their figures to another place on the page that feels more satisfying. Often times through our discussions, familiar roles emerge. One such role is that of the family mediator. The family mediator may typically find himself in the middle of relationship or ferrying information between different individuals in the family group. Because this role may have been comfortable and familiar in settling family conflict or dissipating discord in a family it may also be the role one naturally takes in a new group. If this role is no longer comfortable or is one that does not fit the current situation, through the sculpture they are able to change this role by becoming aware of it and through physically placing their creation in a different place on the page. This awareness opens up greater dialog and can be utilized in facilitating changes. These changes permeate like concentric circles after a stone has been dropped into a pond, affecting our inner world, which can be manifested outwardly.

CHAPTER 9

SHADOWS IN THE BOX
Dioramas and Boxes

In this penultimate chapter, I will discuss working with grief and loss through art and image, a rich and intense field. Through the exploration of the use of dioramas and boxes, I will discuss special considerations for working issues of loss through the metaphorical use of shadow as it relates to this art medium and its historical manifestations and functions. Creating and re-creating containers, home-like environments, enables the retelling of the narrative while also shifting memory and perceptions. Working with boxes in therapy can lend itself instrumentally to both the metaphorical and literal uses of containment and protection when working with this non-linear and multi-faceted form. A box, like a mask, creates a three-dimensional space that provides an interior space and an exterior space. These spaces hold significance when working with raw affect, such as feelings associated with loss, rejection, and disconnection. Mixed media can be utilized with boxes, such as paint, collage, the inclusion of found objects, and assemblage. Simple forms can create complex expressions and monumental works when grouped together. For example, in the work of Louise Nevelson, her assemblage art is often contained within a box and unified by a single color—black, white, or gold—influenced by her personal symbolism. Her "sculpted wood assemblages transcended space and transformed the viewer's perception of art" (The Louise Nevelson Foundation, 2015). Her puzzle-like work was often constructed of everyday objects, held within one or more boxes, and offer a profound study in light, form, and composition, as shown in Figure 9.1. Individual pieces were intimate but, when assembled with others, became monumental. Historically, her work is significant because during the 1960s and 1970s as the feminist movement was evolving, her work broke the "taboo that only men's artwork could be large-scale. Her works initiated an era in which women's life history became suitable subject matter for monumental artistic representation," as she explored industrial materials like wood, plexiglass, aluminum, and steel (The Art Story Foundation, 2015). In her work created with wood, the legs of tables and chairs, T-squares, and necks of canes are transformed into cylinders, cuboids, cones, and volumetric forms coupled with their shadows; these become the language of her art. Friedman (1973) stated, "Only a few basic forms unify the art of all periods, the rest are variations" (p. 11). The cube is one of the unifying fundamental forms.

Nevelson's family emigrated from Russia in the early 20th century, and they struggled with depression and perhaps cultural clashes as part of the Jewish minority in Maine and due to their loss of cultural roots. Her father worked as a wood-cutter before opening a junkyard, and thus, the materials that were commonplace

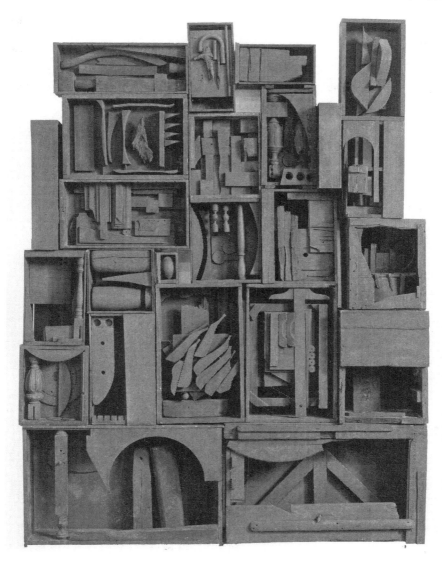

Figure 9.1 Louise Nevelson (1899–1988). *Black Wall.* 1959. Painted wood, 2642 × 2165 × 648 mm. Presented by the Friends of the Tate Gallery 1962. Location: Tate Gallery, London, Great Britain. Photo Credit: Tate, London/Art Resource, NY. Art Credit: © 2014 Estate of Louise Nevelson/Artists Rights Society (ARS), New York.

throughout her childhood became prominent in her artwork as an adult (The Art Story Foundation, 2015). Although a psychobiography of Nevelson is beyond the scope of this text, I can describe that she builds on past experiences in order to create anew. According to Wilson (2013), a Nevelson historian and art therapist, Nevelson believed that the goal of everyone's life is to become a fully individual self, and she strived for this ideal in her inexorably linked personal and creative life. She struggled to find her signature art style for nearly 50 years, returning to the materials familiar to her in childhood and associated with her father.

The boxes in which Nevelson created are not unlike the boxes of the therapeutic intervention of sand tray therapy. Developed by Swiss Jungian analyst Dora Kalss, the sand tray experience provides adults and children a way to construct and portray their psyche, or self. Using miniature figurines placed in a tray filled with sand, it works on the premise that the psyche possesses a natural tendency to heal itself, given the proper conditions. The tray is considered the *vas Hermetis*, a special container or vessel in which alchemical properties were combined, a uterus of spiritual renewal or rebirth (Farrell-Kirk, 2001; CW 13:97). This is like the hermetically sealed vessel in which our psyche and inner world dwell, as described in Chapter 1 and illustrated in Figure 1.16. Here, the heating up and cooling down processes are alive and active in the creative inner psychic life. The figurines and terrain created in the sand represent and express the inner world of the individual and provide opportunities for creative play, setting the tray, or stage, for its unfolding and change. Play that takes place in respectful silence activates the internal archetypal dimension to manifest in the tray. It is believed that silence during the therapy session, much like the work of active imagination, is necessary in order to minimize intrusion or distraction of the sand tray artist's inner dimension and expression. As Friedman (2015) described,

> Since sand play is one of the few therapeutic techniques in which language skills are unnecessary for understanding the expressions of the psyche, it has truly become a cross-cultural method that is now practiced therapeutically worldwide. . . . Sand play now offers us a unique opportunity to view universal, archetypal patterns as well as observe the unfolding development of the individual psyche [n.p.].

The unfolding symbolic work is similar in sand tray and art making with boxes and dioramas. Each provides a container, or vas, in which one must go down into the depths of their psyche and draw forth its potent material, and it can be depicted through arrangements of found or assembled objects or figurines. Jung spoke of the vessel as a *krater*, "a wonderworking vessel," a place where immersion and transformation into a spiritual being take place (CW 13:93) providing experiences to change and reconfigure and demonstrating resiliency in the face of loss and struggle.

Grief and Loss

Loss challenges individuals' ability to carry on the daily functions of life as well as their beliefs and can gnaw at their core sense of self. Grief is a normal reaction to loss, and it often requires years to fully integrate it and resume daily function. Grief and mourning, especially when protracted and debilitating, threatens to transform from melancholy into deep depression and other forms of mental illness, such as substance abuse, phobias, hoarding, or anxiety.

When speaking about loss, it is important to keep in mind that there are multiple reactions to loss and more than one kind of loss, some of which are often overlooked. Tangible losses include times when something, someone, or some ability is lost, unavailable, or diminished from its original capacity. Such losses are recognized in the death of a loved one or pet, or at the end of a marriage.

But sometimes losses are more subtle, like a loss of connection or a relationship rupture, such as might occur in a falling out or disagreement between family members or friends; illness and the loss of health; and diminished ability in physical or cognitive function—these losses are known as ambiguous loss (Boss, 1999). Moving, even for promising reasons, can result in grief over what is lost, such as moving from a house, city, region, or culture. We can also experience loss due to a transition, such as from being an only child to being one of many, or conversely, becoming an only child after the loss of a sibling, which can occur due to divorce or remarriage of parents, and which can lead to a reconfiguration of living arrangements when stepfamilies or intergenerational family reconfigure. Loss can be experienced when adult children move into the role of caretaker as parents or siblings age or become disabled. Many of these types of loss are more easily recognized by family and friends as there exist few community or religious rituals to help buffer the isolation and pain accompanying this type of loss.

Another type of loss that is often unacknowledged and lacks community rituals of support but is nonetheless significant includes perceived loss. Perceived losses are feelings of unmet need or want, or the denial of something deserved. Such losses leave a feeling of ambiguous loss and typically have no culturally sanctioned or group experience to assist in the mourning process. These losses are often only individually experienced, although they may be shared among family members living in the same circumstances. But they are rarely communicated to one another. Although more than one person may share the experience, there is no wake, no sitting Shiva, funeral, or religious service, and no community outpouring of support. Individuals who experience such ambiguous losses often have difficulty recognizing, honoring, and grieving. They may share some of the same responses as being traumatized or neglected but manifest more insidiously. Specific examples include emotional or physical responses, which were not present or present enough, including inadequate attention, affection, compassion, understanding, and empathy. Many of these types of losses lead to emotional and physical responses akin to traumatic response.

Both of these categories of loss—tangible and ambiguous—can be supported through the arts. But before speaking about art's role in grief due to loss, a context for understanding the prevalence of loss and its traumatic effects may be helpful.

To suffer or witness trauma or abuse can create loss, such as disintegration of self, dissolving of trust, and melting way of self-concept and identity. Among the many types of traumas and abuses that are seen in clinical practice are sexual and physical traumas. Tjaden and Thoennes (2000) reported that as many as 25% of women and 7.6% of men have been raped or physically assaulted by a current or former spouse, cohabiting partner, dating partner, or acquaintance at some time in their lifetime and that as many as 1.3 million women and 835,000 men are physically assaulted by an intimate partner each year in the United States. These traumas are assaults not only on the physical body but also on the core of the individual. In their wake, the boundaries of body, mind, and soul become shattered. Physical trauma through abuse, such as domestic situations or violent crimes, is experienced by 15% of university students. Psychological trauma can include experiencing being rejected, degraded, or devalued as a person. It can also include being terrorized, isolated, corrupted, exploited, or denied essential stimulation, emotional responsiveness, or availability by an unreliable caregiver (Bloom, 2000). Traumatic experiences can also occur due to emotional neglect such as typically accompanies parental alcoholism and drug addiction. It is estimated that 28 million children in the United States have one or more parents who are alcoholics. Other forms of trauma include witnessing abuse, experiencing poverty, and homelessness.

Some losses and traumas tend to be overlooked or minimized. For example, surgeries in early childhood often include prolonged separations from family members and require invasive, painful procedures, but the resulting trauma may not be addressed. So too are injuries from auto accidents and house fires, loss of a loved one or pet, breakups from significant others, multiple parental divorces, and stepparents entering and exiting children's lives. Humiliating or deeply disturbing experiences are traumas that can result in losses of identity, self-confidence, and agency, but may not be readily obvious. So is bullying, which can be associated with silencing shame.

The emotional and physical effects of trauma include but are not limited to shock, denial, and disbelief of the situation and its severity. These feelings are not exclusive to the time of the traumatic event but can linger for years. Being in denial about the severity of a molestation or betrayal is not uncommon even decades after the event. Often one comes to believe "it wasn't *that* bad," blames oneself, or questions the actual existence of the event because there are typically no witnesses, and speaking to the perpetrator is not a possibility or is rejected. Self-blame undermines one's self-worth and can quickly lead to pervasive feelings of disconnection, numbness, or alexithymia, the condition of having no words for feelings (Thompson, 2007). Without words and filled with guilt and shame, one may ultimately withdraw further into the isolation and sadness.

Such feelings of sadness and hopelessness can leave individuals feeling powerless over a situation, depressed, anxious, or too fearful to reach out for help. Commonly, they experience mood swings that can include anger, irritability, confusion, and difficulty concentrating. Accompanying physical symptoms can include insomnia, nightmares, heightened startled response, racing heartbeat, and even panic attacks. Additionally, unexplained aches and pains, fatigue, difficulty concentrating, edginess, agitation, and muscle tension are common. When in the throes of profound grief, people have the human need to establish tangible connections to beloved and revered figures, whether real, imagined, or mythical. Thus, is it beneficial to realize that "art is the bridge between the tangible mundane and the intangible realm of the spiritual" (Mauck, 2006, p. 817). Mourning art preserves the tie to the lost person or object while simultaneously altering the relationship and the loss. It memorializes and allows for both letting go and holding on. It has the ability to create incremental order out of the chaos resulting from loss. And it provides a necessary distance from the experience so it can be integrated and consolidated, transforming the loss from a raw experience into a necessary symbolic form.

Historical Uses of Art for Mourning

Art used in the service of mourning is laden with symbolism, as the crushing pain from loss often leaves one without words, and the routines of daily life fall into chaos. An image relies on its ability to consolidate the chaos and renders it into a form and structure, which communicates the complex multiplicities of loss simultaneously. The allegorical engraving *Melancholia I* by Albert Dürer (1471–1528), shown in Figure 9.2, captures the three kinds of virtue in medieval scholasticism—moral, theological, and intellectual—as they reflect the existential nature of life (Metropolitan Museum of Art, 2000). In Medieval philosophy, individuals were thought to be dominated by one of the four humors: blood, phlegm,

Figure 9.2 Albrecht Dürer (1471–1528). *Melancholia I* (1514). Engraving. Credit: Foto Marburg/Art Resource, NY.

yellow bile, and black bile. This concept of the four humors was largely based on the mythology of the Greek gods Apollo, Dionysus, Epimetheus, and Prometheus, and is the basis for some contemporary psychological types. For example, Jung incorporated this concept into his philosophical stance, which was focused on the underlying framework of conscious phenomena and the importance of rounding out the dominant and subordinate functions of the psychological types. These types became the foundation for the Myers-Briggs Personality Test, which considers various factors, like extraversion, to formulate 16 psychological types. The test was created as an easier way for people to use Jung's ideas and identify psychological types without having to sift through his academic theory (The Myers & Briggs Foundation, 2012). This test, like so many other examples of modern psychology, disavows the rich and complex history of psychological theory that has added to its evolution in favor of a truncated understanding of the philosophical perspective.

Melancholy, associated with black bile, was the least desirable of the four humors. It was thought that, "if grief lingers too long, it may turn into a paralyzing depression and that melancholics who succumbed to prolonged depression were likely to become insane" (Wojcik, 2015). The ideas of the Renaissance linked melancholy with creative genius. The symbols Dürer uses in *Melancholia I* echo the ones used in alchemy and mysticism and include the circle and the point. The circle symbolizes eternity, and the point, our place in it. The point within the circle is the concentration of time in the moment, with the circle (eternity) and point (concentration) representing the macro- and microcosms in which we are simultaneously one (Roob, 2006). The main character of the artwork is a winged female personification, like an angel, who can transcend her earthly bonds, with a crown of herbs upon her head. She is surrounded by tools associated with geometry, one of the seven liberal arts, which emphasizes artistic creation and is the one through which Dürer hoped to approach perfection in his own work (Rothschild, 1982). She is also surrounded by the tools of an artisan and is holding a compass, an instrument often associated with imposing order out of chaos. This is also seen in William Blake's (1757–1827) *Newton*, shown in Figure 9.3, and in his etching and watercolor *The Ancient of Days*, shown in Figure 9.4, where his invented

Figure 9.3 William Blake. *Newton* (1795/c. 1805). Color print finished in ink and watercolor on paper, 46.0 × 60.0 cm. Location: Tate Gallery, London, Great Britain, Photo Credit: Tate, London/Art Resource, NY.

deity Urizen (a pun on "your reason") holds a compass over the black emptiness below (Rothschild, 1982) in *The Book of Urizen*, a creation myth.

In *Melancholia I*, the sphere is said to represent the orb of life, the circle of human existence, similar to a mandala, and it contrasts with the permanent and "perfect" logic of the solid geometric form with a faint skull on its face. On the

Figure 9.4 William Blake. *The Ancient of Days, illustration for Europe*, plate 1, 1794, detail. Location: British Museum, London, Great Britain, Photo Credit: Eileen Tweedy/The Art Archive at Art Resource, NY.

wall is a magic square, a four-by-four square in which all the lines of numbers add up to 34, whether they are in columns, rows, or diagonals. The magic square relates to religious, astrological, spiritual, and mystical beliefs. The hourglass is a constant reminder of the sands of time, slipping away until the time of our death— a constant reminder of our temporal existence, the hour glass, coupled with the scale, stresses the importance of what we do with the transient time we are granted in this lifetime. The scale on the wall reminds the viewer of the balance to be maintained in life and a measure of good deeds. It harks back to the weighing of souls, which appeared in Christian art during the Middle Ages and recalls the weighing of the heart on a balance with the feather of truth, a postmortem rite described in Egyptian mythology (Moon, 1997). The skeletal dog on the floor is a sharp reminder of the harshness life holds and our corporal needs and desires.

The bell was an audible demonstration of grief and has been described as saddening the landscape, shadows, and the present sounds from the past (Wojcik, 2015). Bell ringing signified the departure of the soul, and poet-priest John Donne (1572–1631) famously chided people who did not listen to the bell. "No man is an island, entire of itself," he wrote, "Any man's death diminishes me, because I am involved in mankind, and therefore never send to know for whom the bell tolls; it tolls for thee." According to Wojcik (2015), curator of The Museum of Mourning Art at Arlington Cemetery in Drexel Hill, Pennsylvania, bells toll for the deceased as a means to gain entrance into heaven while others pray for the deceased, depending on the religious belief. The bell would ring according to gender and age and would be heard by all townspeople so they could assist the newly deceased soul in finding its way to the afterlife, aided by the prayers of the living. It was desirable to have a great number of funeral attendees to assist in the passage to the other world. The iconography of death and mourning continues to be relevant in modern traditions, customs, and art.

Worshiping relics and bearing relics, such as in lockets, have served to comfort millions throughout the centuries. They have served the purpose of holding onto the lost person while providing containment of and contact with what has been lost. Although commonly seen in Christian practices, the reverence and talismanic properties accorded to such items are not solely archaic or Christian, and through the ages, many cultures and religions have had similar practices and beliefs (Egan, 1993). Amulets on necklaces were worn as a means to ward off evil spirits, as in the popular *bulla*, a hollow pendant used by the Etruscans from the 5th century onward. Consisting of gold or leather, they contained perfume or a charm, protecting children until they reached adulthood (Egan, 1993). Pre-Christian Jews also wore amulets containing the sacred "phylacteries," or *tefillin*, to protect them from harm, and this practice continues among modern day Orthodox Jewish men. *Phylactery* comes from *philare*, "to keep or preserve," and *teras*, "law." Wearing one was believed to keep the wearer safe from witchcraft. This term was used during the Christian era until the 15th century, when the French term *reliquary* replaced *phylactery* (Egan, 1993).

In the 6th and 7th centuries, interring relics of the saints became customary in or under the altar, creating shrines. By the 9th century, reliquaries, small cases or boxes, were apparent, and were placed on top of the altar. Over time, the altars looked less like tables and more like sarcophagi. "The earliest reliquaries were decorated boxes, often of silver or ivory with images having to do with salvation" (Mauck, 2006, p. 830). They were also used as portable alters and even as "speaking" reliquaries, which allowed for explanations of their contents, such as bones or other artifacts of the pious like sandals or other vestments. Like cremation urns, some reliquaries became the last resting places for the bones of saints or nobles. According to Mauck (2006), reliquaries became most popular between the 11th and 13th centuries, and their decorations became their most opulent. In the *Gates of Paradise*, Lorenzo Ghiberti created a reliquary, or casket, shown in Figure 9.5, in Florence in 1446 that was made of copper gilt and champlevé enamel. It looks like a small architectural structure, like a chapel or home for the dead. Smaller-scale coffins may contain the remains of the departed, but perhaps just as important is that they become imbued with the essence of the deceased. A touchstone to return to the object holds the symbolic image of the dead. Thus, reliquaries are as much for the living as for the deceased.

During the period of mourning, wearing rings, cloths, and other decorative arts communicated not only the loss but also the degree of relationship the deceased person had with the wearer and the amount of time that had passed since the death. Rings and brooches woven with the departed's hair were common, and interestingly, as we know now through advances of technology, hair continues to hold the DNA, a human fingerprint as it were, of a person long after death. Like the *relicarios*, miniature devotional jewelry was popular on the Iberian peninsula as well as in the Americas during the Colonial Period, it was also popular in the Philippines and continued to be so through the Victorian Era. Typically, the brooch or ring would have a painting or polychrome enamel on one side with an image devoted to a saint or other deity and hair intricately woven on the reverse and pressed under glass. The frame of the brooch would be metal, such as gold or silver, and could include gems or pearls. Seed pearls were often associated with tears and were routinely included in mourning jewelry. Emerging out of an irritant to the oyster, a pearl forms around a single grain of sand, creating layer upon layer of concentric rings of calcification to produce the pearlescent orb. Similar to the pains of suffering that gather into the layers of life, it is a pearly seed of wisdom

Figure 9.5 Lorenzo Ghiberti (1370–1455). *Reliquary Casket*. Front view. Made in Florence, Italy (1446). Copper gilt, champlevé enamel. 7 1/2 × 7 3/4 × 3 1/4 in. (19.1 × 19.7 × 8.3 cm). The Metropolitan Museum of Art, New York, NY, USA. Credit: Image copyright © The Metropolitan Museum of Art. Image source: Art Resource, NY.

and depth. And it is through loss that there emerges a deepening of character and a more soulful presence. "The flowing pearl," as Jung referred to it (CW 14:317), was equated with the divine water, as seen in Chinese alchemy, which is fluid and mercurial like the psyche (Ronnberg & Martin, 2010). Like the pearl, art materials have inherent useful properties, carrying meaning and significance.

The Adorning Amulet

Making jewelry and devotional objects in a therapeutic setting utilizes the preciousness of the amulet and is popular due to its ease and its ability to be worn and to adorn. One can create charms and beads from clay, or utilize pre-made beads and charms. Clays that can be baked, such as Sculpey™ or Fimo™, are preferable due to their vivid colors, hardness, and durability. I like glass beads because of their heft and significance as opposed to lightweight plastic beads, which may draw infantile associations. Glass beads come in a range of colors and opacity. The brilliant colors, swirls in glass, iridescent sheen, pearly luminance, brilliant gold, and mercurial silver hark back to the raw materials associated with nobility, grandeur, and esteem. The choice of materials in therapy will be influenced by setting, resources, budget, and the standards for acceptable materials, as well as clinical insight. Beads have had roles in beautification rituals as well as a long tradition of signifying wealth and status, as seen in jewelry signifying nobility, marriage, and the previously discussed aspects of death and mourning. Beads and charms can be found tucked into the wrappings of the deceased, or placed in coffins to ensure safe passage into the next life. Bead necklaces and bracelets, due to their ease to create by stringing on a cord or, my preference, using a soft-wire that has been pre-wound into a thin silk cord for easy threading, are an easy, non-threatening way to engage in the arts in a therapeutic context. Amulets hold a potent history and continue to possess magico-spiritual powers for current creators, regardless of religious background.

Beads were once used in trading and commerce and may still be used in gift giving or to strengthen relationships among group members, peers, and family members. It is not uncommon for art projects, such as bead necklaces, to be given to a family member, most often by a child (Congdon, 1994). Hyde (2007) speaks of gift giving as a means of holding communities together in the Pacific Islands, strengthening communal ties, and increasing amicable relations through gifts, such as dowries or other gift-giving traditions. Some gifts were used like currency, but unlike the Western ideal of money, these gifts were meant to be passed along among tribes and holding or saving a gift was unconscionable. In therapy, creating necklaces or bracelets can provide a gentile and tangible reminder of strength and community, even when alone. As a group intervention, creating safety bracelets can provide a touchstone to ensure contemplation, remind the participant of groundedness, or, like a rosary, provide a tangible source for ritual for contemplation and prayer. In a group, I will often have members choose a special bead for each person in the group, a bead that reminds them of that person or seems to *speak to them* in terms of what they may need in their lives. I then invite each participant to ceremonially explain what quality, attribute, or reminder they are "giving" to the other person along with the bead. This group ceremony is like a benediction or blessing. This process is followed by each member incorporating the beads and the blessings, along with many of their own, into a piece of wearable art. Of special note, I have discouraged the creation of anklets because so many of my patients struggle with trauma issues and are working on staying present and grounded. To feel the anklet, one must bring one's foot or feet off the floor, making one hunch over in the fetal position on the floor or chair. Postures that reinforce sitting straight and holding one's head and shoulders high physically translate into increasing feelings of confidence, power, and directness, with increased eye contact, and lessening dissociation and ungroundedness.

The functions of the amulet and reliquary are similar in that they possess holding and containment aspects, which mediate and buffer against the bereavement. Both forms become imbued with the energy or symbolic representation of the loss. The amulet internalizes elements of the loss, holding it embodied within a form that can be carried and transported, whereas the reliquary holds the loss in a displayed, externalized form. The amulet takes the significant aspects of loss and turns them inward, whereas the reliquary makes the inner world visible, creating a home or place for it to rest in the outer world. These two functions are very much a part of boxes used in art psychotherapy.

Therapeutic Uses of Boxes

Like the amulet and reliquary, boxes used in therapy offer mediating and buffering qualities to the artist and viewer while providing a means to remain in contact with the loss. Additionally, there are many benefits to incorporating boxes into therapy because they provide a three-dimensional canvas on which relational space becomes a part of the form. The box is a tangible object that can be manipulated, carried, and held. Like sculpture, turning the box provides different perspectives and experiences of not only the box itself but also the imagery contained on or within its form. The images on the sides of a box are never fully visible at the same time. Light casts shadows into the depth of the box, which can be dramatic when illuminated from above or the side, especially when hung on a wall as in a framed shadow box. Boxes serve to contain and protect. The contents may be concealed or revealed in order to adjust for unacceptable or incompatible matter. If the box has a lid or cover, this is especially true because one can *keep a lid on it*, *put it under wraps*, or *put a lid on something*, as in something simmering under the surface.

Due to its multi-sidedness, the rectangular or square cuboid has planes on which to view work, creating an inherent pacing to the revealing of the contents. The box provides a mystery or secret form to be explored as its multifaceted sides are exposed. The box unites separate planes while also accommodating complex interrelationships, which may sometimes be juxtaposed (Farrell-Kirk, 2001). These juxtapositions can be jarring or can provide rhythmic flow to a piece and its contents. The box is a form that is unified while also holding the separateness of the planes and sides: inside and outside, top and bottom, left side and right side. The box can be deep or shallow, and so the contents may reflect varying degrees of depth, drama, and distance. Boxes serve as sturdy stages for personal dramas. They are a stage onto which mini-microcosms of one's inner life can be projected and played out in the front part of the stage or placed further back and obscured by those things that seem to take front-stage. Just as the amulet allows an invisible element, a lost loved one, or a value to be contained, carried, and related to, the diorama allows the invisible inner world to have a place to be in the outer world.

When working within a group context, individual scenes can be placed together to create a larger construction, much like the interior of a dollhouse or apartment building once the exterior wall has been removed. Collective group work with boxes is a powerful reflection of the ability to simultaneously hold both the individual and the group contexts, without compromising the structure and space. The walls of the box are able to support an individual's boundaries while also being placed in close proximity to others by stacking or arranging them to create a new combined order—a larger assemblage. In the group, the placement of the boxes can be discussed in terms of similar content, repeated themes, or patterns that are visible. If stacking, discussions can include insight into hierarchies, group roles, and leadership styles. If not adhered together, the boxes retain their individual integrity when removed from the group or rearranged. The similar form, the box, gives unity to the group's individual expressions while preserving the individuals' identity. This is different from group work in which the same piece of paper is shared for drawing, as in mural work, because in shared work there is no designated space for the individual but only for the group. There may be times this would be desired, just as there are times that keeping the integrity of the individuals' boundaries within a group context is desired. The latter could be the case for a new group in which members might be tentative about working with others, or for individuals who are working to create or sustain differentiated boundaries with others, or for those whose personal boundaries have been violated in the past and who need the support of the art materials for protection within the group context.

In a new group, while group members are attempting to work out their roles and define leadership, working with boxes allows for more focus on the individual work, so the jockeying for leadership can take a back seat to individual expression. So while the group is present in the work, it becomes a supportive and respectful holder of therapeutic space without members' immediately having to verbally share. Individuals working to create or sustain boundaries are aided by the art form as it physically gives a space in which to work. The rigid sides provide containment and, unlike paper where it may be easy to smear color off the edges, a box demands attention to its boundaries due to its volume. Sometimes the supporting materials, collage, found objects, and paint may create another ring of materials that need to be contained to not spill over onto the neighboring group mate's space. But the place of the psychic work is held within the box. It is recommended that boxes with more weight and substance than a tissue box be used in most cases because the heft in materials will withstand more manipulation and application of paint or found objects. If needed, the walls of the box can be reinforced through the layering of materials or the choice of the type of box that is more substantial, such as a wooden or metal box.

God Boxes

Making God boxes is an intervention that incorporates painting, collage, and decoupage. The God referenced is a higher power or other divine source, as is typical in 12-step recovery programs. The God box uses the intervention *Create a box of those things you would like to surrender to God*. This can include things that one feels powerless over or things one would like to let go of or give up. Typically, these things are depicted on a piece of paper or painted or collaged directly on the interior of the box, while the outside of the box may reflect hope and strength to carry on.

The example of a God box, shown in Figures 9.6 and 9.7, was created with a pre-made box, acrylic paint, and collage. The young woman, Annie, was

Figure 9.6 A God box created by a 20-year-old woman at an eating disorders facility, who worked in muted hues of purple, red, and orange as she depicted on the exterior of her box a reminder to "fight" for the things she wanted to surrender to her God or Higher Power. © 2016 Michelle L. Dean.

Figure 9.7 The interior of the God box revealed conflicted ideals about her commitment and desires or readiness to recover from her anorexia. © 2016 Michelle L. Dean.

20 years of age when she created her God box at an inpatient eating disorders facility. Annie had participated in crew at the collegiate level as the team's coxswain. A vital position, the coxswain provides navigation and typically coordinates the rowers by processing the information of the boat's surroundings and shouting orders to the other eight rowers who are facing backward to the direction they are headed. Coxswains are typically smaller than the other athletes on their team and are, as Annie described, "dead weight" because they don't actually contribute to the rowing, but act as a conduit between the coaches and the teammates and may provide some steering assistance with the rudder. Her role as coxswain and her eating disorder were steadfastly linked. In weight-conscious sports, like wrestling, gymnastics, and dance, there is a tendency to develop eating issues due to the resolute focus on weight and body size, which are often fueled by an extreme, size-focused lifestyle. Annie had started her restrictive eating before she entered college, but the pressure to perform, coupled with intense academics, family discord at home, and her struggle with increasing independence contributed to her difficulty eating. But Annie was a fighter, wanting to do things her way. Her desire to get back to her life and her loyalty to her teammates compelled her to want to leave treatment prematurely and against medical advice. Annie's God box was created on the day of her discharge, and although other group members encouraged her to stay in treatment, she assured the group she was "fine and would not be coming back."

Annie worked diligently, painting the outside of the box in muted hues of purple, red, and orange. On the top of her box she placed the cutout word "fight," a reminder to fight for the things she wanted to surrender to her God or higher power.

"I am a fighter, and I am going to fight for my recovery and for my team once I am discharged," she said.

When she opened the box she said, "I quit my anorexia. . . . I am not going to die for it."

As the group members and I looked at the box, I read what she had written on the interior, "I Quit" was painted on the lid, and "Anorexia: To die for" was scribed below. When read together, "I Quit; Anorexia: To die for" had an opposite meaning than what she said she intended. Annie became flustered and said that she knew what she meant, and reiterated she would not be returning to the treatment center.

Annie was discharged a day later leaving her box behind, saying, "I don't need that damn box, I know what I am going to do."

When I inquired if she would consider taking it with her in order to place images or journal entries describing those things she would like to surrender to her higher power, she turned her back and left.

About three weeks later, Annie returned to treatment. The first thing she said to me upon entering the art therapy room was, "I was so mad at you when I left. But you were absolutely right. I was willing to die for my anorexia and it was going to kill me."

Reassuring her that I was glad she had had a change of mind and was back in treatment, I said, "It was your artwork that told you that you had already quit your recovery and that the anorexia had the potential to kill you."

When she was ready to be discharged this time she took her box as a reminder of what she needed to do and was in a much better place to continue her recovery process on an outpatient basis.

Spiders in the Park

Another way to approach the box is to create a diorama in the container itself as seen in Figure 9.8, *Spiders in the Park*. This image was created by one of our sons

Figure 9.8 Spiders in the Park was created as a means to contain the fear of a previously encountered spider. © 2016 Michelle L. Dean.

after encountering a scary spider on the playground equipment at the park. Using found objects such as popsicle sticks, buttons, yarn, and leftover foil Halloween decorations, he constructed this image when he was about four years of age. He took great delight in placing the clear plastic casing of the premade picture frame over the image, as if containing his fear.

Dioramas were a medium I often utilized when working with young trauma survivors. Working at a rape crisis center, my patients were often children, sometimes as young as two, and the adults I worked with there also benefited from this as well. Using cardboard boxes, cutout figures, and found materials we created scenes, like dollhouses in which to play. With one young girl who was the age of seven, we created elaborate backgrounds and paper dolls and placed them in the boxes. From week to week we used many of the same characters, adding to the repertoire when significant events happened, such as changing backgrounds when a new scene of the story needed to be told or new characters needed to make an appearance in order to serve a function. She added policemen as we neared her trial date, referencing not only the actuality of the legal situation but also invoking the power of the rule of law, a theme which appeared in her work for many months afterward. We created dogs, more than a dozen, until she felt we had enough to create a dog sled team. Being inspired by a film about sled dogs, the captivating hold that the film had on her was its resonance with her own inner conflicts and desires. Her need to recreate winning races, survive daring feats, and perform heroic rescues reflected her own sense of the need to survive and also her desire to be rescued. This ran parallel the dynamics that were being played out with her parents as her mother, an abuse survivor who struggled with addiction, was unable to protect her daughter, my patient, from the incestuous situations in the home. My patient's father fought to gain custody and rescue her from the situation, a process that was complex and contentious at times. The repetition and the familiar characters, which played out their drama in a safe container, allowed for the painful psychic contents of her trauma to have a place to be dramatized, and the narrative could be rescripted when she ready.

Time and again, one witnesses that the availability of an appropriate expressive mode invites psychological contents to be drawn forth onto the stage of creative expression. There the contents, which clearly appear to be the relevant ones to the psychological dilemma, are found to appear and to work themselves out. The metaphor of the container, the simple box, creates such a stage, an empty space that quickly fills up with elements that are themselves invisible but also quite real and seem to wish to have a place to be.

This simple device, like all other art mediums, has its own specific set of attributes and lends itself to different possibilities. Like the amulet and reliquary, boxes used in therapy offer mediating and buffering qualities as they possess holding and containment aspects, which mediate and buffer against bereavement. The forms become imbued with the energy or symbolic representation of the loss. While the amulet embodies elements of the loss, holding within the form the ability to be carried and transported, the reliquary holds a vestige of the loss in an externalized form. The amulet takes the significant aspects of loss and turns them inward, while the reliquary allows the inner word to become visible, creating a home or a place for it to rest in the outer world.

As one can see from the examples offered, the dimensionality and the unique properties of each expressive form offer possibilities for becoming a platform for the expression of relevant psychological issues. Such issues emerge quite naturally, as if waiting for a form to become available in order to serve as its voice. The therapist tuned to the prevailing theme that the patient is carrying, as well as the individual needs and nature of the patient, may step in to provide the means for such expression and gauge the relevancy of the level of engagement with what is expressed. At times it may appear that interpretation and acknowledgment are needed, while at other times one simply helps the process along, like a doula attending to a psychological birth. At still other times, a silent witness is what is most required.

CHAPTER 10

CONCLUSIONS

From the dawn of humanity and our earliest cave paintings to the contemporary use of art in the psychotherapy office, art has possessed intrinsic transformational and spiritual aspects that reflect the human condition. The permutations of its expressions are endless. No book, no matter how comprehensive, will ever account for all the ever-expanding ways that art can be used in the process of psychological healing. As Heraclitus (2001) once remarked,

> The soul is undiscovered,
> though explored forever
> to a depth beyond report [p. 45].

Like the soul, the creative process always springs anew from the well of humanities' creative potential, assuming ever-new forms and, thus, evading exact definition.

Conceptually understanding the historical context, origins, and functions of art and its many forms is imperative for grounding and comprehending its application in the psychotherapy process. Art making, as a naturally arising human activity, corresponds to our need to express our condition, intrinsically and extrinsically, and so it is naturally related to psychological process and understanding. This understanding assists in how we see and exist in our own context; hence, it is meaningful to know how forms of art functioned in their own specific historical contexts. Although these contexts are not literally the same, they remain paradigmatically so. Forms and materials of art have specific attributes that lend themselves to specific functions. Working with images in an art psychotherapy process, as noted in Chapter 4, is especially helpful for mediating external experience, especially those experienced as overwhelming or traumatic. Art making provides a context for the handling of such difficult psychic materials.

Creativity arises from clusters of experiences. Technological advances, changes in societal attitudes, personal histories, and the like give shape to different understandings of art. Understanding such changes assists us in seeing our relationship to art, how we see art's potential, and what our immediate cultural prejudices may blind us to. Art therapy, as a profession, grew out of healing traditions involving the arts with a history that precedes and exceeds that of modern medicine. Within these traditions, the arts were valued for their transformative and healing aspects. As such, they were grounded in something profoundly human. Art forms, like archetypal forms, arise from a primal, or what was historically considered a divine, source.

The isolated implementation of a task or procedure that ignores the fact that each and every such procedure exists within a broader context, a fact we begin to understand more clearly through the lens of historical example, runs the risk of asserting its relevance at the cost of what actually is contextually appropriate. Without historical context and understanding, there is not only a split or disconnect between therapist and patient but also splits within the therapist and patient. These splits are prime for projection and for the insertion of a biased and possibly intrusive technique.

Firsthand knowledge of the process of making and utilizing the arts as a living discipline is essential. The practice of utilizing art in a psychotherapy context must be alive, not deadened with standards or research that does not enhance the quality of the experience. Art making by its nature, adds value through experience. Acknowledgment of aesthetics, defined by its ability to elicit feelings, and cultural ideals is essential to utilizing art in psychotherapy, which runs counter to objectivity. The aesthetic dimension carries the capacity to engage, and thus, the mirroring element is invoked. This mirroring becomes the individual's response to a cultural attitude or pattern (Dallett, 2008; Woodman, 1980). Art bridges differences through communication, enhancing mutual understanding in the contexts of both psychotherapy and society, generally. For art psychotherapists, patients, and a culture, this means "cultivating new skills and enlarging our scientific horizons so that there is room for the creativity that is a part of our everyday experience of living" (Goodwin, 2007, p. 31).

The work of employing the arts in psychotherapy is about honoring the individual in his or her immediate context, which both makes sense and is valuable. The art provides a means to bridge individual and cultural deficits. It is a means to build a "relationship with our imaginative life [,which] is an absolutely crucial part of any authentic and effective individual or collective liberation" (Taylor, 1992, p. 113). Societies need to support the arts for they are the carriers of culture, delivering value, appreciation, and empathy. Art in therapy should not be a set of coveted techniques, although they are often called interventions, but instead should cover an orientation and attitude toward everything that is creative in life. For it is the nature of imagery and creativity, like Hermes, to transcend boundaries: to dissolve, recreate, and redefine them. Although art therapy shares the distinctive quality of defying easy definition (Dean, 2011a) it is a means of restoring creativity and wellness to individuals, families, communities and society by connecting to the inner world of knowing through images.

APPENDIX A: VENDORS AND SUPPLIERS FOR ART MATERIALS

Cheap Joe's Art Stuff
Discounted art supplies
http://www.cheapjoes.com

Dick Blick Art Materials
Professional and student grade materials
http://www.dickblick.com

Hollander's
Book-binding supplies
http://www.hollanders.com

Jerry's Artarama
Artist friendly, low prices
http://www.jerrysartarama.com

Nasco
Sells school supplies, farm and ranch products, art materials, health care trainers, educational and teacher resources, senior care items, and more
http://www.enasco.com

Rex Art
International art supplier
http://www.rexart.com

S & S Arts & Crafts
Educational, art, therapy rehab supplies and games
http://www.ssww.com

Utrecht
Art supplies, student and professional grade
http://www.utrechtart.com

APPENDIX B: RECIPES FOR BOOK BINDING AND PASTE PAPERS

Flour Paste

4 tablespoons rice flour
3 tablespoons wheat flour
3 cups water
½ teaspoon glycerin
1 teaspoon dish detergent

Cook the flours with a little water over medium heat; continue to add water until it resembles thin custard. Remove from heat and add the glycerin and detergent to keep the paste smooth and pliable.

Cornstarch Paste

Mix ¼ cup cornstarch with ¼ cup water until well blended. Heat over medium heat while adding an additional cup of water until it resembles custard. Add ½ cup of water to thin.

Methylcellulose

Mix 1 teaspoon into 1 pint of cold water (hot water does not work as it prevents it from "melting"). Let stand overnight or longer. It does not go bad, so make extra and store in a sealed container (e.g., Mason jars) for whenever needed.

APPENDIX C: THEMES FOR WEB WRITING

These themes are written in the center of the circle and may include archetypal images as well as other issues or concerns.

Self
Body
Mother
Survivor
Hate
Depression
Addiction
[Name of the] illness
Body image
Threshold
Shadow
Peace
Love
Hero
Recovery
Survivor
Child
Happiness
Seed
Beginning
Ending
Father
Marriage
Death
Birth
One
New
Together
Apart
Home

REFERENCES

American Psychiatric Association. (2013). *Diagnostic and statistical manual of mental disorders* (5th ed.). Washington, DC: Author.

Anderson, L.W., & Krathwohl, D.R. (2001). *A taxonomy for learning, teaching, and assessing: A revision of Bloom's taxonomy of educational objectives*. New York, NY: Addison-Wesley Longman.

Argon, G.C. (1965). Painting. *Encyclopedia of World Art* (Vol. X). London, England: McGraw-Hill Publishing.

Arieti, S. (1976). *Creativity: The magical synthesis*. New York, NY: Basic Books.

The Art Story Foundation. (2015). Louise Nevelson. Retrieved from http://www.theartstory.org/artist-nevelson-louise.htm

Avrin, L. (1991). *Scribes, script and books: The book arts from Antiquity to the Renaissance*. Chicago, IL: American Library Press.

Bach, S. (1990). *Life paints its own span: On the significance of spontaneous pictures of severely ill children*. Zürich, Switzerland: Daimon Verlag.

Baer, D. (n.d.). Why Bill Gates bought da Vinci's notebooks. Retrieved from http://www.fastcompany.com/3009718/bottom-line/why-bill-gates-bought-da-vincis-notebooks

Bagilhole, R. (1983). *Practical printmaking*. London, England: Chartwell Books.

Bardot, H. (2008). Expressing the inexpressible: The resilient healing of client and art therapist. *Art Therapy: Journal of American Art Therapy Association, 25*(4), 183–186.

Bechtel, A. (2009, January). *Rewriting life stories: The altered book as a tool of transformation*. Presented at The Delaware Valley Art Therapy Association Annual Conference: The Lens of Transformation: Envisioning Therapeutic Change Through Art Therapy, Philadelphia, PA.

Belkofer, C.M., & Konopka, L.M. (2008). Conducting art therapy research using quantitative EEG measures. *Art Therapy: Journal of the American Art Therapy Association, 25*(2), 56–63.

Belkofer, C.M., Vaughan Van Hecke, A., & Konopka, L.M. (2014). Effects of drawing on alpha activity: A quantitative EEG study with implications for art therapy. *Art Therapy: Journal of the American Art Therapy Association, 31*(2), 61–68.

Berry, P. (2008). *Echo's subtle body: Contributions to an archetypal psychology* (2nd ed.). Putnam, CT: Spring Publications.

Bjorklund, G., & Krebs, M. (1985). Nation at risk of children at risk? *Education Week, 4*, 24.

Black, C. (Ed.). (2011). *The art of insanity: An analysis of ten schizophrenic artists*. Chicago, IL: Solar Books

Bloom, S.L. (2000). The neglect of neglect, part 1. Email from America, *Psychotherapy Review, 2*(2), 208–210.

Boorsch, S., & Orenstein, N.M. (1997). The print in the north: The age of Albrecht Dürer and Lucas van Leyden. *The Metropolitan Museum of Art bulletin, 54*(4).

Boss, P. (1999). *Ambiguous loss: Learning to live with unresolved grief*. Cambridge: Harvard University Press.

British Museum. (n.d.). William Morris, *Initial D*, a design for a woodcut. Retrieved from http://www.britishmuseum.org/explore/highlights/highlight_objects/pd/w/william_morris,_initial_d.aspx

Brooke, S. L. (1995). Art therapy: An approach to working with sexual abuse survivors. *The Arts in Psychotherapy, 22*(5), 447–466.

Brooke, S. L. (2004). *Tools of the trade: A therapist's guide to art therapy assessments.* Springfield, IL: Charles C. Thomas Publishers.

Buk, A. (2009). The mirror neuron system and embodied simulation: Clinical implications for art therapists working with trauma survivors. *The Arts in Psychotherapy, 36*(2), 61–74.

Bungay, S. (1987). *Beauty and truth.* Oxford, England: Oxford University Press.

Burlingame, G. M., Fuhriman, A., & Mosier, J. (2003). The differential effectiveness of group psychotherapy: A meta-analytic perspective. *Group Dynamics: Theory, Research, and Practice, 7*(1), 3–12. doi: 10.1037/1089-2699.7.1.3

Calisch, A. (1989). Eclectic blending of theory in the supervision of art psychotherapists. *The Arts in Psychotherapy, 16,* 3743.

Cameron, J. (1992). *The artist's way: A spiritual path to higher creativity.* New York, NY: G. P. Putnam's Sons.

Cameron, W. B. (1963). *Informal sociology: A casual introduction to sociological thinking.* New York, NY: Random House.

Campbell, J. (1968). *The masks of God: Creative mythology.* New York, NY: The Viking Press.

Carrigan, J. (1993). Ethical considerations in a supervisory relationship: A synthesis. *Art Therapy: Journal of the American Art Therapy Association, 10*(3), 130–135.

Cartwright, R. (2010). *The twenty-four hour mind: The role of sleep and dreaming in our emotional lives.* Oxford, England: Oxford University Press.

Chalquist, C. (2013). Why I am not a member of the American Psychological Association. Retrieved from http://www.chalquist.com/apa.html. Excerpted from Engaged psychology: Past, present, prospects. *Journal of Holistic Psychology, 3.*

Chambala, A. (2008). Anxiety and art therapy: Treatment in the public eye. *Art Therapy: Journal of the American Art Therapy Association, 25*(4), 187–189.

Chandraiah, S., Anand, S. A., & Avent, L. C. (2012). Efficacy of group art therapy on depressive symptoms in adult heterogeneous psychiatric outpatients. *Art Therapy: Journal of the American Art Therapy Association, 29*(2), 80–86.

Chastel, A. (1961). *The genius of Leonardo da Vinci: Leonardo da Vinci on art and the artist.* New York, NY: The Orion Press.

Chilton, G. (2007). Altered books in art therapy with adolescents. *Art Therapy: Journal of the American Art Therapy Association, 24*(2), 59–63.

Chilton, G. (2013). Art therapy and flow: A review of the literature and applications. *Art Therapy: Journal of the American Art Therapy Association, 30*(2), 64–70.

Chu, J. A. (1991). The repetition compulsion revised: Reliving dissociated trauma. *Psychotherapy, 28,* 327–332.

Congdon, K. C. (1990). Normalizing art therapy. *Art Education, 19,* 21–24, 41–43.

Congdon, K. C. (1994). Democratizing art therapy. In M. O. Jones (Ed.), *Putting folklore to use* (pp. 136–149). Lexington: KY: University Press of Kentucky.

Cooper, D. E. (Ed.), Lamarque, P., & Sartwell, C. (Advisory Eds.). (1997). *Aesthetics: The classic readings.* Oxford, UK: Blackwell Publishing.

Craig, E. (1998). Metaphysics. In E. Craig (Ed.), *Routledge encyclopedia of philosophy.* London, England: Routledge. Retrieved from http://www.rep.routledge.com/article/N095

Cubberley, E. P. (1920). *The history of education: Educational practice and progress considered as a phase of the development and spread of the Western Civilization.* Boston, MA: Houghton Mifflin Co.

Dallett, J. O. (2008). *Listening to the rhino: Violence and healing in a scientific age.* New York, NY: Aequiteas Book from Pleasure Boat Studio: A Literary Press.

de Botton, A., & Armstrong, J. (2014). *Art as therapy.* London, England: Phaidon Press, Ltd.

de Vries, A., & de Vries, A. (2004). *Elsevier's dictionary of symbols and imagery.* Amsterdam, Boston: Elsevier.

Dean, M. L. (2006a). Creative destruction: Art based interventions with eating disordered clients who self-injure. *The 16th Renfrew Center Conference,* Philadelphia, PA.

Dean, M. L. (2006b). Preserving the self: Art psychotherapy applications with eating disordered clients who self-injure. The American Art Therapy Association Conference, New Orleans, LA.

Dean, M. L. (2008). Preserving the self: Treating eating disordered individuals who self-injure with art therapy. In S. Brooke, *The creative therapies and eating disorders* (pp. 56–82). Springfield, IL: Charles C. Thomas Publisher, LTD.

Dean, M. L. (2009, July). Libellus: Little books & other bindings. Presented at The Media & Techniques Workshop Series, Oreland, PA.

Dean, M. L. (2010a, June). Creating meaning through relationships. Artsblog Green papers. *Americans for the Arts.* Retrieved from http://blog.artsusa.org/2010/06/15/creating-meaning-through-relationships/

Dean, M. L. (2010b, June). Hardening of the categories leads to art disease. Artsblog Green papers. *Americans for the Arts.* Retrieved from http://blog.artsusa.org/2010/06/14/hardening-of-the-categories-leads-to-art-disease/

Dean, M. L. (2011a, January). Growing the profession: The American art therapy perspective. Retrieved from http://blog.americansforthearts.org/2011/01/04/growing-the-profession-the-american-art-therapy-perspective

Dean, M. L. (2011b, July). Therapeutic art journals: Advance practice course. Presented at The American Art Therapy Association, Washington, DC.

Dean, M. L. (2013). Cultural considerations of eating disorders through art therapy. In P. Howie, S. Prasad, & J. Kristel (Eds.), *Using art therapies with diverse populations: Crossing cultures and abilities* (pp. 277–288). London and Philadelphia: Jessica Kingsley Publishers.

Dean, M. L. (2015). Printmaking: Reflective and receptive impressions in the therapeutic process. In D. Gussak & M. Rosal [Eds.], *The Wiley handbook of art therapy.* Hoboken, NJ: Wiley Blackwell.

della Barba, E. (2013). The ex-voto in Italy: The history of ex-voto jewellery [sic] and painting in Italy. *Swide.* Retrieved from http://www.swide.com/art-culture/italian-traditions/the-history-of-ex-voto-jewellery-and-paintings-in-italy/2013/09/02

Diamond, S. A. (1996). *Anger, madness, and the daimonic: The psychological genesis of violence, evil and creativity.* New York, NY: State University of New York Press.

Duignan, B. (Ed.). (2010). *The 100 most influential philosophers of all time.* New York, NY: Britannica Educational Publishing.

Dunn-Snow, P., & Joy-Smellie, S. (2000). Teaching art therapy techniques: Mask-making, a case in point. *Art Therapy: Journal of the American Art Therapy Association, 17*(2), 125–131.

Durkin, J., Perach, D., Ramseyer, J., & Sontag, E. (1989). A model for art therapy supervision enhanced through art making and journal writing. In H. Wadeson, J. Durkin, & D. Perach (Eds.), *Advances in art therapy* (pp. 391–432). New York, NY: John Wiley.

Earley, M. L. (1999a). Art therapy: Body image, media & art. The American Art Therapy Association Conference, Orlando, FL.

Earley, M. L. (1999b). Art therapy with eating disordered clients. The Renfrew Center Conference, Philadelphia, PA.

Edinger, E. (2008). The tragic hero. In M. Heyneman (Ed.), *The inner journey: Myth, psyche, and human spirit* (pp. 32–44). Sandpoint, ID: Morning Light Press.

Egan, M. J. (1993). *Relicarios: Devotional miniatures from the Americas.* Santa Fe, NM: Museum of New Mexico Press.

Eitner, L. (1961). Drawing. *Encyclopedia of world art* (Vol. IV). London, England: McGraw-Hill Publishing.

Elder, G. R. (1996). *An encyclopedia of archetypal symbolism* (Vol. 2). The body. The Archive for Research in Archetypal Symbolism. Boston, MA: Shambhala.

Eliade, M. (1961). Divinities. *Encyclopedia of world art* (Vol. IV). London, England: McGraw-Hill Publishing.

Elkins, D. N. (2007). Empirically supported treatments: The deconstruction of a myth. *Journal of Humanistic Psychology, 47*(4), 474–500.

Ellmann, R. (Ed.). (1969). *The artists as critic: Critical writings of Oscar Wilde.* New York, NY: Random House.

Fabricius, J. (1976). *Alchemy: The medieval alchemists and their royal art.* London, England: Diamond Books.

Farrell-Kirk, R. (2001). Secrets, symbols, synthesis, and safety: The role of boxes in art therapy. *American Journal of Art Therapy, 39,* 88–92.

Favazza, A. R. (1996). *Bodies under siege: Self-mutilation and body modification in culture and psychiatry* (2nd ed.). Baltimore, MD: Johns Hopkins.

Finkelstein, D., & McCleery, A. (2002). *The book history reader.* New York, NY: Routledge.

Finkelstein, D., & McCleery, A. (2005). *An introduction to book history.* New York, NY: Routledge.

Fish, B. J. (2008). Formative evaluation research of art-based supervision in art therapy training. *Art Therapy: Journal of the American Art Therapy Association, 25*(2), 70–77.

Franklin, M. (2010). Affect regulation, mirror neurons, and the third hand: Formulating mindful empathic art interventions. *Art Therapy: Journal of the American Art Therapy Association, 27*(4), 160–167.

Freud, S. (1933). *New introductory lectures on psychoanalysis: Standard edition.* London, England: Hogarth.

Freud, S. (2010). *Selected papers on hysteria and other psychoneuroses* (A. A. Brill, Trans.). New York, NY: The Journal of Nervous and Mental Disease Publishing Company (Original work published 1912).

Friedman, H. (2015). What is sandplay therapy? C. G. Jung Institute of Los Angeles. Retrieved from http://www.junginla.org/education/what_is_sandplay

Friedman, M. (1973). Quotes. *Nevelson wood sculptures* by Martin Friedman, Walker Art Center. Retrieved from http://www.louisenevelsonfoundation.org/pdf/quotes.pdf

Gadamer, H. G. (2012). *Truth and method* (2nd ed.) (J. Weinsheimer & D. G. Marshall, Trans.). London and New York, NY: Continuum International Publishing Group.

Gantt, L. (1998). A discussion of art therapy as a science. Art Therapy: *Journal of the American Art Therapy Association, 15*(1), 3–12.

Gantt, L., & Tabone, C. (1998). *The formal elements art therapy scale: The rating manual.* Morgantown, WV: Gargoyle Press.

Gantt, L., Tinnin, L. W., & Williams, K. (1993, November). Exploring common ground: Contributions from related fields. Panel presented at the American Art Therapy Association Conference, Atlanta, GA.

George, A. (2014). Jung in the Garden of Eden: A myth of the transformation of consciousness. *Depth insights: Seeing the world with soul: A scholarly e-zine for Jungian and depth psychology community.* Retrieved from http://www.depthinsights.com/Depth-Insights-scholarly-ezine/jung-in-the-garden-of-eden-a-myth-of-the-transformation-of-consciousness-arthur-george-j-d/

Gold, J. (1985). Cartesian dualism and the current crisis in medicine—a plea for a philosophical approach: Discussion paper. *Journal of the Royal Society of Medicine, 78,* 663–666.

Goldblatt, D., & Brown, L. B. (2011). *Aesthetics: A reader in philosophy of the arts* (3rd ed.). Boston, MA: Prentice Hall.

Goodwin, B. (2007). *Nature's due: Healing our fragmented culture.* Edinburgh: Floris Books.

Green, B. L., Wehling, C., & Talsky, G. J. (1987). Group art therapy as an adjunct to treatment for chronic outpatients. *Hospital and Community Psychiatry, 38*(9), 988–991.

Greenberg, M. S., & van der Kolk, B. A. (1987). Retrieval and integration of traumatic memories with the "painting cure." In B. A. Van der Kolk (Ed.), *Psychological trauma* (pp. 191–215). Washington, DC: American Psychiatric Press.

Grottanelli, V. L. (1961). Drawing. *Encyclopedia of world art* (Vol. IX). London, England: McGraw-Hill Publishing.

Gussak, D., & Rosal, M. [Eds.]. (2015). *The Wiley handbook of art therapy.* Hoboken, NJ: Wiley Blackwell.

Hakim, J. (2004). *The story of science: Aristotle leads the way.* Washington, DC: Smithsonian Books.

Hardy, D. (2005). Creating through loss: How art therapists sustain their practice in palliative care. In D. Waller & C. Sibbett (Eds.), *Facing death: Art therapy and cancer care* (pp. 185–198). Berkshire, England: Open University Press.

Hargreaves, J. (2009). *A little history of dragons.* New York, NY: Walker & Company.

Hass-Cohen, N. (2003). Art therapy mind-body approaches. *Progress: Family Systems Research and Therapy, 12,* 24–38.

Hass-Cohen, N. & Carr, R. (Eds.). (2008). *Art therapy and clinical neuroscience*. London, England: Jessica Kingsley Publishers.
Hayes, J. A., Yeh, Y. J., & Eisenberg, A. (2007). Good grief and not-so-good grief: Countertransference in bereavement therapy. *Journal of Clinical Psychology, 63*(4), 345–355.
Heraclitus. (2001). *Fragments* (B. Haxton, Trans.). New York, NY: Penguin Group.
Herzog, W. (Director), & Nelson, E., Ciuffo, A., Harding, D., Hobbs, J., McKillop, D. (Producers). (2010). Cave of forgotten dreams [Motion picture]. France: Creative Differences, History Films, Ministère de la Culture et de la Communication, Arte France, Werner Herzog, Filmprodukton, More4.
Hess, E. H. (1958, March). "Imprinting" in animals. *Scientific American Offprints, 198*(3), 2–8. Retrieved from http://www.columbia.edu/cu/psychology/terrace/w1001/readings/hess.pdf
Hogan, S. (2001). Withymead Britain's first therapeutic community dedicated to art therapy. In S. Hogan (Ed.), *Healing arts: The history of art therapy* (pp. 220–289). London, England: Jessica Kingsley Publishers.
Hones, M. J. (1995). Clinical application of the "scribble technique" with adults in an acute inpatient psychiatric hospital. *Art Therapy: Journal of the American Art Therapy Association, 12*(2), 111–117.
Hurwitz, A., & Day, M. (2001). *Children and their art: Methods for the elementary school*. Fort Worth, TX: Harcourt College Publishers.
Hustvedt, S. (2011, April). Three emotional stories: Reflections on memory, the imagination, narrative, and the self. Presented at Arnold Pfeffer Center for Neuropsychoanalysis at the New York Psychoanalytic Institute. Neuropsychoanalysis Foundation. Retrieved from https://www.youtube.com/watch?v=iZfxgEFDuLc
Hyde, L. (2007). *The gift: Creativity and the artist in the modern world*. New York, NY: Vintage Books.
Jung, C. G. (1963). *Memories, dreams, reflections*. New York, NY: Vintage Books.
Jung, C. G. (1966a). The practice of psychotherapy: Essays on the psychological transference and other subjects (R. F. C. Hull, Trans.). In H. Read et al. (Series Eds.), *The collected works of C.G. Jung* (Vol. 16). Princeton, NJ: Princeton University Press (Original work published 1958).
Jung, C. G. (1966b). Two essays on analytical psychology (R. F. C. Hull, Trans.). In H. Read et al. (Series Eds.), *The collected works of C.G. Jung* (Vol. 7, 2nd ed.). Princeton, NJ: Princeton University Press (Original work published 1948).
Jung, C. G. (1967). Alchemical studies (R. F. C. Hull, Trans.). In H. Read et al. (Series Eds.), *The collected works of C.G. Jung* (Vol. 13, 2nd ed.). Princeton, NJ: Princeton University Press (Original work published 1957).
Jung, C. G. (1968a). The archetypes and the collective unconscious (R. F. C. Hull, Trans.). In H. Read et al. (Series Eds.), *The collected works of C.G. Jung* (Vol. 9, 2nd ed.). Princeton, NJ: Princeton University Press (Original work published 1959).
Jung, C. G. (1968b). *Man and his symbols*. New York, NY: Dell Publishing Company.
Jung, C. G. (1969). The structure and dynamic of the psyche (R. F. C. Hull, Trans.). In H. Read et al. (Series Eds.), *The collected works of C. G. Jung* (Vol. 8, 2nd ed.). Princeton, NJ: Princeton University Press (Original works published 1943 & 1928; 2nd ed. 1935).
Jung, C. G. (1970a). Civilization in transition (R. F. C. Hull, Trans.). In H. Read et al. (Series Eds.), *The collected works of C.G. Jung* (Vol. 10, 2nd ed.). Princeton, NJ: Princeton University Press (Original works published 1957, 1959, & 1933).
Jung, C. G. (1970b). Mysterium conjunctions: An inquiry into the separation and synthesis of psychic opposites in alchemy (R. F. C. Hull, Trans.). In H. Read et al. (Series Eds.), *The collected works of C.G. Jung* (Vol. 14, 2nd ed.). Princeton, NJ: Princeton University Press (Original work published 1955 & 1956).
Junge, M. (2010). *The modern history of art therapy in the United States*. Springfield, IL: Charles C. Thomas.
Kalshed, D. (1996). *The inner world of trauma: Archetypal defenses of the personal spirit*. London, England: Routledge.
Kapitan, L. (2010). The empathic imagination of art therapy: Good for the brain? *Art Therapy: Journal of the American Art Therapy Association, 27*(4), 158–159.

Kaplan, F. F. (1998). Scientific art therapy: An integrative and research-based approach. *Art Therapy: Journal of the American Art Therapy Association, 15*(2), 93–98.

Kaplan, F. F. (2000). *Art, science and art therapy: Repainting the picture.* London, England: Jessica Kingsley.

Kellogg, R. (1970). *Analyzing children's art.* Palo Alto, CA: Mayfield Publishing Co.

Kellogg, R., & O'Dell S. (1967). *The psychology of children's art.* New York, NY: CRM-Random House Publication.

Kettenmann, A. (2000). *Frida Kahlo: Pain and passion.* Köln, Germany: Taschen.

Kielo, J. B. (1991). Art therapists' countertransference and post-session therapy imagery. *Art Therapy: Journal of the American Art Therapy Association, 8*(2), 14–19.

Kinsella, T. (2011, December). Querying and queering in the virgin: Iconography and iconoclasm in the art of Friday Kahlo. Paper presented at the Chicano/a conference in UCC. Retrieved from https://www.academia.edu/764865/Querying_and_Queering_the_Virgin_Iconography_and_Iconoclasm_in_the_Art_of_Frida_Kahlo?

Klorer, G. (2014). "Ribbons of Hope" update. Retrieved from http://missouriarttherapy.blogspot.com/2014/09/ribbons-of-hope-update.html

Kugler, (2008). Psychic imaging: A bridge between subject and object. In P. Young-Eisendrath & T. Dawson (Eds.), *The Cambridge companion to Jung* (pp. 77–91). Cambridge, England: Cambridge University Press.

Landgarten, H. (1994). Magazine photo collage as a multicultural treatment and assessment technique. *Art Therapy: Journal of the American Art Therapy Association, 11*(3), 218–219.

Lear, J. (1999). *Open minded: Working out the logic of the soul.* Cambridge, MA: Harvard University Press.

Leavy, P. (2013). *Fiction as research practice: Short stories, novellas, and novels.* Walnut Creek, CA: Left Coast Press.

The Louise Nevelson Foundation. (2015). Biography. Louise Nevelson Foundation. Retrieved from http://www.louisenevelsonfoundation.org/biography.php

Lowenfeld, V. (1965). *The nature of creative activity.* London, England: Routledge & Kegan Paul (Original work published 1939).

Lowenfeld, V., & Brittain, W. L. (1987). *Creative and mental growth* (8th ed.). New York, NY: Macmillan Publishing Co.

Lusebrink, V. B. (1990). *Imagery and visual expression in therapy.* New York, NY: Plenum Press.

Lusebrink, V. B. (2004). Art therapy and the brain: An attempt to understand the underlying processes of art expression in therapy. *Art Therapy: Journal of the American Art Therapy Association, 21*(3), 125–135.

Lusebrink, V. B. (2010). Assessment and therapeutic application of the expressive therapies continuum: Implications for brain structures and functions. *Art Therapy: Journal of the American Art Therapy Association, 27*(4), 168–177.

Maguen, S., & Litz, B. (2012). Moral injury in veterans of war. *PTSD Research Quarterly, 23*(1), 1–6. Retrieved from http://www.ptsd.va.gov/professional/newsletters/research-quarterly/v23n1.pdf

Malchiodi, C. A. (2003). Art therapy and the brain. In C. A. Malchiodi (Ed.), *Handbook of art therapy* (2nd ed., pp. 16–24). New York, NY: Guilford Press.

Marques da Silva, N., Congdon, K. G., Salvatori, M. R., & Alves de Oliveira, J. C. (2010). Requesting miracles: Votive offerings from diverse cultures. Winter Park, FL: Alice & William Jenkins Gallery at Crealdé School of Art.

Mauck, M. (2006). Visual arts. In G. Wainwright & K. B. Westerfield Tucker (Eds.), *The Oxford history of Christian worship* (pp. 817–840). Oxford, England: Oxford University Press.

Maurer-Mathison, D. V. (1993). *Decorative paper.* New York, NY: Illustrated Books.

McCafferty, J., Kwak, K., Dean, M. L., & Kane, J. (2007). Eating disorders: A collaborative approach to treatment. In *The American Art Therapy Association Conference Proceedings* (Vol. 38, pp. 80). Albuquerque, NM: The American Art Therapy Association.

Meshcheryakova, K. (2012). Art therapy with orphaned children: Dynamics of early relational trauma and repetition compulsion. *Art Therapy: Journal of the American Art Therapy Association, 29*(2), 50–59.

Metropolitan Museum of Art. (2000). Albrect Dürer Melencolia I (43.106.1). *Heilbrunn Timeline of Art History*. New York, NY: The Metropolitan Museum of Art. Retrieved from http://www.metmuseum.org/toah/works-of-art/43.106.1

Meyer, L. (1992). *Black Africa: Masks sculpture jewelry*. Paris, France: Terrail.

Miller, A. (2012). Inspired by *El Duende*: One-canvas process painting in art therapy supervision. *Art Therapy: Journal of the American Art Therapy Association, 29*(4), 166–173.

Moon, B. A. (Ed.). (1997). *An encyclopedia of archetypal symbolism: The archive for research in archetypal symbolism* (Vol. 1). Boston & London: Shambhala.

Moon, B. L. (2007). Dialoging with dreams in existential art therapy. *Art Therapy: Journal of the American Art Therapy Association, 24*(3), 128–133.

Moon, B. L. (2008). *Introduction to art therapy: Faith in the product* (2nd ed.). Springfield, IL: Charles C. Thomas.

The Myers & Briggs Foundation. (2012). C. G. Jung's theory. Retrieved from http://www.myersbriggs.org/my-mbti-personality-type/mbti-basics/c-g-jungs-theory.asp

Naumberg, M. (1987). *Dynamically oriented art therapy: Its principles and practices*. Chicago, IL: Magnolia Street Publishers.

Neumann, E. (1974). *Art and the creative unconscious: Four essays*. Bollingen Series LXI. Translated from the German by Ralph Manheim. Princeton, NJ: Princeton University Press.

Nissen, D. (2008). Stalking the feral artist: A series of monoprints in which the artist has an unforeseen encounter with Habuman. *Jung Journal: Culture & Psyche, 2*(4), 17–33.

Olmert, M. (1992). *The Smithsonian book of books*. Washington, DC: Smithsonian Books.

Paracelsus. (n.d.). BrainyQuote.com. Retrieved from http://www.brainyquote.com/quotes/quotes/p/paracelsus170321.html

Peterdi, G. (1959). *Printmaking: Methods old and new*. New York, NY: The Macmillan Company.

Phillips, J. (2003). The use of art therapy in impacting individual and systemic issues in foster care. In D. J. Betts (Ed.), *Creative arts therapies approaches in adoption and foster care: Contemporary strategies for working with individuals and families* (pp. 143–151). Springfield, IL: Charles C. Thomas.

Pifalo, T. (2002). Pulling out the thorns: Art therapy with sexually abused children and adolescents. *Art Therapy: Journal of the American Art Therapy Association, 19*(1), 12–22.

Plato. (1974). The allegory of the cave. In *Republic* (pp. 240–248). Harmondsworth, England: Penguin Books.

Ponteri, A. K. (2001). The effect of group art therapy on depressed mothers and their children. *Art Therapy: Journal of the American Art Therapy Association, 18*(3), 148–157.

Read, H. (1962). *The meaning of art*. London, England: Faber & Faber Limited.

Read, H. (1966). Psychology of art. *Encyclopedia of world art* (Vol. XI). London, England: McGraw-Hill Publishing.

Read, H. (1977). *The art of sculpture*. Bollingen Series XXXV. 3. Princeton, NJ: Princeton University Press.

Rehavia-Hanauer, D. (2003). Identifying conflicts of anorexia nervosa as manifested in the art therapy process. *The Arts in Psychotherapy, 30*(3), 137–149.

Rockwell, P., & Dunham, M. (2006). The utility of the Formal Elements Art Therapy Scale in assessment for substance use disorder. *Art Therapy: Journal of the American Art Therapy Association, 23*(3), 104–111.

Ronnberg, A., & Martin, K. (2010). *The book of symbols: Reflections on archetypal images*. Cologne, Germany: Tashen.

Roob, A. (2006). *The Hermetic Museum: Alchemy & mysticism*. Köln, Germany: Tashen.

Ross, J., & Romano, C. (1972). *The complete Printmaker: The art and technique of the relief print, the intaglio print, the collagraph, the lithograph, the screen print, the dimensional print, photographic prints, children's prints, collecting prints, print workshop*. New York, NY: The Free Press.

Rothschild, D. M. (1982). Lorenzo Bartolini's Demidoff Table. *Metropolitan Museum Journal, 17*.

Rowland, S. (2015). Jung, art and psychotherapy re-conceptualizing by the symbol that joins us to the wildness of the universe. *International Journal of Jungian Studies, 7*(2), 81–93.

Rubin, J. A. (1984). *Child art therapy: Understanding and helping children grow through art* (2nd ed.). New York, NY: Van Nostrand Reinhold.

Rubin, J. (2001). *Approaches to art therapy: Theory and techniques*. New York, NY: Brunner-Routledge.

Rubin, J. (2010). *Introduction to art therapy: Sources & resources*. New York, NY: Routledge.

Salvatori, M. R. (2015). Ex-votos: Stories of miracles. Retrieved from http://www.mariolinasalvatori.com/?p=12

Schaefer, C. (2009). *Frida Kahlo: A biography*. Westport, CT: Greenwood Press.

Schaper, E. (1992). Taste, sublimity, and genius: The aesthetics of nature and art. In P. Guyer (Ed.), *The Cambridge companion to Kan.* (pp. 367–393). Cambridge, England: Cambridge University Press.

Schaverien, J. (1992). *The revealing image: Analytical art psychotherapy in theory and practice*. London, England: Jessica Kingsley Publisher.

Schulz-Weidner, W. (1967). Shamanism. *Encyclopedia of World Art* (Vol. XIII). London, England: McGraw-Hill Publishing.

Schut, H. A. W., de Keijser, J., van den Bout, J., & Stroebe, M. S. (1996). Cross-modality grief therapy: Description and assessment of a new program. *Journal of Clinical Psychology, 52*(3), 357–365.

Shamdasani, S. (Ed.). (2009). *Red book: Liber novus. C.G. Jung* (M. Kyburz, J. Peck, & S. Shamdasani, Trans). New York and London: W. W. Norton & Company.

Shorter, E. (1992). *From paralysis to fatigue: A history of psychosomatic illness in the modern era*. New York, NY: The Free Press.

Solomon, R. C. (1989). *Introducing philosophy: A text with integrated readings* (4th ed.). San Diego, CA: Harcourt Brace Jovanovich, Publishers.

SoulCollage®. (2015). The history of SoulCollage®. Retrieved from http://www.soulcollage.com/about-soulcollage

Springham, N. (2008). Through the eyes of the law: What is it about art that can harm people? *International Journal of Art Therapy: Inscape, 13,*(2), 65–73.

Stanford. (2005). Epistemology. *The Stanford Encyclopedia of philosophy*. Retrieved from http://plato.stanford.edu/entries/epistemology/

Stone, A. (2015, February). How art heals the wounds of war: In making a mask, soldiers who suffer brain injuries put a face to their pain. *National Geographic*. Retrieved from http://news.nationalgeographic.com/news/2015/02/150213-art-therapy-mask-blast-force-trauma-psychology-war

Strauss, V. (2015, January). Report: Requiring kindergartners to read—as Common Core does—may harm some. *The Washington Post*. Retrieved from http://www.washingtonpost.com/blogs/answer-sheet/wp/2015/01/13/report-requiring-kindergartners-to-read-as-common-core-does-may-harm-some/

Taylor, J. (1992). *Where people fly and water runs uphill: Using dreams to tap the wisdom of the unconscious*. New York, NY: Warner Books.

Thien, M. (2015, May). Why Hong Kong is clamping down on creative writing. *The Guardian*. Retrieved from http://www.theguardian.com/books/booksblog/2015/may/18/why-hong-kong-is-clamping-down-on-creative-writing

Thompson, J. (2007). *Blocked imagination—Emptied speech: A brief account of the alexithymia concept*. Australia: Soul Books.

Tjaden, P., & Thoennes, N. (2000). *Extent, nature, and consequences of intimate partner violence*. Washington, DC: U.S. Department of Justice. Retrieved from http://www.ojp.usdoj.gov/nij/pubs-sum/181867.htm

Travers, P. L. (2008). The world of the hero. In M. Heyneman (Ed.), *The inner journey: Myth, psyche, and spirit* (pp. 2–9). Sandpoint: ID: Morning Light Press.

Ulman, E., & Levy, B. (1992). An experimental approach to the judgment of psychopathology from paintings. *American Journal of Art Therapy, 30*, 107–112.

van der Kolk, B. A. (1994). The body keeps the score: Memory and the evolving psychobiology of posttraumatic stress. *Harvard Review of Psychiatry, 1*(5), 253–265.

van der Kolk, B. A., & Greenberg, M. S. (1987). The psychobiology of the trauma response: Hyperarousal, constriction, and addiction to traumatic reexposure. In B. A. Van der Kolk (Ed.), *Psychological trauma* (pp. 63–89). Washington, DC: American Psychiatric Press.

Vernworn, M. (1914). *Ideoplastische Kunst*. Mill Valley, CA: Enthnographic Arts Publications.

von Franz, M. L. (1980). *On divination and synchronicity: The psychological meaning of chance*. Toronto, Canada: Inner City Books.

von Franz, M. L. (1995). *Creative myths* (Revised ed.). London, England: Shambhala.

Wadeson, H. (1980). *Art psychotherapy*. New York, NY: Wiley & Sons.

Wallace, I. L. (2004). From the Garden to Eden and back again: Pictures, people and the problem of the perfect copy. *Angelaki, 9*(3), 137–155.

Waller, D. (Ed.). (2002). *Art therapies and progressive illness: Nameless dread*. New York, NY: Brunner-Routledge.

Wampold, B. E. (2001). *The great psychotherapy debate: Models, methods, and findings*. Mahwah, NJ: Lawrence Erlbaum Associates.

Weiss, P. (1976). *Simple printmaking*. New York, NY: Lothrop, Lee & Shepard.

White, L. M. (2002). *Printmaking as therapy: Frameworks for freedom*. London, England: Jessica Kingsley Publishers.

Wilson, L. (2013). Creativity and self-hood. Conference proceedings of the Delaware Valley Art Therapy Association, Malvern, PA.

Winick, S. (2013, December). Einstein's folklore. *Library of Congress*. Retrieved from http://blogs.loc.gov/folklife/2013/12/einsteins-folklore

Winnicott, D. (1971). *Playing and reality*. London, England: Routledge.

Wojcik, Elizabeth (Curator) in discussion with author, at The Museum of Morning Art at Arlington Cemetery, February 2015.

Wojtkowski, S. (2009). Jung's "art complex." *Archive for Research in Archetypal Symbolism (ARAS)/Art and Psyche Online Journal, 3*. Retrieved from http://aras.org/sites/default/files/docs/00028Wojtkowski.pdf

Woodman, M. (1980). *The owl was a baker's daughter: Obesity, Anorexia Nervosa and the repressed feminine*. Toronto, Canada: Inner City Books.

Yalom, I. D. (1983). *Inpatient group psychotherapy*. New York, NY: Basic Books.

Yalom, I. D. (1985). *The theory and practice of group psychotherapy* (3rd ed.). New York, NY: Basic Books.

Zhang, J. (2014). Powerful self-portraits reveal artist's descent into Alzheimer's disease. *My Modern Met*. Retrieved from http://www.mymodernmet.com/profiles/blogs/william-utermohlen-alzheimers-self-portraits

INDEX

Italicized page numbers refer to figures.